Walter Steuart, Church of Scotland

Collections and Observations

Concerning the worship, discipline, and government of the Church of Scotland

Walter Steuart, Church of Scotland

Collections and Observations
Concerning the worship, discipline, and government of the Church of Scotland

ISBN/EAN: 9783337291556

Printed in Europe, USA, Canada, Australia, Japan

Cover: Foto ©Lupo / pixelio.de

More available books at **www.hansebooks.com**

AND
OBSERVATIONS

Concerning the Worſhip, Diſcipline, and Government of the CHURCH of SCOTLAND.

In Four BOOKS.

By WALTER STEUART of PARDOVAN.

Unto which are added,

The Form of Proceſs in the Judicatures of the Church, with Relation to Scandals and Cenſures;

AND

The Second Book of Diſcipline; or, Heads and Concluſions of the Policy of the Kirk, approved of by Act of Aſſembly 1581:

A NEW EDITION.

EDINBURGH:
Printed for J. DICKSON and C. ELLIOT.
M,DCC,LXXIII.

PREFACE.

IT was the happiness of Scotland, very early, perhaps as early as the apostolic age, to receive the light of the glorious gospel: and although, as was the case with the rest of the Christian world, this light came to be greatly obscured, by the ambitious incroachments of the church of Rome; yet it is evident, that in Scotland it was never entirely extinguished. For, in some of the remoter parts of our country, in some of those very islands which we are now apt to consider as the seats of ignorance and barbarity, lived a people, remarkable for simplicity of manners, purity of behaviour, and unaffected piety towards God. These never submitted to the usurpations of the Papal tyranny; and these were " the little leaven which afterwards leavened the whole lump." Of their number, a Columbus and a Kentigern were famous in the fifth century, and a Clemens and Sampson, in the seventh.

And even in the tenth age, when the darkness of corruption and error had greatly increased, we are told, there were some godly men in Scotland, who taught the true doctrine of Christ's atonement, and continued to exercise their functions apart by themselves, without acknowledging the authority of those who assumed a spiritual power over God's heritage. But it was not till about 400 years after this, that any thing of a general reformation began to appear. Then " indeed waters broke forth in our wilderness, " and streams in our desert." Nor was all the cruelty of bigotted zeal able to destroy this heavenly plant; but, watered by the blood of a Resby, a Hamilton, and a Wishart, it grew stronger and stronger, till thousands flocked to its refreshing shade, and took shelter under its branches.

To support and animate these, and carry on the glorious work so happily begun, providence raised up a man of apostolic piety and resolution, whose zeal awakened the attention, and whose prudence conducted the zeal of his countrymen, in shaking off the Romish yoke. Every one will immediately perceive, that I speak of the famous John Knox, that great instrument of our reformation, whose name will be precious to latest ages.

The civil dissensions which then prevailed in the country, did not a little befriend the reformation. And the bold attempt of the Popish clergy to get the whole power into their own hands, on the death of James V. opened the eyes of many who till then had remained insensible; while the hope of enriching themselves with the revenues of the church, made others ready to join in abolishing Popery. And thus, from different principles, a barrier was formed in defence of the reformation, which all the fraud and cruelty of the Queen-Regent, or the address and destructive charms of her unfortunate daughter, were never able to overturn. Nay, those very measures which they took for crushing the Protestant interest, by the tender mercies of our God, proved the means of establishing it, and hastened the overthrow of the Papal power in this country. So that, in 1560, the essential doctrines of genuine Christianity were publicly acknowledged by the states of the kingdom, and the corruptions of the church of Rome condemned.

Hitherto the struggle principally had been about the doctrines of religion, as of the first and greatest importance; but these being now in some measure secured, our reformers turned their attention to the government of the church, which, under the Papacy, had become a system of worldly power and interest, and, instead of promoting religion, tended to excite and strengthen some of the worst passions in the human mind.

A plan for the worship and government of the church was accordingly drawn up, not merely in conformity to the church at Geneva, as one of our modern historians asserted; but such a plan as to our pious ancestors appeared most agreeable to the mind of God in scripture, and the practice of the primitive church.

It is true, this plan was widely different from that of the church of Rome. In it there was nothing to gratify ambition or avarice; but an amiable, a grand simplicity runs through the whole; such as suited the worship of the humble Jesus, and the nature of that kingdom which is not of this world.

But although our reformers thus freely gave up with all in the Romish church which could please a sensual mind, it was no part of their opinion, that the worship of God should be mean and grovelling, or the ministers of religion be rendered incapable of discharging the duties of their functions, by poverty, or depend upon the changeable humours of people for their subsistence. Though they gave up with all views of living in affluence upon the revenues of the church, and did not look upon these as the property of the clergy; yet did they esteem them a fund sacred to religious purposes, to be employed in supporting the clergy with decency, maintaining the poor, and educating the youth of the nation.

So that Knox, and the other leading instruments of the reformation, were very far from encouraging that dilapidation of church-revenues

revenues which afterwards took place. Nor were they the persons, whatever has been alledged, who were for demolishing the very fabrics of the churches, and all that was decent and cleanly in the places of public worship. No: the first was often done in direct opposition to their warmest remonstrances, by the lower class of people, who had long groaned under the oppressive tyranny of the monks and Popish clergy; while those of higher rank, who had the revenues of the church in their hand, could scarce be prevailed upon to employ them in a way which would prevent the other.

But although this form of worship and government was embraced by the friends of the reformation in Scotland, and practised by them, so far as their situation would allow; yet it was not till the year 1592, that it received the sanction of civil authority, and became the national order. And even when the Presbyterian church seemed thus established, her tranquillity was but of short duration: for there remained in the country a strong party, who, either retaining a secret regard to Popery, or thinking it prudent to recede as little as possible from the old practice, were for adopting that form of church-government which had been established in England. The people of this persuasion continued with great keenness to oppose Presbytery: and though they could not, for some time, procure an absolute repeal of the laws in its favour; yet, by repeated innovations, they gradually destroyed their effect, till at last they got a kind of mixed Episcopacy substituted in its place, which continued to be the form of the church in this country till the breaking out of the civil wars.

The true Presbyterians, still very numerous in Scotland, having now appeared with their usual zeal in support of civil liberty, were well intitled to the countenance of the parliament; whereas the friends of the hierarchy, both in Scotland and England, had rendered themselves and their opinions obnoxious, by supporting the crown in those arbitrary and unconstitutional measures which first inflamed the nation. This occasioned the calling together that assembly of divines, which, about the 1648, met at Westminster: An assembly which, whether we consider the number, learning, or piety, of the persons who composed it, may well be compared with the ancient councils. This venerable body, after a long and candid examination, agreed to the scheme of doctrines, and the form of worship and government, contained in their confession of faith and directory, which is, in substance, the same with what had been established in the beginning of the reformation. This

confession

confession and directory was soon after received by the church of Scotland; which had now recovered something of its former power, and continued, if not to flourish, at least to exist, till the Restoration; when the King, forgetting all the promises made during his afflictions, and the services done him by the Scots Presbyterians, abolished their government, and permitted a most cruel persecution to be carried on against them; because they would not abjure all their known principles, conform to the Episcopal government, and acknowledge him head of the church. This persecution in Scotland continued during the whole reign of Charles II. and King James his brother, whose open attachment to Popery, and pursuit of arbitrary measures, at last awakened the zeal of the nation, and produced that ever-memorable revolution in 1688, which, as Voltaire elegantly expresses it, may well be called the *Æra of British liberty*. The happy consequences of this change the Presbyterians in Scotland immediately felt, not only in respect of civil property, but also in the full establishment of that worship and government in the church, to which they had discovered a most steady attachment during a cruel persecution of eight and twenty years.

Let me now adduce a few testimonies for the church of Scotland, which may be found in a little book, intitled, *The Government and Order of the Church of Scotland*, printed at Edinburgh *in anno* 1641, and reprinted there by the society of stationers, for George Mossman *in anno* 1690. I wish every minister in Scotland had one of them. It was done by the pains of a generous English gentleman, who was very inquisitive into the order and constitution of our Church, who tells he was strongly drawn to the liking of this church, by the testimonies given to the reformation thereof by some most famous witnesses which he relates.

The *first* is, of that worthy Scots martyr Mr George Wishart. " This realm shall be illuminated with the light of Christ's gospel, " as clearly as ever was a realm since the days of the apostles. " The house of God shall be builded in it, yea it shall not lack, " whatsoever the enemy imagine to the contrary; the very top- " stone, the glory of God shall evidently appear, and shall once " triumph in despite of Satan: But alas, if the people shall be af- " ter unthankful, then fearful and terrible shall the plagues be " that after shall follow." *Hist. of the Church of Scotland*, p. 108.

The *second* is, of Beza, after he had visited Scotland, writing to John Knox, epist. 79. " This is a great gift of God, that you " have brought into Scotland together, pure religion and good or-
" der

" der, which is the bond to hold fast the doctrine. I heartily
" pray and beseech for God's sake, hold fast these two together,
" so that you may remember that if one be lost, the other cannot
" long remain. As bishops brought forth Popery, so false bishops,
" the relicts of Popery, shall bring in to the world Epicurism.
" Whosoever would have the church safe, let them beware of this
" pest. And seeing you have timely dispatched it in Scotland, I
" beseech you never admit it again, albeit it flatter with shew of
" the preservation of unity, which hath deceived many of the
" best of the ancients.

The *third* is, of the body of the confession of faith, p. 6. " It
" is the rare privilege of the Church of Scotland before many, in
" which respect her name is famous, even among strangers, that
" about the space of fifty-four years, without schism, let be heresy,
" she hath kept and holden fast unity, with purity of doctrine.
" The greatest help of this unity through the mercy of God, was,
" that with the doctrine, the discipline of Christ and the apostles,
" as it is prescribed in the word of God, was by little and little
" together received ; and according to that discipline so near as
" might be, the whole government of the church is disposed : By
" this means all the seeds of schisms and errors, so soon as they be-
" gin to bud, and shew themselves in the very breeding and birth,
" were smothered and rooted out. The Lord God out of his in-
" finite goodness grant unto the king's most gracious Majesty,
" to all the rulers of the church, to the powers that are the nur-
" sers of the church, that according to the word of God, they
" may keep perpetually that unity and purity of doctrine."

The *fourth* is, of King James VI. (*Basil. Dor. to the reader.*)
" The religion professed in this country, wherein I was brought
" up, and ever made profession of, and wishes my son ever to con-
" tinue in the same, as the only true form of God's worship, &c.
" I do equally love and honour the learned and grave men of ei-
" ther of these opinions, that like better of the single form of po-
" licy in our church, than of the many ceremonies of the church
" of England, &c. I exhort my son to be beneficial to the good
" men of the ministry, praising God that there is presently a suf-
" ficient number of good men of them in this kingdom, and yet
" are they all known to be against the form of the English Church."
And in the assembly 1590, his Majesty praised God, " for that he
" was born to be a king in the sincerest church in the world, where
" religion was most soundly and sincerely professed." Before his
Majesty went to England, it has been oft heard what was his ver-
dict

dict of the English service. As also when he was settled in England, what was his answer to the Bishop of Bath, when he inquired how it came to pass, that there were not errors and heresies in the church of Scotland wherewith their church was plagued? He said, "The order and government of that church, was such "as guarded against all these; for so soon as any error appear- "ed, the kirk-session took notice of it; if it was too hard for "them, it came to the presbytery, and from that to the synod, "and at last to the general assembly, and nothing could escape "them."

The *fifth* is, Brightman, our own countryman, joineth the churches of Helvetia, Swevia, Geneva, France, Holland, and Scotland, all together into one church, for the counter-pain of the church of Philadelphia. "Because" saith he, "they al- "most live by one and the same laws and manner of government, "as touching any matter of moment; neither doth the distance "of place break off that society, which the conjoining of mind "and good-will coupleth together." Having thus joined them into one church, he subjoineth concerning it: "Loath would I be "to provoke any man to envy, or to grieve him with my words; "yet this I must say, there is no place where the doctrine sound- "eth more purely, the worship of God is exercised more uncor- "ruptly, where more faithful diligence of the pastors doth flou- "rish, or more free and willing obedience is given by the people, "nor yet where there is greater reverencing of the whole religion "among all orders." And afterwards saith, "Neither doth it "only keep the doctrine of salvation free from corruption: but it "doth also both deliver in writing, and the exercise in practice "that sincere manner of government, whereby men are made "partakers of salvation." This in his *Commentary on the Revelation*, iii. 7.

To these may be added, what upon the one hand is said by these of the separation in their first petition to King James, insert in their apology to the doctors of Oxford. "We are willing and "ready to subscribe to these grounds of religion published in the "confession of faith, made by the church of Scotland, hoping in "the unity of the same faith to be saved by Jesus Christ, being also "like minded for, and with other reformed churches in points of "greatest moment."

And upon the other hand, that the meeting of ministers for interpreting scripture, like unto their presbyteries, were allowed by Arundel, Hutton, and Matthew, three archbishops in England,
and

PREFACE.

and proved very profitable in the northern parts for increase of knowledge both in ministers and people.

But all these, faith that gentleman, and the like testimonies, were to me but like the saying of the woman of Samaria to her countrymen, till I did more fully understand the constitution and order of that church; then did I believe, not because of their testimonies, but because I did see and know, and from that which I have seen and do now know. "When I have walked and gone round "about that church, when I have told the towers thereof, mark- "ed well her bulwarks, and considered her palaces," I may without offence affirm three things.

1. "That God hath not dealt so with every nation." If envy would permit, I might say, *any nation*, as he hath dealt with them, whereof no cause can be given but his own good pleasure. He sheweth mercy and maketh the sun to shine on whom and where he will, and of him, and through him, and for him, are all things.

2. It is no wonder though that nation stand to the defence of their reformation: Had the Lord been pleased to bless us with the like at the time of our reformation, we would not have been so unwise as to make exchange of it with Prelacy; we would have forsaken all things rather than to have forsaken it. It is more strange that any should have been found amongst them at any time, to speak or do against their own church. For, faith Cicero, *offic. l.* 1. "But after you have with your reason and mind, made a general "survey of all societies, there is none more grave, more dear than "that which each one of us hath with this country; parents are "dear, children, friends, familiars, are dear: But our native "country alone taketh all these within their compass: for which "what good man will doubt to die, could his death serve her "for good. So much the more detestable is their barbarity, who "hath with all kind of wickedness rent asunder their native "country, and both are and have been exercised in overturn- "ing her from the very foundation." If a patriot speak so of his country, a citizen so of his republic, what should the Christian, born, baptised, and bred in Scotland, think and say, if he has been born there, not only to this mortal, but to that immortal and everlasting life. No children on earth have better reason to say, *We are not ashamed of our mother*, and it were to be wished that the saying were reciprocally true.

3. Having the pattern of all the reformed churches before us, and this example so near unto us, what need we to stand amazed, as not knowing what to chuse? To abide that which we have

been, is neither profitable nor possible; to conjoin the two in one, is but the mixture of iron and clay, and must needs make the distemper greater. It were well for us, and no other thing well for us can I see, that laying aside our high conceit of ourselves, and the low esteem of other reformed churches, we would resolve to follow them as they follow Christ, and not to despise the government of Christ, because they seem to be but mole-hills: but to conform to them because they are conformed to Christ, *and to the pattern shewed in the mount.*

Such is the high esteem in which our excellent ecclesiastic constitution has been held by the most eminent persons of different ranks, both at home and abroad: And as the following collections (wherein the fullest view of its tendency to promote the great ends of religion in the spiritual and eternal welfare of those who shall embrace it, is exhibited, that ever has been published,) are now become so scarce, that a copy of them has been with difficulty procured for many years, the publisher judged a new edition of them would be no unacceptable service to the public.

PREFACE

To Pardovan's Collections.

IT was matter of regret, especially about the beginning of our happy Revolution in the year 1689, that the judicatures of this church, very much wanted fixed and established rules, for directing their proceedings; or, though they had them, yet they lay so scattered and hid, that intrants to the holy ministry, and the younger pastors, yea even some among the more aged of that sacred order, were too much strangers to them. The consideration whereof, did chiefly move me to set about this work: And if my endeavours herein, may but a little contribute to the benefit or service of the office-bearers and guides of this church, it is a reward greater than I deserve. And till a better compend be composed, these collections are humbly offered, to be recommended by professors to their students: For, except this subject be studied and understood by ministers and elders, their memories may well be burdened with their duty, but their judgements, till then, shall still remain ignorant and unsatisfied about it.

Now, as for those of our neighbour churches in this and the other island, who now differ from us, I hereby present them with that form of the house of God in Scotland, with which their pious, wise, and learned predecessors did once so passionately desire uniformity. So that whenever it shall please our great and good God to animate their successors with the like spirit, they may fall about building conform to this pattern. Not that I propose this work as the deed of the Church of Scotland, or of any judicatory therein; only in so far as what is collected or observed in it, shall be found supported by their acts or universal customs.

The materials of these collections, and in particular, of what is said on that title concerning parochial visitations by presbyteries, were chiefly gathered from, and lay scattered among the old and late manuscript and printed acts of general assemblies: The overtures concerning discipline, transmitted by them to presbyteries, the directory for worship and church-government, and the constitutions of some other churches have been helpful to the completing of the composure. Besides, I thought it not improper to add, here and there, some hints of civil laws, which I hope the reader will not find unuseful or impertinent, seeing there are some circumstances

cumstances concerning the worship of God, and the government of his church, common to human actions and societies, which are to be ordered by the light of nature and Christian prudence, according to the general rules of the word.

I have divided these collections into four books. The *first* treats of church-government, which principally concerns her office-bearers and judicatures. The *second* is concerning the worship of God and sacred things, with what relates to the maintenance thereof. The *third* and *fourth* books treat of church-discipline; the one concerning errors and scandals; and the other about the method of reclaiming and censuring the erroneous and scandalous.

CONTENTS.

PARDOVAN'S COLLECTIONS.

BOOK I.

Tit.	Page.
I. Of the election and ordination of pastors	1
II. Of transportation and admission of ministers	14
III. Of acts of transportability, of dimissions, and missions, and colleague ministers	20
IV. Of expectants, as also of students and bursars	23
V. Of schoolmasters and instructors of youth	30
VI. Of doctors and professors of theology	32
VII. Of ruling elders	34
VIII. Of deacons	35
IX. Of moderators of church-judicatures	38
X. Of clerks, readers, and precentors	39
XI. Of church-sessions	41
XII. Of presbyteries	44
XIII. Of parochial visitations by the presbytery	47
XIV. Of provincial synods	53
XV. Of extraordinary synods, and general assemblies	56
XVI. The order of the rolls of church-judicatures, and ranking of church office-bearers, and of her registers	74
XVII. Of visitations of schools and universities.	77
XVIII. Of a general council of protestants	80

BOOK II.

I. Of lecturing, preaching, catechising, public prayers before and after sermon, singing of psalms, and ministerial benediction	82
II. Of family-worship	87
III. Of baptism	90
IV. Of the Lord's supper	97

Tit.	Page.
V. Of the folemnization of marriage	107
VI. Of vifitation of the fick	114
VII. Of burial of the dead, lyke-wakes, and dirges	117
VIII. Of minifterial vifitation of families	118
IX. Of fanctification of the Lord's day; and obferving faft and thankfgiving days	121
X. Of collections and recommendations for the poor	126
XI. Of provifion for fchools and univerfities	ib.
XII. Of the immunity and union of churches	128
XIII. Of churches, church-dikes, manfes, yards, glebes, bells, utenfils, ornaments, books, and high roads to churches	130
XIV. Of tithes, ftipends, and mortifications	134

BOOK III.

I. Of apoftacy, and atheiftical opinions of deifts	142
II. Of papifts, quakers and Bourignionifts	143
III. Of fchifm, and prelacy, and of the laws and acts for preventing innovations and errors	150
IV. Of witches and charmers	158
V. Of blafphemy, curfing, profane fwearing, and lottery	163
VI. Of the profanation of the fabbath. Of not obferving faft and thankfgiving days. Of withdrawers from, and difturbers of the public worfhip of God, and obfervers of fuperftitious days.	165.
VII. Of flandering and affaulting of minifters, beating and curfing of parents, and injuries perfonal and real	169
VIII. Of bribery, partiality, and negligence of judges	172
IX. Of deforcement of church-officers	173
X. Of murder, parricide, duels, and felf-murder	174
XI. Of inceft, adultery, bigamy, rapes, fornication, *et de venere monftrofa*.	180
XII. Of penny bridals, promifcuous dancing, ftage-plays, immodefty of apparel, drunkennefs, tippling, and acts in general againft profanenefs.	185
XIII. Of theft, facrilege, ufury, falfehood, beggars and vagabonds	191
XIV. Of art and part	195

BOOK IV.

Tit.   Page.

I. Of scandals and church-discipline in general. Of the method of proceeding with the scandalous, and how scandals are to be tabled before church-judicatures   197

II. Of the transaction and prescription of scandals   204

III. Of libels, probation, and citation   205

IV. Of the vocational and personal faults of ministers and probationers, how they are censured, and of the method of proceeding to censure, and of reponing them against these censures   216

V. Of sentences and their reviews. Of declinatures, references and appeals.   229

VI. Of the order of proceeding to excommunication   233

VII. Of the order of proceeding to absolution.   240

FORM of PROCESS in the Judicatures of the Church.

Chap.   Page.

I. Concerning church-government, discipline, scandals, and censures in general   243

II. Concerning the entering of processes, citation of parties and witnesses, and taking depositions, and anent fugitives from discipline   244

III. Concerning swearers, cursers, profaners of the Lord's day, drunkards, and other scandals of that nature   248

IV. Concerning the sin of fornication, adultery, and scandalous carriage tending thereto   249

V. Concerning appeals from a kirk-session to a presbytery, &c.   252

VI. Concerning processes which natively begin at the kirk-session, but are not to be brought to a final determination by them   254

VII. Concerning processes against ministers   255

VIII. Concerning processes in order to the censure of the greater excommunication   258

IX. Concerning the order of proceeding to absolution   261

The Second Book of Discipline.

Chap.	Page.
I. Of the kirk and policy thereof in general, and wherein it is different from the civil policy	264
II. Of the policy of the kirk, and persons and office-bearers to whom the administration is committed	266
III. How the persons that bear ecclesiastical functions are to be admitted to their office	267
IV. Of the office-bearers in particular, and first of the pastors or ministers	269
V. Of doctors, and their office, and of the schools	270
VI. Of elders and their office	271
VII. Of elderships, assemblies, and discipline	272
VIII. Of the deacons and their office, the last ordinary function of the kirk	275
IX. Of the patrimony of the kirk, and distribution thereof	ib.
X. Of the office of a Christian magistrate in the kirk	276
XI. Of the present abuses remaining in the kirk which we desire to be reformed	277
XII. Certain special heads of reformation which we crave	280
XIII. The utility that shall flow from this reformation to all estates.	283

Want of discipline shewn to be a great cause of the present corruption of Christians. By Professor Ostervald. 285

COLLECTIONS
AND
OBSERVATIONS
Methodized, &c.

BOOK I.

TITLE I.

Of the Election and Ordination of Pastors.

§ 1. OUR Lord Jesus Christ hath instituted a government and governors ecclesiastical in his house, with power to meet for the order and government thereof: and to that purpose the Apostles did immediately receive the keys from the hands of their Lord and Master Jesus Christ, who hath, from time to time, furnished some in his church, with gifts for government; and with commission to exercise it when called thereunto. And it is also agreeable to, and warranted by the word of God, that some others, besides those who labour in the word and doctrine, be church-governors, to join with the ministers of the word, in the government of the church, and exercise of discipline: which office-bearers, reformed churches do commonly call *Ruling Elders*. It is likewise agreeable to the same word, that the church be governed by several sorts of judicatures, such as, kirk-sessions, presbyteries, provincial and general assemblies; all which have power, one in subordination to the other, to call before them any persons within their own bounds,

The intrinsical power of the church, the divine warrant and power of her judicatures, pastors, and elders, asserted.

whom

whom the ecclesiastical business, which is before them, doth concern, either as party or witness; see cap. 1. act 11. assem. 1707. The church of Scotland, by this article, denies the independency of presbyteries and provincial synods, as much as they do the independency of a single congregation. But till the churches become all of one mind in the Lord, and civil rulers become her nursing fathers, in their several independent kingdoms and governments, it would seem, till these good days come, the churches are to manage their own affairs independently upon each other; not that this independency proceeds either from scripture, or the nature of the church, but from restraint and misunderstandings. See the last title of this book.

The various names given to pastors, and why. Titles of dignity in the church favour of Popery.

§ 2. Pastors, bishops, and ministers, are they who are appointed to particular congregations: in respect whereof, sometimes they are called pastors, because they feed their congregations; sometimes bishops, because they watch over their flocks; sometimes ministers, because of their service; sometimes also presbyters or seniors, for the gravity of manners which they ought and are supposed to have. See Polity of the Kirk, cap. 4 By the act of Assembly, December 17. 18. 1638, art. 19. seeing the office of diocesan or lordly bishop is removed and abjured by this kirk, it is thought fit that all titles of dignity, favouring more of Popery than of Christian liberty, as chapters, with their elections and consecrations, abbots, priors, deans, archdeacons, preaching deacons, chanters, sub-chanters, and others, having the like title, be no more used hereafter, under pain of church-censure.

Intimation for the electors to meet, is made by the presbytery, but ordinarily upon their application. A few applying, stops the jus devolutum.

§ 3. When the presbytery are well informed that a parish, for the most part, is unanimous to elect a fit person to be their pastor, then they are to appoint one of their number to preach on a Lord's day in the vacant congregation, and, after forenoon's sermon, to intimate, that elders, heritors, magistrates, and town-council, (when that vacancy happens in a burgh royal), and heads of families, do meet at the church on such a week day, (being always ten free days after the intimation), in order to the electing of a fit person to supply their vacancy. Which order seemeth most agreeable to that apostolical practice, Acts vi. 3. " Wherefore, brethren, look ye out among you seven

" men of honest report, full of the Holy Ghost, and
" wisdom, whom we may appoint over this business."
And the presbytery, for ordinary, waits till the electors
apply to them for that intimation; which application will
stop and interrupt the *jus devolutum*, (of which hereafter),
although it be made by a few electors, because their meeting to apply hath no convener

§ 4. By the act of Assembly August 4. 1649, the kirk-session is to meet and proceed to the election, and it doth most properly belong to them, as the representatives of that congregation, to look out for a fit person to be their pastor. But seeing the heritors (especially such as reside in the parish) and magistrates, with their town-council, in burghs, are the most lasting, as well as the most considerable heads of families, on whose satisfaction and assistance the comfortable living of ministers may much depend, the 33d act, sess. 2. of King William and Queen Mary's parliament hath joined them (being Protestants) with the elders, in subscribing of calls to ministers. It is to be minded, that both session and town-council do subscribe personally as the heritors do. By the above-mentioned act of Assembly, no person, under the censure of the kirk, is to be admitted to vote in the election of a minister. By the 6th act of the 4th session of King William and Queen Mary's parliament, all persons whosoever, giving voice in calling of ministers, are, at their meeting appointed for that effect, to swear the oath of allegiance, and subscribe the same, with the assurance.

Who are habile electors, who not; and what makes a call legal.

§ 5. By that same last-mentioned act of parliament, it is enacted, That if application be not made by the elders and heritors of the parish, to the presbytery, for the call and choice of a minister, within the space of six months after the vacancy, that then the presbytery may proceed to plant a minister *tanquam jure devoluto*. See § 3. *sub finem*. And that forecited act of Assembly 1649, appoints, where the congregation is disaffected or malignant, the presbytery to provide them with a minister. Where a parish, or its greater part, is remiss or erroneous, and therefore will not, or delays to call a minister, the presbytery, in that case, by their power from Christ, may give a mission or call to a particular person, and ordain him

When a presbytery may plant a' vacancy *tanquam jure devoluto*.

him to labour in the work of the ministry among that people; by virtue whereof, he hath right to enjoy both office and benefice. By the 18th canon *concilii Antiocheni*, it is determined, " Si quis ordinatus non ierit in parochi-
" am ad quam est ordinatus, non sua quidem culpa, sed
" propter populi recusationem, vel aliquam aliam causam,
" quæ a se non oritur is sit et honoris et muneris parti-
" ceps."

The meeting of electors; the election itself; the call signed; the power of the absent electors accresceth to these present.

§ 6. When the day is come on which the electors were appointed to meet, by the above-mentioned order of intimation, the minister, whom the presbytery ordered to moderate at the election, having ended sermon, and dismissed the congregation, except these concerned, is to open the meeting of electors with prayer; and thereafter they proceed to vote the person to be their minister, as they are called upon by the session-clerk, who is also clerk to that meeting: which vote being taken and carefully marked, the moderator is to pronounce the mind of the meeting, *viz* That a call be given to the person named; which the clerk is to have ready drawn up to be read and signed by them in presence of the moderator. The meeting of electors having been convened upon the presbytery's intimation, if either heritors, elders, or town-council, be wanting or absent, their power accresceth to these present, they having all had the lawful advertisement given them, and none of these distinct bodies has a negative upon another.

Form of a call.

§ 7. We the heritors, elders, and magistrates of the town-council of   being destitute of a fixed pastor, and being most assured by good information, and our own experience, of the ministerial abilities, piety, literature, and prudence, as also of the suitableness to our capacities of the gifts of you Mr A. B. preacher of the gospel, or minister at C. have agreed, with the advice and consent of the parishioners foresaid, and concurrence of the Rev. presbytery of D. to invite, call, and intreat: Likeas, We, by these presents, do heartily invite, call, and intreat you, to undertake the office of a pastor among us, and the charge of our souls. And further, upon your accepting of this our call, promise you all dutiful respect, encouragement, and obedience in the Lord. In witness whereof, &c.

§ 8. There-

§ 8. Thereafter the moderator is to atteſt, that, conform to the preſbytery's appointment, he did moderate at the meeting of electors, the plurality, or all whereof preſent, made choice of Mr A B. to be their paſtor at ſuch time and place. Which atteſtation he is to ſign upon the call. See § 33. In caſe there be a parity among the electors votes, (that is, when they ſplit or divide in their calling of two perſons), then the moderator muſt either be allowed the caſting vote, or elſe application muſt be renewed to the preſbytery to convene the electors a ſecond time. *The atteſtation of a call; and what is to be done, if the electors divide in voting.*

§ 9. The right of patronage, according to Streinius's *Summa juris canonici*, is a power to preſent a fit perſon to a vacant church-benefice: which right is acquired ſeveral ways; as, 1. When one gifts ground to build a church upon. 2. If, with conſent of the biſhop, one build a church. 3. If one beſtows upon a church, or mortifies to thoſe ſerving the cure thereat, ſome conſiderable maintenance. Theſe three ways are contained in that known verſe, "Patronum faciunt, dos, ædificatio, fundus." The 4th way is, An immemorial cuſtom of preſenting. 5. By a privilege and gift thereto derived from the Pope *Patronages deſcribed, and how acquired at firſt.*

§ 10. The right of patronages with us in times of the late Prelacy became ſo twiſted with other ſecular intereſts, that it was expreſsly avowed and pleaded for as a part of a man's private patrimony, the rights whereof he had ſettled and confirmed to him and his heirs, as thoſe of his other eſtate, by charters under the ſeals, and might lawfully ſell and diſpoſe of it, and from which he could not be excluded without injuſtice; theſe rights were then tranſmitted according to the common degrees and rules of blood. *Patronages, how conſidered under Prelacy.*

§ 11. This church maintains, That the patron's pretended privilege of a negative intereſt in the call and maintenance of miniſters, is a ſinful and wrongous uſurpation, without warrant from the word of God, deſtructive of the true liberties and intereſt of the church, and moſt ſcandalouſly offenſive to all ranks of Chriſtians therein. This is gathered from their writings and ſermons, and act of Aſſembly Auguſt 4. 1649. *The opinion of this church of it.*

§ 12. The miniſter who moderated the call, and theſe commiſſioned to proſecute the ſame, ſhall next preſbytery- *Call preſented and approved.*

ry-day present the call to them. If they find no ground to demur upon granting their concurrence, then they are to grant the same, which the clerk is to signify upon the call. But if they find grounds to delay or refuse their approbation, in that case these are to be particularly condescended upon in their records: Thus the presbytery is vindicated from arbitrary procedure, and parties concerned have access to make answer for themselves.

Calls prosecuted to expectants or ministers.

§ 13. If the call be to a probationer within the presbytery's bounds, then the presbytery is to put him upon trials, in order to ordination. But if he be under the inspection of another presbytery, then the presbytery to whom the call was first presented, and with which they have concurred, is to write, or send one of their number, together with the parish commissioners, and desire that presbytery where the probationer resides, to concur with them in offering the call to him, and injoining him to repair to the bounds to which he is called, and there submit to the ordinary trials, in order to ordination. How the call should be prosecuted to a fixed minister, see in the following title.

Calling and entry of a minister is to be directed by the presbytery.

§ 14. It is to be remembered, that no probationer or minister, is to receive any call to a vacant congregation, but from the hands of the presbytery to which they belong; for, it is by their determination that the calling and entry of a minister is to be ordered and concluded. K. William and Q. Mary's parl. sess. 2. cap. 23.

Ordination described: no ministerium vagum.

§ 15. Ordination is the solemn act of the presbytery, setting apart a person to some publick church-office: For this see the Directory. It is agreeable to the word of God, and very expedient, that such as are to be ordained ministers be designed to some particular church, or other ministerial charge; See the Directory and Heads of the Polity of the Kirk; as also the 10th act, chap. 1. of the French church-discipline; wherein they agree, that ministers shall not be ordained, without assigning them a particular flock.

Mens gifts should be suited to their posts.

§ 16. By the same article, ministers must be fit for the flocks which shall be assigned unto them; and by the act of Assembly 1596, ratified December 1638, it is determined, That because men may be fit for some places, who are not meet for others, the principal places are to be provided with men of most worthy gifts; and none are to accept

cept of a greater charge than they are able to difcharge. Indeed, when a minifter is endowed with prudence, and hath love and refpect from his people, a greater charge will be eafier to him than to another.

§ 17. On a probationer's accepting of the call of a parifh, which is underftood to be done when he fubmits himfelf to the presbytery to undergo his trials in order to ordination, he is by them to be tried, as when he was licenfed, (for which fee that title), except the homilies and previous catechetic trials. When the presbytery is fatisfied of his trials, they fend one of their number to preach in that congregation, and after forenoon's fermon, to intimate to them, that the probationer whom they have called to be their minifter, his edict was now to be ferved. Which edict, after reading by him or the precenter, is to be affixed by the bedal upon the moft patent church-door: The tenor whereof is as follows. *Trials of an intrant to the miniftry; and ferving of his edict.*

§ 18. This prefbytery having received a call from the parifh of   to Mr A. B. preacher of the gofpel, to be their minifter, and finding the fame orderly proceeded, and the faid Mr A. B. having undergone all the parts of his trial, in order to his ordination; and the prefbytery upon the whole judging him qualified to be a minifter of the gofpel, and fit to be paftor of this congregation, have refolved to proceed, unlefs fomething occur which may juftly impede the fame: and therefore do hereby give notice to all perfons, efpecially the members of this congregation, that if any of them have any thing to object, why the faid Mr A. B. fhould not be admitted paftor here, they may repair to the prefbytery, which is to meet at   the   day of   with certification, that if no perfon object any thing that day, the prefbytery will proceed without further delay. *Form of an edict.*

§ 19. The prefbytery meeting, as it was appointed by the preceding, for receiving the execution of the edict, which ought to be ten free days after ferving of the fame, the minifter who was appointed to preach at ferving of the edict, is to give an account of his diligence, and return the edict indorfed by himfelf or the precenter and bedal; then the prefbytery is to order their officer, three feveral times, at the moft patent door of the church, to give notice, That if there be any there who has any thing to object againft the perfon called his being their minifter, they may come and *The edict returned and executed.*

and do it to the presbytery; with certification, as in the edict.

Ordination-day set, and intimated: and what day most convenient for the fast.

§ 20 If there be no material impediment found, the presbytery is to name a convenient day within less than ten days; if it can be, for their meeting to ordain the candidate at the church of the congregation to which he is to belong. The day appointed for his ordination, is to be intimated from the pulpit on the Lord's day preceding, inviting all to be present, and telling them that they are to set apart that day as a fast to be by them observed with more than ordinary supplication, for the assistance and blessing of God upon the ordinance of Christ, and labours of his servant. But the ordination-day is more proper for thanksgiving than fasting, and experience may confirm us herein: for we find, that on the account of some things convenient to be done that day, another before were fitter to be observed for the fast.

Popular ordination condemned from acts vi. 3.

§ 21. Our church doth condemn any doctrine that tends to support the peoples power of ordaining their ministers: for by the 5th act of Assembly 1698, upon information that a divine of the church of England, had in his sermon charg'd them as corrupters of the word of God, who to favour popular ordinations, had caused that passage of scripture Acts vi 3. " Whom WE may appoint over this business," to be printed, " Whom YE may appoint," &c. they did unanimously disclaim the above-mentioned error of the press, and did declare, they did not own any other reading of that text to be according to the original, but " Whom WE may appoint," &c.

The ordination-sermon, and preface to the action.

§ 22 The ordination-day being come, conform to the presbytery's appointment, one of their number preacheth; the subject of whose sermon should be concerning the qualifications of ministers, and the reciprocal duties betwixt them and their people. The sermon, prayer, and praises after sermon, being ended, the minister from the pulpit is to shew the occasion of that day's meeting, and all the steps of the presbytery's procedure hitherto with respect to that affair.

The questions to be answered by the intrant before imposition of hands, or, his ordination engagements.

§ 23. Then the minister calls on the intrant, who, in face and audience of the congregation, is to answer to these following questions: 1. If he doth believe the scriptures of the Old and New Testaments, and the truths therein contained,

contained, to be the word of God? 2. If he doth own, and will adhere unto the confession of faith, and catechisms of this church, and doctrine therein contained, as being founded on, and consonant to the holy scriptures? 3. If he will be faithful and zealous in maintaining all the truths of the gospel, the unity of the church, and peace thereof, against all error and schism whatsoever, notwithstanding of what trouble or persecution may happen? 4. If he do likewise own and will adhere to the worship, discipline, and government of this church, as being founded on, and consonant to the holy scriptures? 5. If he hath been led in his designing the work of the ministry, by a single and sincere love to God, and aim at his glory in the gospel of his son, and not by filthy lucre, and the motives of worldly gain, as the great inducement moving him to the ministerial work? 6. If he hereby engage to be diligent and assiduous in praying, reading, meditating, preaching, administring the sacraments, catechizing, and exercising of discipline, and in performing all other ministerial duties toward the people committed to his charge? 7. If he resolves to own his ordination to the holy function of the ministry, and to continue in duty, notwithstanding of any trouble that may arise in the church hereafter? *vide Quæ.* 3. 8. If he will humbly and willingly submit himself unto the admonitions of his brethren, and discipline of this church? Lastly, If he will take care that he himself and his family shall walk unblameably, be examples to the flock, and adorn the profession of the gospel by their conversation?

§ 24. In the most conspicuous place of the church, and near to the pulpit, a table and seats being placed where the brethren of the presbytery, the heritors and elders of the congregation, with the magistrates and council, when in burghs royal, are to sit, together with the intrant, so that all the ministers may conveniently give him imposition of hands, and the others may take him by the hand, when thereunto called: the minister is to come from the pulpit to the foresaid place, where the intrant kneeling, (for the more decent and convenient laying on of hands) and the brethren standing, he, as their mouth, in their Master's name and authority, doth in and by prayer set the candidate apart (not only the minister who prays, but all the brethren that conveniently can, laying their hands upon

The place where, and the manner how, ordained.

his head) to the office of the ministry, invocating God for his blessing to this effect:

Directory for ordination prayer.

§ 25. Thankfully acknowledging the great mercy of God in sending Jesus Christ for the redemption of his people, and for his ascension to the right hand of God the Father, and thence pouring out his spirit, and giving gifts to men, apostles, evangelists, prophets, pastors, and teachers, for the gathering and building up of his church, and for fitting and inclining this man to this great work, and to intreat him to fit him with his Holy Spirit, to give him, who, in his name, is set apart to his holy service, to fulfil the work of the ministry in all things, that he may both save himself and the people committed to his charge.

The right hand of fellowship; he is saluted as minister: the conclusion of the work.

§ 26. The prayer being ended, the minister who moderates in the action, and thereafter all the ministers of the presbytery, takes the person ordained by the right hand, saying unto him, we give unto you the right hand of fellowship, to take part of the ministry with us. Then the heritors, elders, and magistrates, when in burghs, should salute him as their minister, in taking him by the right hand, as a testimony of their acceptance of him. Then the minister returning to the pulpit, after having had a short and pertinent exhortation, both to the minister and people, he is by solemn prayer to commend both pastor and flock to God's grace. Then he is to sing a part of a Psalm, such as 132. from verse 1. and dismiss the congregation, with pronouncing the blessing.

Form of an act of ordination and admission.

§ 27. The whilk day the presbytery of   met at the kirk of   considering that there had been a call presented upon the   day of   unto them, from the heritors, elders, and parishioners of the said parish of   to   preacher of the gospel, to be their minister: To which call the said presbytery of   their concurrence was sought by the said parish, within the bounds of which presbytery the said parish lies; and with which call the said presbytery did concur, as their act thereanent, dated &c bears: likeas, conform to the acts and constitutions of this church, observed in the like cases, and at the desire of the said parish, the said presbytery did put the said   then only a probationer, to all the parts of his trial for the ministry, as is usual, wherein he was approven to the satisfaction of the said presbytery. After which,

which, the presbytery of   did cause serve his edict at the said church of   in the due and orderly form, on a Sabbath day, being the   day of   whereby it was publicly intimate to the said congregation, that in case any person had any thing to object against the said Mr   why he should not be ordained and admitted minister to the said charge of   they might apply themselves to the said presbytery of   which was to sit at the   day of   where they should be fully heard; with certification as effeirs. And accordingly, the brethren of the presbytery met at   the day aforesaid, and the edict being returned indorsed, and all parties concerned in the said congregation being lawfully called, and none compearing to object against the said ordination and admission, therefore, the said presbytery did determine to meet at the kirk of   upon the   day of   in order to the ordination and admission of the said Mr   to the said parish, and appointed Mr   minister of the gospel at   within their bounds, to preach at the said admission and ordination. Which being accordingly performed, the brethren met presbyterially, taking the whole matter to consideration, as said is, did then and there, in due order, and all requisite formalities, solemnly ordain, admit, and set apart, by imposition of hands and prayer, the said Mr   in face of the whole congregation there present, to the sacred order of the ministry, in the said congregation and parish; and afterwards was received to ministerial communion by the brethren of the ministry, and by the heritors and elders as their minister. This is extracted, &c.

§ 20 While the church doth enjoy peace, and is at full liberty, it is very reasonable that the above comely order should be observed; but in troublesome times, and in cases of great necessity, ministers must be ordained without particular relation to a parochial charge, otherwise there shall be no ordination in times of persecution. By act 4. chap · of the French church-discipline, it is declared, That in such extraordinary cases, a minister of the gospel may be ordained by three ministers: but in times of peace, by no fewer than seven, and in case the colloquy consist of fewer, it shall call in some of the neighbouring ministers to accomplish that number. *Ordination sub cruce, and quorum for ordination.*

§ 19.

§ 29. You will find the old manner of electing and ordaining of ministers at the beginning of our Reformation, in Knox's forms, prefixed to the old Psalms, that it was performed without imposition of hands, and without a nursery of expectants: which notwithstanding was an ordination both valid and lawful, especially in that infant-state of this reformed church.

The manner of election and ordination at our Reformation.

§ 30. By the d and d articles, chap. 1. of the French church-discipline, the bishops, curates, priests, and friars, among the Popish clergy, turning Protestants, were to be re-ordained by imposition of hands. And in the sixth session of Assembly 1690, the moderator is allowed and authorised to declare, in their name, that they would depose no incumbents simply for their judgement about the government of the church, nor urge re-ordination upon them.

Re-ordination of Popish clergy, and Episcopal incumbents.

§ 31. None are allowed to enter the ministry, under the age of twenty-five years, except such as the synod or Assembly judge fit for the same: see Assem. 1638, 1647, and 1704, session 10. Other churches have likewise very much regarded the age of intrants to the ministry; for by the 4th *canon concilii sexti in Trullo*, it is said, "sanctorum divinorumque patrum nostrorum canon in his quoque valeat, ut presbyter ante trigesimum annum non ordinetur etiamsi sit homo valde dignus;" which canon agrees with the 11th *concil. Neocæsar*. This church hath likewise a special regard to the literature of intrants, (of which more afterwards), and it is generally esteemed an essential accomplishment, that they should have the Latin tongue: for you will see in the supplement to Calderwood's history, that in the Assembly 1575, it was ordained, That none should be admitted ministers, except such as can interpret and speak congruous Latin, unless the General Assembly, for their singular gifts and graces, found cause to dispense therewith. Accordingly they have, both of old and of late, dispensed therewith; particularly the Assembly 1708, appointed the presbytery of Sky, after trial of his other qualifications, to ordain one to be minister at St Kilda, who wanted the Latin tongue.

The age and literature of those to be ordained.

None having the Irish language, to be settled in the lowlands; or those born on the north side of Tay, to be settled in the south.

§ 32. By the 6th act of Assembly 1699, ministers and probationers having the Irish language, are not to be settled in the low country, till the highland places be first provided: and by the 16th session of the same Assembly, presbyteries

presbyteries are to be censured who settle any probationer in the south who was born on the north side of Tay (except it be in the case of a call given to such probationers by the city of Edinburgh) till they have been twelve months in the north, without receiving a call there; in which case they are free to come south, and accept of a call; and any north-country probationer, who shall be otherwise settled, is *ipso facto* transportable. And no doubt the same certification may be extended against ministers and probationers, having the Irish language, that are settled in lowland congregations, contrary to the foresaid act, conform to the 11th act of Assembly 1708.

§ 32. By the 16th act of Assembly 1697, for the more expeditious planting of the north, the agent of the kirk, or any person deputed by him, is authorised to prosecute calls from the north side of Tay, and other presbyteries there mentioned, to any minister belonging to any parish on the south side of Tay: but as for parishes in the south of Scotland, they prosecute calls thus: After the call hath been signed and attested, as in sect. 8. the moderator is to propose to the meeting, that they appoint some of their number, not only to present their call to the presbytery, for their approbation and concurrence, but to prosecute the same till it be brought to an issue: which commission is to be signed by the moderator and session-clerk, in respect that all the deeds of that meeting are recorded in the session-books. *How calls are prosecuted from the north, and how they differ from the ordinary method.*

§ 34. By the 13th act of Assembly 1697, upon a letter from the commander in chief of his Majesty's forces, it is recommended to the respective kirk-sessions where the forces are quartered, to provide them with convenient seats for hearing, and to inspect them as they do other parishioners. And the commission of the General Assembly, upon application from the chief commanders, is to settle ministers in regiments belonging to this kingdom: but when the commission is not instructed to receive such applications, then, no doubt, they are to be made to the presbyteries. Thus we see that ministers do not receive their warrant to take oversight of a regiment, as colonels and other officers do their commissions from the Sovereign. *The army, by whom to be inspected, and how to be fixed with ministers.*

§ 35. By the 13th act of Assembly 1708, it is transmitted as an overture to presbyteries, that when the sufficiency *Differences about intrants, how composed.*

cy of intrants to the holy ministry is contested in the presbytery that ordains them, that in this case the presbytery shall refer the whole affair to the respective synods, and that the synod shall appoint some of their number to examine *coram* such intrants, and give directions to the presbyteries in such cases.

TITLE II.

Of Transportation and Admission of Ministers.

Transportation described.

§ 1. TRansportation or translation is an authoritative loosing of a minister's relation to one charge, and a making up of that same relation betwixt him and another, done for the greater good of the church. This act hath no resemblance to the dissolving of the relation itself betwixt a minister and the church, as in the censure of deposition; but it only resembles a master's taking one from labouring in such a part of his vineyard, to continue the same work in another part thereof.

Calls must be managed and directed by the presbytery.

§ 2. No minister is to receive or entertain a call from another congregation, till it come to him by his own presbytery. And any man transporting himself to another congregation, deserves both to be loosed from his own charge, and debarred from entering into the other; the canonists, upon this title do thus determine, " Qui enim sua propria " authoritate ad aliam se transfert ecclesiam, priore relicta, " & suam amittit & ab aliena repellitur. Vide Petri Biar- " noy examen juridicum "

How a presbytery proceeds in presenting a call.

§ 3. The presbytery having heard, by word or petition, these commissioned from the vacant congregation to prosecute the call, and after sustaining their commissions, and finding the call, as to what appeareth at present, to be orderly, and the reasons thereof not without some ground and weight, they are thereafter, at the same diet, to deliver their call, by their moderator, to the minister desired to be transported, with the reasons thereof, and to summon him, *apud acta*, to appear before the presbytery; the time for compearance being at least fifteen free days thereafter.

The ordinary method for citing in transportations.

§ 4. If the minister called be absent from the presbytery, then the call, with the reasons thereof, or rather a double of both, attested under the clerk's hand, are to be
delivered

delivered to him by the presbytery-officer, either perfonally, or at his dwelling-houfe, together with a citation for him and his parifh to appear *ut fupra*.

§ .. A. B. moderator, &c Forafmuchas, the heritors, elders, &c. of the parifh of   have appli d to us for our warrant and precept to cite Mr C. D minifter at   and the parifhioners thereof, to hear and fee the faid Mr C. D. tranfported in manner, and to the effect under-written, conform to a call given him by the faid parifh: Herefore, we require you, that upon fight hereof, ye pafs, and lawfully fummon the faid Mr C. D. perfonally, or at his dwelling-place: And ficklike, all and fundry the parifhioners of the faid parifh of   by open reading hereof, and affixing a juft copy of the fame, at and upon the parifh-kirk door, upon a Sabbath-day before noon, immediately after fermon and pronouncing the bleffing, all upon fifteen free days warning, to compear before the faid prefbytery, within the kirk of   upon the day of   next to come, in the hour of caufe, with continuation of days, to hear and fee the faid Mr C. D. tranfported, by fentence of the faid prefbytery, from the faid parifh of   to the faid parifh of   to ferve in the work of the miniftry thereat; or elfe to alledge a reafonable caufe to the contrary: with certification to them, if they fail, they fhall be holden as confenting to the faid tranfportation; and the faid prefbytery will proceed to do therein according as they fhall find juft. And this our precept you are to return duly execute and indorfed. Given at   by A. B. *Pibri Cls.*

Form of a fummons of tranfporta-tion.

§ 0. If the prefbytery have ground to fear that their officer may meet with moleftation or oppofition in executing of their fummons, the General Affembly, for preventing of deforcement and profanation of the Sabbath, by their 7th act, 1704, ordains the minifter himfelf, being cited *apud acta* by the prefbytery, or, if abfent, by the prefbytery's letter, to be prefent at the day appointed for hearing the caufe: whereof the minifter is appointed to give advertifement from the pulpit, to his elders, heritors, &c; in fhort, to all that were concerned in calling him, that if any of them has a mind to defend their right to him, they may be prefent at the prefbytery on fuch a day. For which caufe the minifter is appointed to communicate unto them the

How, in extraordinary cafes, a parifh is to be cited.

Call and reafons muft be imparted to the parifh.

the call, and the reasons thereof, transmitted to him: but this he ought also to communicate in all ordinary citations, if he intends the parish should defend their right and possession. As for this extraordinary way for citing a parish, there was more need for it at the beginning of our happy Revolution, when there were few ministers and expectants, and many competing vacancies: But now when the churches are generally planted, and seeing there is such a plentiful nursery of hopeful probationers for supplying the few remaining vacancies, there is rather ground to fear that there be competing different calls from one parish, than of calls from distinct parishes to one man: But if it should happen that neither minister nor parish compear, then the presbytery is to grant certification against them, by holding them as consenting to the desired transportation.

Extraordinary citations rarely needed in a well planted church.

What done in the case of non-compearance.

§ 7. By the 6th act of Assembly 1694, it is recommended to vacant parishes, That they do not attempt a transportation, till they first seriously essay and follow other means of providing themselves; which is indeed the speedy way to increase the number of labourers in the Lord's vineyard, and to continue others at the place appointed for their work.

Vacancies must first essay to call probationers.

§ 8. By that same act of Assembly, all debates in processes of transportation, must be managed with that meekness and brotherly kindness, as becometh parts and members of the some body of Christ, and that they represent their reasons and answers with perspicuity and brevity.

How debates in transportations should be managed.

§ 9. And to prevent contentious appeals in such matters, it is ordained by that act, That if both the competing parishes be within the same presbytery, in that case the presbytery's decision shall be obeyed; or if the parishes be in different presbyteries, and both presbyteries in the same synod, in that case the decision of the synod shall take effect. But with certification, that the respective judicatures appealed from shall be censured, if they be found to have malversed; and, on the other hand, if any be found unnecessarily to pursue appeals and complaints, they shall be severely censured therefor.

Rash appealers in transportations, when to be censured.

§ 10. By the 5th act of Assembly 1702, the parish craving transportation, is to satisfy the judicature if there be a legal stipend, and a decreet therefor. It were to be wished that the church were truly and better informed of the quantity

Every benefice should be recorded.

quantity and circumstances of every benefice within the nation, that so they might be directed to apply accordingly; and, for that end, let presbyteries be appointed to give in an exact account of these within their bounds, that the same may be insert and regisirate in the books of the General Assembly, conform to the act August 31. 1647.

§ 11. Actual ministers, when transported, are not to be tried again, as was done at their entry to the ministry: but only the presbytery, in which the calling parish lies, shall judge of his gifts, from what they have heard of him in the exercise thereof, whether they be fit and answerable for the condition and disposition of that congregation. There are abilites requisite to make one a fit minister for some considerable parishes, which are not so necessary to one in a small private parish. Eminent congregations are such, where are universities, towns and burghs, places of noblemens residence, or frequency of Papists. See Assem. August 2. 1642, interpreting the act 1596, concerning the trial of ministers, ratified December 17. 1638, and § 10. tit. 1. *How the suitableness of mens gifts is to be tried, and what is meant by eminent congregations.*

§ 12. As there useth to be solemn prayer at the fixing of a ministerial relation to a certain charge, so when that is changed and carried into another, it is very fit, as is used, that light and direction should be sought in such a weighty and concerning matter to the church, from the glorious God and blessed Head thereof, and that immediately before the judicature enter upon the process. *Prayer is to be made before entering upon the process of transportation.*

§ 13. The which day, anent the summons touching   and anent the citations given to the said Mr A. B. and his said parishioners, to have compeared before the said presbytery, at certain days now bypast, with continuation of days; the said summons, and all parties having interest, being called in presence of the said presbytery; and last of all, upon the day and date of their presents, the said pursuers compeared by   their commissioner; and the said Mr A. B. and his parish of   being lawfully summoned, and they compearing; the said presbytery having heard and considered the call given to the said Mr A. B. by the said parish of   and the reasons produced by the pursuers for inforcing the said transportation; and also having maturely considered the good and advantage of the church in the said transporta- *Form of an act of transportation.*

tion, and being well and ripely advised in the haill premisses; the said presbytery (after calling upon God for light and direction) by their vote, have transported, and hereby transports the said Mr A. B. from the said parish of   to the said parish of   to serve in the work of the ministry, as their lawful pastor thereat, and appoints Mr C. D. minister of·   to declare the said kirk of   vacant upon Sabbath the   day of   conform to the acts, practice, and constitutions of this church used in the like cases

How to proceed when two parishes lie in different judicatures.

§ 14. If the congregation to which the minister is called doth lie in the bounds of another presbytery, then the presbytery to which he belongs does only transport him, declares his kirk vacant, and appoints him to wait for, and obey the orders of the presbytery where the charge lies to which he is transported, as to the time of his admission thereto. But if both parishes lie within the bounds of the judicature which transports, then they appoint the time of his admission also.

Ministers without flocks, how admitted.

§ 15. If the minister called had not any relation to a particular charge in the church, then the presbytery hath nothing to do but admit him after the former steps of call and edict, &c.

The manner of admitting ministers.

§ 16. When a minister, formerly ordained, comes to be admitted minister in such a congregation, the same is performed by the presbytery in face of the congregation, with the same solemnities of an ordination; only there is no re-imposition of hands, nor any thing that is peculiar or essential to ordination; and the only questions needful are these: 1. If he does adhere unto, and promise, in the Lord's strength, to perform his ordination-engagements? 2. If he hath had any indirect hand in his own transportation or admission to this parish? 3. If he doth now accept of the charge of this parish, and promise, in the Lord's assistance, to discharge all the parts of the ministerial function among them faithfully?

The form of an act of admission.

§ 17. The presbytery of   being met at the parish-kirk of   conform to an appointment made by the said presbytery, dated   to the effect under-written, taking to consideration, that the present magistrates, town-council, heritors, and elders of the said burgh and parish of   had given a call to Mr A. B. minister of the gospel,

gospel, inviting him to be their minister: And sicklike, That the said call had been orderly presented to the said presbytery, and by them sustained; and also, that the said call had been accepted by the said Mr A. B. and that thereupon the said presbytery had appointed the said Mr A. B. his edict to be served upon Sabbath the   day of and also appointed a meeting of the said presbytery for his admission, to be held this present day and place. The said presbytery being now met conform to the said appointment, and having seen and considered the said edict duly and orderly served and indorsed, and returned conform to the practice of this church, did cause thrice publicly call all having or pretending to have interest, to compear and propone their objections, if they any had, against the said Mr A. B. his life, doctrine, or qualifications, or against the foresaid call, and the procedure thereon, above mentioned, why he should not be admitted lawful minister of the said burgh and parish: but none compeared to object thereagainst. Likeas thereupon after sermon preached, conform to appointment of the said presbytery by Mr C. D. minister at   the said presbytery did, in presence of the whole congregation there assembled for the time, admit, receive, and appoint the said Mr A. B. to be minister of the foresaid burgh and parish, according to the order and practice of this church. And sicklike, the magistrates, town-council, heritors, and elders of the said burgh and parish, did take the said Mr A. B. by the hand, in testimony of their receiving him to be their minister. Extracted forth of the records of the said presbytery, by   &c.

§ 18. Acts of ordination and admission by the presbytery, are in place of presentation, collation, and institution, and serve for them all, as a sufficient and legal title to the benefice.

The effect and use of ordination and admission acts.

§ 19. Some things there are which may debar a man's entering into the ministry, and may be reason enough for the church to shut the door upon him, such as some mistakes and escapes offensive in the life, that may proceed from rashness, weakness, ignorance, or want of prudence: yet when once he is admitted, and entered, the like escapes will not be found sufficient to depose and thurst him out;

Impediments to admission, not always grounds for deposition.

for,

for, "Multa impediunt matrimonium contrahendum, quæ non dirimunt contractum."

TITLE III.

Of Acts of Transportability, of Demissions, and Missions, and Colleague Ministers.

The ground for, and method of prosecuting this act.

§ 1. WHEN a minister labours under insupportable grievances in a parish, whereby his ministry is rendered unedifying to the people, and uncomfortable to himself; in these circumstances (all other means having been essayed and proved ineffectual for redressing his grievances) the pastor doth apply to the presbytery for an act of transportability. Whereupon they appoint one of their number to preach at that kirk, and after forenoon's sermon to advertise the parish, being the defenders, to appear before the presbytery, on such a day, and there hear and see their minister obtain that act in his favours, or otherwise to propone reasons in the contrary. After hearing of both parties, their brother's complaint being found relevant and verified, an act of transportability is granted.

The nature and import of this act.

§ 2. By which act the presbytery looseth their brother's relation to that parish as fixed minister thereof, and declares, that through their direction and inspection, he is capable to receive a call to any other charge, without their being called as having any interest: yet, in the mean time, till such an occasion of removal be offered, they do appoint him to exerce his ministry in that parish; whereby his right to intromit with the benefice continueth as formerly, the act of transportability being occasioned through the peoples fault. But this act will be but rarely sought in a well planted church: And, without granting it, the presbytery may use innocent and prudent methods for obtaining a call to their grieved brother from some vacant parish, which will as effectually answer the end as such an act can do. Upon the whole, this practice hath been but rare, and its expediency, to say no more of it, is disputed by many.

The causes and stile of demission.

§ 3. It is in the church's power to accept of demissions or not, as they find the grounds of them to be. They use to run in these terms, I Mr A. B. minister at C. for such causes,

causes, demit my ministry at the said parish of C. purely and simply into the hands of the presbytery of D. declaring, that for my part, the said parish shall be held vacant, and that it shall be free to the parish and presbytery, after due intimation hereof, by warrant of the presbytery, to call and plant another minister therein; and consents that this be recorded in the presbytery books, "ad futurum rei me-"moriam". In witness whereof I have subscribed thir presents at &c.

§ 4. Which demissions being received by the presbytery, they are thereupon to appoint one of their number to preach at that kirk, and after forenoon sermon to make intimation of the acceptation of the demission, and the presbytery's order thereon, to declare the kirk vacant. The execution whereof being reported to the presbytery, and recorded by them, they are to proceed and plant that parish, as they do other vacant congregations. *The effect of a demission upon intimation.*

§ 5. When the vacancies are many, and the ministers in some part of the church so few in number, that it exceeds the power of classical or provincial Assemblies, in whose bounds they lie, to supply them, then the General Assembly who is concerned in these bounds, as parts of the national church, doth appoint ministers by way of mission to supply these vacancies: for this see the acts of several late Assemblies for supplying the north, and the instructions given to their commissions concerning that affair. As also, by appointment of this church, ministers have been transported, ordained, and sent in mission to the Scots African and Indian company's colony in Caledonia in America. *In what case the national Assembly sends ministers in mission.*

§ 6. Upon petition from the most part of the Scottish nation in the north of Ireland, in their own name, and in name of the rest of the Protestants there, to the General Assembly in the years 1642, 1643, and 1644, representing the extreme necessity they had of more ministers, and how this church had formerly supplied other churches in Germany and France. The Assembly being willing to sympathise with every member of Christ's body, although never so remote, much more with that plantation which was a branch of their own church, they did for some years send ministers in mission to supply there, as may be seen by the printed acts in the years above named. But in Assembly 1690, sess. 8. they decline to send any ministers to Northumberland, *In what cases they send to other churches.*

upon

upon a petition from some in that country, in respect that these people do not belong to this national church.

Churches should send to the Heathens.

§ 7. As it is the constant prayer and hope of the reformed churches, that the kingdom of Christ may and shall be enlarged, by sending the gospel to the rest of the Heathen; so, in testimony of the sincerity of these hopes and prayers, they must be joined with suitable endeavours for spreading the gospel among them. This church hath not that happy opportunity, and invitation of concurring Providence to forward that work that some other churches have, through our want of foreign plantations, and by being injuriously dispossessed of what we had, as the thirty-eight minute of the proceedings in parliament 1701 doth complain.

When a colleague is needful. Aged and sick ministers should have both maintenance and a colleague.

§ 8. When a parish, though not of so great extent as to require a new erection, becometh so numerous, that albeit a minister's voice may easily reach them all, the seats being conveniently placed; yet he is not able alone to discharge the other ministerial duties, with that exactness and ease which pastors of ordinary parishes may do, it is but reasonable, in that case, to join a yoke-fellow with him. By the act of Assembly July 30. 1641, it is declared, That old ministers and professors of divinity, shall not by their cessation from their charge, through age and inability, be put from enjoying their old maintenance and respect. This doth likewise agree with the 48th act, chap. 1. of the French church-discipline; and by the book of policy, chap. 7. when ministers, through age, sickness, or other accidents, become unmeet to do their office, in that case, their honour should ramain to them, their kirk should maintain them, and others ought to be provided to do their office: Thus they still enjoy double honour, viz. reverence and maintenance.

Colleagues must share both office and benefice.

§ 9. When a parish findeth work for two ministers, and they divide the same equally between them, nothing can be reasonably alledged against sharing of their wages from the parish accordingly; except it be said, that he who gets the first call to the greater benefice, will from that take advantage to keep possession thereof: which practice, however it may receive protection from strict law, yet justice, which is mixed with equity and kindness, condemns it, seeing his helper or second is to be always as fit for the same charge as he, as is appointed by Assembly 1646, in the first remedy proposed against the corruptions of the ministry.

§ 10. When he who had the greater stipend (it having been neglected at his entry to oblige him to divide the same equally with his colleague) is now removed by death, or otherwise, then the parish is not obliged to allow the surviving colleague to succeed to and uplift the first stipend, except he be content, and engage to amend his predecessor's manners, which if he refuse to do, at the sight of his callers and the presbytery, then let him only enjoy the stipend to which he was called. But the most effectual way and proper season for obliging colleagues to share their benefices, is thus to be done at their calling and admission: Insert in the call, that as he is to be one of the ministers of such a parish, so he is to have the half of the stipend: and let his ordination and admission act carry that same qualification: But colleagues, of consent, may prevent this. *To which the parish may oblige them, how, and when.*

§ 11. By the act of Assembly December 17. 18. *anno* 1638, one of the ministers, without advice of his colleague, is not to appoint diets of communion nor examination, neither to hinder his colleague from catechizing, (to wit, from house to house), and using other religious exercises, as oft as he pleaseth. But now the kirk-session doth direct as to these diets, for communion especially. *Public ministerial work is to be perform'd by mutual consent, and private diligence not to be hindered.*

§ 12. Colleagues are to apply themselves to doctrine, according to the gifts wherein they most excell, and as they shall agree betwixt themselves; see Directory for preaching the word. *How they are to apply their gifts.*

TITLE IV.

Of Expectants, as also Students and Bursars.

§ 1. THE presbytery is not only to hinder those whom they know to be unfit, from entring upon their trials; but also they are to look out for, and stir up such whose gifts are promising, to submit themselves unto trial, and that albeit the one were a professed student of theology, and the other were not. *Who they are that the presbytery should encourage to enter upon trials.*

§ 2. Before any presbytery invite students to pass their trials, they are to be satisfied as to the soundness of their
principles,

Wherein the presbytery is to be satisfied before they invite students to enter upon trials.

principles, and of their sober, grave, prudent, and pious behaviour. And it is appointed, that such persons shall produce, before the presbyteries who admit them to trials, sufficient testimonials from the ministers of the parishes where they lived, and from the legally established presbyteries in whose bounds they resided, and also from the professors of divinity; see the 10th act of Assembly 1694; as also, by an act of the Assembly thereafter, it is recommended to presbyteries, before any be admitted to trials, that they see their testimonials of their passing their course in philosophy, and their obtaining their degrees of masters of arts in some university. And by the 13th act of Assembly 1696, probationers that apply to presbyteries are not only to bring sufficient testimonials, but also a letter of recommendation from a person known to the presbytery. And by the 5th act of Assembly 1705, testimonials from professors of theology, in favour of such as are to enter upon their trials, are not to be regarded by presbyteries, unless they bear their knowledge of these they recommend to trials, as to their moral and pious carriage, as to their progress in their studies, and their promising parts, and of their good affection to the government of church and state, and fitness to serve the church.

Expectants trials.

§ 3. The trials of a student, in order to his being licensed to preach the gospel, do consist in these parts, 1. the homily, which is a discourse upon some text of holy scripture assigned unto him by the presbytery, and delivered before them in private. 2. The exegesis, which is a discourse in Latin upon some common head of divinity appointed him by the presbytery, and delivered before them, at which time also he gives in the substance of his discourse, comprised in a short thesis or doctrinal proposition in paper, which he is to defend, at the presbytery's next meeting, against two or three ministers who are appointed to impugn his thesis. 3. The presbyterial exercise and addition: the exercise gives the coherence of the text and context, the logical division, and explanation of the words, clearing hard and unusual phrases, if any be, with their true and proper meaning according to the original language, and other parallel places of scripture, proposing and answering any textual questions that occur, and then a plain and short paraphrase upon the text: this is ordinarily the work of one half hour. The addition gives the doctrinal propofitions or truths, which, without ftraining, may be deduced from the text fo explained, with reafons, applications, and pertinent improvement and application, as the other half hour will allow. 4. A lecture, or expofition of a large portion of fcripture, ordinarily a whole chapter. 5. A popular fermon. Thefe three peices of exercife, viz. prefbyterial exercife, lecture, and popular fermon, are to be in the pulpit before the people. 6. He is to be tried in his knowledge of the original languages, by interpreting a portion of the Greek New Teftament, *ad aperturam libri*, and reading and expounding a portion of fome Pfalm in Hebrew. Of his knowledge of facred chronology, ecclefiaftic hiftory, efpecially of our own church, anfwering extemporary queftions, of the meaning of hard places of fcripture, on heads of divinity, polemic or practical, on cafes of confcience, on church-government and difcipline, and is likewife to be tried as to his piety, prudence, and former godly converfation, act of Affembly January 30. 1698.

§ 4. By the 10th act of Affembly 1704, prefbyteries are appointed to lay it on fome of their number to examine the ftudents in their own prefence upon the feveral heads of divinity, and the government of the church, and to know what reafon they can give of their faith, and if they can anfwer to fome principal objections of adverfaries againft it, and that previoufly to all other parts of their trial. From all which it appears, that from the beginning of trials, to the time they are licenfed to preach the gofpel as probationers for the miniftry, they are a full half year exercifed in order thereto, allowing the ordinary meetings for prefbyteries to be once a month. Which time for trials will yet be longer, if we confider the 13th act of Affembly 1708, appointing private trials concerning his fenfe and experience of religion, yet previous to all thefe mentioned. *Some trials are previous to thefe.*

§ 5. By the 3d act of Affembly 1697, the commiffioners from the feveral prefbyteries within this church, are to bring in an account to the General Affembly yearly, of all expectants or probationers for the miniftry. As alfo, of all ftudents who attend leffons of theology in univerfities, and perform the exercifes enjoined them there, that their names may be read in open Affembly, and recorded in their regifter: *Expectants and ftudents names to be recorded in the Affembly books.*

ſter: Which is a mean to bind all candidates for the miniſtry to a circumſpect walk, that the church may receive good impreſſions of them.

Form of an act licenſing one to preach the goſpel, and his teſtimonial, and recommendation.

§ 6. At   the   day of   The which day the preſbytery of   taking to their conſideration, that in obedience to ſeveral acts of General Aſſemblies made anent trials in order to preaching, they had upon the   day of   received ſufficient teſtimonials in favours of Mr A. B ſtudent in divinity, and that thereupon they had appointed ſome of their number to make ſearch and inquiry into the literature and behaviour of him the ſaid Mr A. B. Which brethren having upon the   day of   reported, That according to the appointment foreſaid, they had privately taken trial of his knowledge in divinity, and of what ſenſe and impreſſion he had of religion upon his own ſoul; and that they had cauſe, from what they found in the foreſaid trial, to judge him fit to be received and entered upon public trials, in order to his being licenſed. Whereupon they, the ſaid presbytery, had admitted the ſaid Mr A. B. upon probationary trials, who having, in all the uſual parts thereof, at divers times thereafter, acquitted himſelf to their ſatisfaction and approbation; therefore they did and hereby do LICENSE the ſaid Mr A B to preach the goſpel of Chriſt as a probationer for the miniſtry within their bounds, he having in their preſence undertaken the uſual engagements appointed by the acts of this church. Extracted &c. Nota, theſe engagements are here omitted, *brevitatis cauſa, vide* § *ſeq.* At his removal out of the bounds of the presbytery where he was licenſed, his teſtimonial is in this form. At   the   day of   The which day, the presbytery of   do teſtify and declare, That Mr A. B. preacher of the goſpel, has, ſince his being licenſed by them, preached ſeveral times, both at their appointment, and the deſire of particular brethren within the bounds, to their ſatisfaction; and that his carriage, ſo far as they know, hath ſince that time been pious, exemplary, and edifying, as became a preacher of the goſpel, and that he hath been obſequious to all their appointments; therefore they do by theſe preſents recommend the ſaid Mr A. B. accordingly to any presbytery where God in his providence ſhall caſt his lot, for all due and ſuitable encouragement from them. Extracted, &c.

§ 7.

§ 7. By the 10th act of Assembly 1691, it is appointed, that when persons are first licensed to preach, they shall oblige themselves to preach only within the bounds, or by the direction of that presbytery which did licence them; and they shall also, by promise and supplication, engage themselves, that they shall be subject to the said presbytery, or to any other church-judicature, where in Providence they shall have their abode, and that they shall follow no divisive course; which engagement is to be insert in the body of their licence. Vide lib. 3. tit 8. § 11. *A probationer's engagements when licensed.*

§ 8. By that same act it is appointed, that when they are removing from that presbytery which did licence them, they shall carry with them an extract of their licence, and a testimonial of their carriage, which they are to produce to some presbytery constituted by the legal establishment, or at least to some minister therein, before they preach within that bounds; which minister is not to employ them, except in his own pulpit, till he give notice thereof to the presbytery at their next meeting. And they are then to require the same subjection and orderly carriage from them, during their abode in that bounds, to which they were engaged to the presbytery by which they were licensed. *What presbyteries or parishes a probationer may preach in, and when to renew his engagements.*

§ 9. And in case any probationers shall have their licences suspended or recalled, for error in doctrine or malverse in conversation, then intimation shall be made thereof by the judicature which hath so censured them to the neighbouring judicatures, or where they shall understand the said probationers are, that so none may employ them to preach. *How sentences against them should be intimated.*

§ 10. And, lastly, by the same act it is declared, That probationers are not to be esteemed, by themselves or others, to preach by virtue of any pastoral office, but only to make way for their being called unto a pastoral charge. *They have no pastoral office*

§ 11. It is the laudable practice of some presbyteries, to licence no probationers till they acquaint their neighbouring presbyteries, that such persons are passing their trials before them. And upon a return, that they know nothing that should impede their being licensed, then they proceed. *Before licensing, other presbyteries acquainted.*

§ 12. Every presbytery, consisting of twelve ministers, is appointed to maintain a bursar (that is, one out of the common purse) and where the number is fewer than twelve, they shall be joined to another presbytery. See act of Assembly, Aug. 7. 1641. *Each presbytery must maintain a bursar.*

The quantity, fund, collection, and continuance of a bursar's maintenance.

§ 13. Every burfar muſt have yearly paid him an hundred pounds Scots at leaſt, the fund whereof ought to be the panalties exacted of delinquents, and fcandalous perſons, by the civil magiſtrate, and by him delivered to the kirk-feſſions. But if that fail, then the kirk-boxes in theſe preſbyteries are to be proportionally ſtinted by them, according to the number of communicants in each pariſh; which maintenance of an hundred pounds is to be collected by the moderator, of the which the ſeveral ſynods are to take account, and their books are to bear the report thereof to the General Aſſembly. It is alſo appointed, that the abode of burfars at fchools of divinity exceed not four years. Vide act of Aſſembly, Feb. 7. 1645.

Qualifications of burſars, and how they are to be tried.

§ 14. By the ſame act, burſars of theology are appointed to bring with them yearly from the univerſities, teſtimonials of their good behaviour and proficiency: and that none be chofen for burfars by presbyteries, but ſuch as are of good report, and have paſt their courſe of philoſophy; and their qualifications are to be tried likewife before they go to univerſities, conform to acts of Aſſemblies 1647, 48, and 49. And by the 5th act of Aſſembly 1705, it is ordained, that in no pariſh the miniſter recommend youth to be taught in Latin upon charity in any grammar-ſchool, but ſuch as be dexterous in reading, and can write, and ſuch as he judges to be of virtuous inclinations; which trial is to be in preſence of ſome elders, and no ſchoolmaſters are to teach any upon charity, but upon ſuch recommendations. Item, it is ordained that preſbyteries appoint a committee of their number yearly to examine poor ſcholars in grammar-ſchools, that ſo none of them be ſuffered to proceed to colleges, with an eye to burſaries, but ſuch as are of good behaviour, and proficients in the Latin: and miniſters are to recommend none to burſaries not ſo qualified: and maſters of colleges are to lauriate no burſars, but upon clear evidence of ſufficient learning and good behaviour, after ſtrict examination.

Poor ſtudents tho' not burſars, are to be inſpected by preſbyteries.

§ 15. For the better breeding of young men to the miniſtry, who are not able to maintain themſelves at univerſities, (nor perhaps find that favour as to get burſaries), preſbyteries where ſuch reſide are appointed to direct their ſtudies. Act June 18. Aſſem. 1646.

§ 16.

§ 16. In order to the advancement and increafe of the knowledge of God in the highlands, by the act of Affembly 1701, it is recommended to feveral fynods to maintain a burfar of theology, having the Irifh language, out of their own purfes. And by the 13th act of Affembly 1704, in refpect the lowland presbyteries be-fouth Tay are competently planted, and that the promoting of knowledge in the highlands is of common concern, therefore it is appointed, that the one half of all burfaries of the presbyteries be-fouth Tay be beftowed on ftudents having the Irifh, at leaft the half thereof: which act is to continue at leaft for four years, and longer, if there fhall be found need. And by the 5th act of Affembly 1707, contributions, and erecting of focieties for the maintenance of poor fcholars, are to be encouraged by judicatures, and the commiffions of Affemblies. *Burfars having the Irifh language encouraged.*

§ 17 By the act of Affembly February 7. 1645, it is appointed, that notwithftanding of any progrefs any may pretend to have made privately in their ftudies, yet in the college they fhall not at firft enter to any higher clafs than that wherein the Greek language is taught; and being entered, they fhall proceed orderly through the reft of the claffes, untill they finifh the ordinary courfe of four years; and otherwife, that none be admitted to the degree of mafter of arts, unlefs the faculty of arts find him to be of extraordinary learning. *None muft leap over the Greek clafs, but finifh the four years courfe before degrees.*

§ 18. By that fame act it is appointed, that none be allowed to enter the Greek clafs, but fuch who are found can make congruous themes in Latin, and are not to be promoted to an higher clafs, till it be found that they underftand what was taught them in the lower. The annual examination of ftudents at the firft fitting down of colleges, looketh as if fomething like this were intended: but the beft effects that fuch examinations do ordinarily now produce, may be the doing of juftice upon fome poor ignorant ftudents, in keeping them back from advancing to higher claffes: and as for the reft who pay the mafters their ordinary dues, they are only thereby excited to be at more than ordinary pains for fome few days. It is a piece of juftice done to the world, that thofe who are to gain and live by their learning, fhould not, under that pretence, be fuffered to impofe upon men by ignorance or craft; for what *Nor doth any advance to an higher clafs, till his profiting in the lower does appear.*

what a great deal of hurt are immoral, ignorant, crafty, and idle scholars, capable to work in their generations? Let them be directed and obliged to serve their time in some honest vocation, where the want of so much knowledge cannot do so great prejudice; otherwise, it is highly reasonable they should study to have accomplishments, and a conversation suitable to the profession and character they bear in the world

Such as remove to other colleges, must carry testimonials with them.

§ 19. By that same act, none who have entered to one college should be admitted to any class in another, than that wherein he was, or should have been in the college from whence he came; nor be admitted without testimonials from the former masters, both concerning his literature and dutiful behaviour, that so these who have been rejected or removed as unworthy or ignorant by one college, may not be admitted or promoted in another. And

Who are to be employed by professors in theological exercises.

in order to the better education of young men for the ministry, by the 22d act of Assembly 1696, it is recommended to professors of divinity, that they require of such students, as they employ in any exercises, testimonials from universities where they have studied, and the places where they have lived.

Universities must instruct on the Sabbath-day.

§ 20. By the act of Assembly August *ult.* 1647, it is recommended to universities to take an account of all their scholars on the Sabbath-day, of the sermons, and of their lessons on the catechism.

TITLE V.

Of Schoolmasters, and Instructors of Youth.

Qualifications of such as bear office in schools by acts of parliament and Assembly.

§ 1. BY the 17th act of King Will. and Queen Mary's parliament, it is ordained, That no professors, principals, regents, masters, or others, bearing office in any university, college, or school, within this kingdom, be either admitted or allowed to continue in the exercise of their said functions, but such as do acknowledge and profess, and shall subscribe the Confession of Faith, and swear the oath of allegiance, (and now they must subscribe the same, with the assurance, *vide* act 6. parl. 1693.), and withal shall be found of a pious, loyal, and peaceable conversation, and of good and sufficient literature and abilities for their

respective

respective employments, and submitting unto the government of the church now settled by law. And by the 10th act of Assembly 1700, all presbyteries are appointed to take special, particular, and exact notice of all schoolmasters, chaplains, governors, and pedagogues of youth within their respective bounds, and oblige them to subscribe the Confession of Faith; and in case of continued negligence, (after admonition), error, or immorality, or not being careful to educate these under their charge in the Protestant Reformed Religion, the presbytery, with respect to schoolmasters, is to apply to the civil magistrates of burghs, and heritors in land-ward; and with respect to governors, chaplains, and pedagogues, to their masters, for removing such persons from these offices: and if this be not remedied by them, that the presbytery, with respect to schoolmasters, apply to the commission of parliament for visitation of schools and colleges: And it is appointed, that an account be given in every half year to the presbytery, by ministers, what schoolmasters, chaplains, governors, and pedagogues, are in their respective parishes And by the 15th act of Assembly 1706, such as have power of settling schoolmasters, are to prefer thereto men who have past their course at colleges, and have taken their degrees, before others who have not, *cæteris paribus.*

§ 2. By the act of Assembly, December 17. 18. 1638, presbyteries are to see that schools in land-ward parishes be settled with able men, for the charge of teaching the youth public reading, and precenting of the psalm, and the catechising of the common people. Which teaching of the youth I understand to be teaching to read, write, and know the principles of religion, according to the act of Assembly August 3. 1642; and by that same act, every presbytery seat and burgh is to have a grammar-school. *The work of a land-ward schoolmaster.*

TITLE VI.

Of Doctors, and Professors of Theology.

The sentiments of this church about the doctor's office. He is no pastor as such.

§ 1. According to the fifth chapter of the Policy of the Kirk, in the General Assembly 1581, the office of the doctor or catechiser, is one of the two ordinary and perpetual functions that travel in the Word. He is to open up the mind of the Spirit of God simply, without such applications as the ministers use. They are such properly who teach in schools, colleges, or universities: But to preach unto the people, to administer the sacraments, and to celebrate marriage, do not pertain to him, except he be called and ordained thereto. If the pastor be qualified for it, he may perform all the parts of the doctor's office, that being included in the pastoral. By the 2d article, chap. 11. of the Discipline of the French church, a doctor in the church cannot preach nor administer the sacraments, unless he be both doctor and minister. And when the General Assembly, February 10. 1645, ratifies the propositions sent to them from the Assembly of Divines at Westminster, concerning church-government, and ordination of ministers, they expresly provide, that the present ratification shall be noways prejudicial to the further discussion and examination of one of the articles or propositions, which holds forth, that the doctor or teacher hath power of the administration of sacraments, as well as the pastor.

Catechists, or doctors, should teach in colleges and in large parishes.

§ 2. Though the office of a deacon is included in the office of a ruling elder, yet it is fit that some be appointed deacons, distinct from that of the elder; so, albeit the office of a doctor be included in that of the pastor, yet it were very fit that some not in the sacred order of the ministry were ordained and set apart to teach and catechise the people, especially in large and incommodious parishes, (See § 3. of the preceeding title,) as well as in schools and colleges.

Synods are to report to the Assembly the names of scholars fit to be professors.

§ 3. By the act of Assembly February 13. 1645, for encouragement to scholars for professions in schools, it is recommended to synods, to try who within their bounds most probably may be for a profession in the schools, and report their names to the General Assembly, that they may be ſtirred up, and encouraged by them to frame their ſtudies for ſuch places. This cumulative power doth noways prejudge or hinder the faculty of an univerſity (which hath power and right to elect) from doing of the ſame. It were to be wiſhed, that this cuſtom of ſynods, reporting to General Aſſemblies the names of ſuch as are fit to be profeſſors, were again revived, and more exactly practiſed; for it would prevent the tranſporting of miniſters to be only teachers or maſters in univerſities, which is an appointing of him to exerciſe the office of a doctor, and diſpenſing with him from preaching of the word, and adminiſtrating of the ſacraments: Which diſpenſation, or the looſing of which tie, if it be a favour, it can never be impoſed upon any paſtor without his own conſent: but if it be a puniſhment, it can be inflicted upon none without their fault. It is liker a commutation of offices than a tranſportation: or if he ſtill continue to be a paſtor, his paſtoral talent is thereby but much hid in a napkin. By the 3d article, 2d chap. of the French church-diſcipline, doctors and profeſſors of divinity ſhall be elected and tried by the ſynods of the province where the academies are.

No paſtor can be compelled to give himſelf to teaching and leave his paſtoral charge.

§ 4. By the 5th chap. of the Policy of the kirk of Scotland, the doctor, being an elder, is to aſſiſt the paſtor in the government of the kirk. And by the act of Aſſembly Auguſt 4. 1643, profeſſors of theology cannot be elected commiſſioners to General Aſſemblies, except they be miniſters; ſo that, as doctors, they are not ruling elders, and the Aſſembly conſiſts of none but paſtors and elders: therefore, as doctors, they cannot be members of church judicatures for government and ruling; ſee §. 1. huj. tit.

The doctor as ſuch no ruling elder, nor as meer doctor, can be member of Aſſemblies.

§. 5. By the act of Aſſembly June 18. 1646, profeſſors of divinity are deſired to preſent their dictates to the next General Aſſembly; but they declined at that time to make any act about it for the future, till further conſideration.

Profeſſors dictates may be reviewed by General Aſſemblies.

TITLE VII.

Of Ruling Elders.

Why called ruling elder.

§ 1. HE is called a ruling elder, because to rule and govern the church is the chief part of his charge and employment therein; and albeit he may act as a deacon, yet his principal business is to rule well, and it belongs not to him to preach or teach.

Election of elders.

§ 2. If there be a total vacancy of ministers and elders in a parish, the presbytery should intimate to the heads of families, to meet with some of their number on an appointed day, and then name elders. But if the masters of families do not keep the appointment, then the presbytery are to nominate and chuse the persons to be elders. In case the vacancy be not total, then the minister and elders do chuse such as should be added to their own number from among the heads of families, and the fittest and most experienced of them may be supposed to be among the deacons; see Assembly August 1. 1642.

Their trial.

§ 3. The trial is to be by the minister and eldership of the congregation; or, in case of the want of these, by the presbytery; and they are to be tried both with respect to their conversation, and also of their knowledge in the principles of religion, and their ability and prudence for government.

Serving of their edict.

§ 4. Before ordination of elders, the names of the persons nominated and tried in order thereto, are to be publicly intimate to the congregation; whereby all are required, in case of their having any objection that is relevant and true against their ordination, to represent the same to the kirk-session.

Ordination of elders.

§ 5. Their ordination is to be by the minister of the congregation; or by one from the presbytery, in the case above supposed, in presence of the congregation, upon a Lord's day after sermon is ended in the forenoon: at which time, the minister calling upon the persons chosen to be elders, they are to be interrogate concerning their orthodoxy, and to be taken solemnly engaged, to adhere to, and maintain the doctrine, worship, discipline, and government of the

the church, and to lay themselves furth, by their office and example, to suppress vice, cherish piety, and exerce discipline faithfully and diligently. Then the elders chosen, still standing up, the minister is next, by solemn prayer, to set them apart, *in verbis de præsenti*. After prayer the minister is to exhort both elders and people to their respective duties.

§ 6. In case an elder change his residence, by removing into another congregation, if the session, upon a savory report concerning him, shall think fit to add him to their number; then, if he be content to accept, his edict is to be served, and he is thereafter admitted into the session; his qualifications having been tried already in the congregation where he was ordained. *Their admission.*

§ 7. As the pastors and doctors should be diligent in teaching, and sowing the word of God, so the elders should be careful, in seeking after the fruit thereof among peoples lives. They are to assist the pastor in the examination of them that come to the Lord's table, and in visiting the sick: They should cause the acts of Assemblies to be obeyed: They should be diligent in admonishing all men of their duty, according to the rules of the Evangel. And things that they cannot correct by private admonition, they should bring to the eldership. See the Heads of the Policy of the Kirk. *Duties of elders more private.*

§ 8. By the ecclesiastic remedies against profaneness, enacted in the Assembly August 10. 1648, it is appointed, that every elder have a certain bounds assigned him, that he may visit the same, every month at least, and to report to the session what scandals and abuses are therein, or what persons have entered without testimonials: and it were fit, that then some time were set apart for prayer: and it were also fit that elders should always keep an exact list of all examinable persons within their quarters, and thereunto put marks, to distinguish communicants from the ignorant and scandalous, and the poor and indigent from such as need not. *They have particular bounds of the parish (called quarters in Scotland) assigned them to visit monthly, and report*

§ 9. The duties of elders which are more public are these which lie upon them in the Assemblies of the church; in which ruling elders have right to reason and vote in all matters coming before them, even as ministers have: for to General Assemblies, their commissions bear them to the same *Their more public duties yet restricted.*

same power with pastors. Howbeit, by the practice of our church, the execution of some decrees of the church doth belong to the pastors only; such as, the imposition of hands, the pronouncing the sentences of excommunication and absolution, the receiving of penitents, the intimation of sentences and censures about ministers, and such like. In short, the elder is to speak nothing to the church from the pulpit.

<small>Number of elders, and their continuance.</small>

§ 10. The number of elders in every congregation is to be more or less, according to the number of people therein, and plenty of fit and qualified persons for that charge; and when they are once lawfully called to the office, they may not leave it again, while their gifts and abilities for discharging the same do continue. Albeit in some congregations, such a number of elders may be chosen, so as one part of them may relieve another for a reasonable time, from the burden and exercise of their office, as was done among the *Levites* under the law. See the book of Policy, chap. 6.

TITLE VIII.
Of Deacons.

<small>How the word deacon is taken: the office described. The session censurable that wants them.</small>

§ 1. THE word Deacon is sometimes largely taken for all that bear office in the ministry, and spiritual function in the church: but commonly it is taken for that ordinary and perpetual ecclesiastical office in the kirk of Christ, to whom the collection and distribution of the alms of the faithful, and ecclesiastical goods do belong. See chap. 8. of the Policy of the kirk: Where it follows, that, seeing this office is of divine institution, it is an unwarrantable omission in some congregations, that either they put no difference betwixt elders and deacons, or else they neglect to appoint any to the office of a deacon. See tit. 6. § 2. I do not think it reasonable or very consistent, for any to be zealous against adding to the kinds of officebearers of Christ's appointment, while they are active in or connive at the diminution of any of them. If it be said, the elder is a deacon, I answer, albeit the pastor includes the office of doctor, elder, and deacon, yet seeing these are of divine institution, reverence is in so far due unto it

as

as to set up these distinct offices: as nothing should be added to the divine institution, upon pretence of imagined decency or order in the invention, so nothing ought to be diminished therefrom, upon pretence that some things in the institution are needless or superfluous.

§ 2. As to what respects the election, trial, ordination, admission, continuance, and number of deacons, the same method may be used about them, as was done concerning elders, *mutatis mutandis*. {*Their election, &c. the same with elders.*}

§ 3. The duties of deacons may be reduced to these heads collected from Mr Guthrie's treatise of elders and deacons, and the heads of the Policy of the kirk. {*Duties of deacons.*} 1. That they take exact notice of the poor, and that they timeously make their case known to the session, to the end their straits may be relieved, and so their breaking out into begging may be prevented. 2. They are to collect and receive that supply for the poor, which the members of that congregation, or strangers, shall be inclined to offer. 3. That the money so received be faithfully delivered to the session, according to whose judgement and appointment the deacons are to distribute the church-goods. In which matters they have a decisive vote with the elders: but in other cases their opinion is only consultative, and they may be always present. 4. That they take care of orphans and idiots, and such as want knowledge and ability to dispose of, and order the things that concern their food and raiment. 5. They are to take care that what belongs to the poor be not dilapidated, or misapplied. 6. They are to acquaint the ministers and elders of the sick within their quarters, that so they may be visited, and, if need be, supplied. 7. By the 9th chapter of the Policy of the kirk, deacons were not only to collect and distribute the ordinary alms, but all the church-goods, teinds, &c. and uplift and pay to the ministers their stipends. This were indeed a work proper for their office, an ease to the minister, and would prevent much noise and offence that is raised when charges to make payment are given, either at their own instance, or in name of their assignees or factors. 8. They may be employed to provide the elements, to carry them, and serve the communicants at the Lord's table.

TITLE

TITLE IX.

Of Moderators of Church-judicatures.

<small>It is convenient the moderator be a minister. His work and power.</small>

§ 1. SEeing the moderator is frequently called to exercise the power of order, as solemn public ecclesiastic prayer, at least twice every session, to wit, at its first opening, and then at its closing, authoritative exhortation, rebuke, direction, it is convenient the moderator be always a minister: But if any affect this office, he should be opposed in his ambitious purposes. The person chosen to be a moderator should be of such abilities that he can discharge the following work, viz. He is to look on himself as the mouth of the meeting; he is to take on him authority, yet looking on it as theirs, not his; he is to see all the rules for decency and order, prescribed by the judicature, exactly kept and observed; he is to acquaint the judicature of all the affairs that lie before them, and may propose the most speedy method how to dispatch them; he is to keep the members from interrupting one another, and from speaking among themselves, or from directing their discourse to any other than to himself; he should likewise keep members, in their speaking, close to the present business; any thing that is spoken impertinently, he is calmly to resent it, according to its demerit, that greater heats may be prevented and diverted; lastly, after the matter hath been fully reasoned on all hands, then he is briefly to resume the substance of what hath been spoke, and thereupon state the vote, and put the question. If the vote be equally carried, then the moderator, (who never votes but in that case) may cast it: and if he be *non liquet*, then the question may be put again at some other time. The moderator may likewise, upon any extraordinary emergency, by his circular letters, convene presbyteries and synods, before their ordinary time of meeting: So may the moderator of the last General Assembly, only they should be sure to have sufficient ground, and so cautious, as to have a multitude of counsellors to warrant and support their adventure.

<small>No assessors to our moderators.</small>

§ 2. Our judicatures chuse no assessors to their moderators, only he ordinarily prevails with, or invites the most experienced to sit near him, that he may have them ready to direct and advise him; and, in absence of the present moderator, his predecessor in that chair moderates; and, in case of his absence, the eldest minister.

§ 3. There is no constant moderator but in kirk-sessions, where the minister moderates *ex officio*; and if there be colleagues, they moderate by turns. Every presbytery, before they fall about business, chuse one of their brethren to be moderator, who continues for six months, from one provincial synod to another; but the moderators of synods and assemblies are changed at every new synod and assembly. The manner of chusing the moderators of these judicatures is thus: A list is proposed by the former moderator of two or three; which list is ordinarily approved, with the addition of one or two more; out of which list, the candidates having first, by turns, given their voice, and removed, the moderator is chosen by the suffrages of the ministers and elders, and set in the place of the former moderator.

No constant moderator, but in kirk-sessions. The manner of their election.

§ 4. It is the privilege of all the members of any free judicature, to propose a vote, and have it put to the question, provided it be seconded by another member, and that although both the moderator and other members should oppose the motion.

The privilege of members.

TITLE X.

Of Clerks, Readers, and Precentors.

§ 1. Every judicature of the church is to have a clerk of their own chusing, to record their acts. They are, I think, as free courts as any councils of royal burghs, on whom the imposing a clerk is declared to have been contrary to law, by the meeting of estates 1689. At his admission, he is to give his oath *de fideli*, and continues either during pleasure or life, as they please to make it: But in case neither of these be clearly expressed in his act of admission, then it is to be understood only during pleasure, because all judicatures are still supposed to retain their liberty to dismiss servants when they will, unless a surrender or restriction of that liberty be proven.

A clerk, his election, admission, and continuance.

§ 2. Acts

How far extracts are probative.	§ 2. Acts and deeds under clerks hands are probative writs, and the warrants thereof are presumed; yet so, as if they be recently quarrelled, the warrants must be produced. No wise clerk will give an extract till the minutes of that diet have first been read. The extracts prove what was done by the judge, or what was said or alledged by parties, but they do not prove that the things alledged were true, except in so far as the instructions thereof are expressed. See Stair's Institut. page 688.
A clerk is not to be declined.	§ 3. Albeit clerks be very near of kin to parties, yet considering the knowledge and faithfulness, that in charity is supposed to be in church-judicatures, it may be thought that they will rather over-rule their clerk, than he them; and therefore he cannot be declined. In inferior civil courts, where frequently there is but one judge, and it is known the clerk doth commonly excel him in knowledge, in which case a declinator should be sustained, and another appointed to be clerk to that process in his place, who is not of near kin to the party.
The first rise of readers. They are now ceased.	§ 4. At the beginning of the Reformation, when there was such a scarcity of ministers, and few of the people could either read themselves, or had ever heard the word of God publicly read in their own language; our reformers, in the year 1605, did appoint men to read the Common Prayers and Scriptures, till these churches should be furnished with ministers: but now, seeing there is such an increase of knowledge, and plenty of teachers, there is no public reading of the word, except by such as are licensed, or ordained to preach it, and can help the hearers to understand the meaning thereof.
Precentors, their office.	§ 5. Precentors, or chanters, are they who begin and order the tune of the psalm that is to be sung, and thereby direct the church's music: By the vulgar sort they are yet called readers, though improperly. They are in most congregations clerks to the kirk-sessions; see book II. tit. 1. § 25.
Beddals, their office and qualifications.	§ 6. Beddals, or beedles, are by our judicatures called officers. They are to the church what the *apparitores* were to civil courts, viz. *magistratum ministri, qui eorum jussa exequuntur,* so called, *quia præsto sunt, obsequunturque magistratibus.* At their admission they give their oath *de fideli,* because their executions bear faith. They should be

be persons of a blameless life, and were affected to the church establishment, who will not discover the secrets of the judicature; and they should also be such as can read and write.

TITLE XI.

Of Kirk-sessions.

§. 1. ALbeit in a session the minister is moderator *ex officio*, as hath been said, yet he hath by right no more power thereby than the moderators of other church-judicatures. See the act of the General Assembly December 17. 1638, anent voting in kirk-sessions; ministers moderating therein are not to usurp a negative voice over the members of his session; and where there are two or more ministers in one congregation, that they have equal power in voting, that one of them hinder not the reasoning or voting of any thing, being agreeable to the acts and practice of the kirk; and, even in that case, voting and reasoning upon any subject can never be hindered, it being inconsistent with the liberty of a free court to be impeded or compelled: But the debate may perhaps furnish ground for a protestation or appeal. See tit. 8. § 6.

No minister must usurp over the session.

§ 2. The kirk-session consists of one or more ministers, and of the elders of the congregation; and it is most convenient they meet weekly, on a week-day, after sermon; for, on the Sabbath, matters of civil right, such as discharging of the almoner's intromissions, securing of money, or ordering of diligence for recovering the same, ought not to be treated or concerted by any man, and far less by church-guides, whose office it is to check that profanity in others. The deacons are always present, not for discipline, but for what relates to their own office. Ignorant and scandalous persons are to be put off, and kept off from kirk-sessions. See act of Assembly, August 10. 1648.

Constituents of a session, and time of their meeting.

§ 3. The matters treated by them, are what concern church-discipline, and the worship of God in that congregation, as, what days of the week are meetest for assembling to public worship, and what hour on the Lord's day before and after noon; when it is seasonable for parochial fasts and thanksgivings; what times are fittest for catechi-

Matters treated by them.

sing and visiting of families; how often, and when the Lord's supper is to be celebrated. They are likeways to inquire into the knowledge and spiritual state of the members of the congregation, whom they are to admonish or encourage as they see cause, and to exclude from the Lord's table all who are found ignorant or scandalous.

According to what rule.

§ 4. In the ordering of all which matters, nothing is to be done by them, but what is according to the settled order and practice of this church: and if there be any new or difficult emergency that causeth doubting or hesitation, the matter is to be referred to the presbytery, for their direction and authority.

Secret confessions not to be propaled, except in what cases.

§ 5. By the 5th chap. 28th and 30th articles of the French church-discipline, consistories shall not give certificates to magistrates by act or otherwise, nor shall particular members of consistories discover unto any the confessions of penitents, which voluntarily, or by admonitions given them, shall have confessed their faults unto them, except it be in the case of treason. And as for crimes which shall be disclosed to ministers by those who desire counsel and consolation, they are injoined not to reveal them to magistrates, fearing least blame should be drawn on the ministry, and sinners for the future should be discouraged to come to repentance, and make confession of their faults, which shall stand good in all crimes confessed, except it be treason. It should be considered that none of the reformed churches of France had the happiness always to have those of their own religion to be their constant judges; and the reputation of the Protestant religion was not tenderly treated, nor duly regarded, when consistorial delations against their brethren were made to Popish judges, 1 Cor. vi. 1. "Dare any of you, having a matter against " another, go to law before the unjust, and not before the " saints?" in these times, when the church's enemies have power and authority: But now, when the civil judges own the same way of God with the church, what should hinder them to inform the magistrate against delinquents, both to their and others terror.

Privy censure in sessions and how to be managed.

§ 6. In every session there ought to be twice in the year privy censures of the members, clerk, and beddal. The ministers undergoing their privy censures in the presbytery, are not to undergo them before the session. In the managing

naging of this censure, the members are one after another to be removed, and then the rest of the members declare what they have observed concerning the conversation of him removed, and of his diligence and prudence in his station. It is to be remembered by all church-judicatures, at their privy censures, that no member judicially delate another, unless secret satisfaction hath been sought and refused. After elders, deacons, clerk, and beddal, have past their censure, each of them, as they are called in, is either to be admonished before all, or others impowered to do it privately; or else they are to be encouraged as need requireth.

§ 7. By the act of Assembly August 19. 1639, the books of kirk-sessions are to be presented once a year to the presbytery, that they may be tried by them; or when there is a visitation of the parish by the presbytery. Assembly August 10. 1648. *Session-books to be tried by the presbytery yearly.*

§ 8. By the act of Assembly February 12. 1645, it is recommended to every kirk-session, to buy the printed acts of the Assembly, and presbyteries are ordained to crave account thereof, and synods are to crave account from presbyteries. And it is added to this act, by the 18th of the Assembly 1705, that the agent for the kirk in all time coming, after every Assembly, so soon as the acts thereof shall be printed, transmit as many copies of the same to every presbytery as there be parishes therein, and both presbyteries and sessions are ordained, at their first meeting after receiving the said acts, to cause read so many of them as are of public concern, in order to their observing thereof; and all this to be upon the charges of the several presbyteries and sessions. *Each session is to have the acts of Assembly read, and to observe them.*

§ 9. By the 4th article of the 5th chapter of the French church-discipline, it shall not be permitted to establish other council for any church-business whatsoever; and if in any other church, there shall any other council be established different from the consistory, it shall forthwith be suppressed: Nevertheless, the consistory may sometimes call to its aid such of the church as shall be thought convenient, and that the ecclesiastical matters be treated of only in the place where the consistory doth assemble. They have lately erected in England societies for reformation of manners, not without some seeming success against vice and immorality, *The kirk-session is sufficient alone for reformation of manners in a parish, having the magistrates concurrence.*

morality, which is commendable and requisite there, until the discipline and government of their church be more pure, and better reformed: But for the church of Scotland, as now established, to imitate that example, beside that it might become an introduction to innovations, it would resemble a vain youth's bringing wide-sleeved coats in fashion, because some persons of quality, who had a distemper in their arms, were necessitated to cause make them wide for their own ease. The author of the Stage condemned, page 45. proves stage-plays to be condemned in scripture by this argument, that which God hath appointed sufficient means to accomplish, it is unlawful for men to appoint other means to accomplish it. But God hath appointed sufficient means for recommending virtue and discountenancing vice, without the stage: *Ergo*, it is unlawful for men to appoint the stage for recommending virtue and discountenancing vice. And the same argument, *mutatis mutandis*, militates against these new lay-societies for reformation of manners in the church.

TITLE XII.

Of Presbyteries.

The constituents of a presbytery, their quorum, and time of meeting.

§ 1. THis judicature consists of all the pastors within the bounds, and one ruling elder from each parish therein, who receives a commission from the eldership to be a member of the presbytery, and represent them there till the next synod be over: Thus twice a year there are new elections of the ruling elders. The number of parishes associated in presbyteries, for their mutual help, is determined by authority of the national synod, December 1°. 18. 1638, article 8. as the adjacency of the congregations, and the easiness of travelling doth best allow. Where there are collegiate ministers, that session may send as many ruling elders. The directory for government saith, That to perform any classical act of government or ordination, there shall be present, at least, a major part of the ministers of the whole *classis*. Presbyteries should meet every third week, and oftner, if business require it: But of this see § 3. of this title.

§ 2. Every

§ 2. Every meeting of a presbytery is to begin with a **Presbyterial exercises and common head** sermon by one of the brethren appointed formerly for that effect, upon a text assigned him by them, except when probationers or intrants supply the pulpit in their public trials. The half of the time allowed for this presbyterial exercise is to be taken up in the explicatory and analytic part of the text, and in answering textual and critical questions and difficulties; this part of the work is called *making*, and requires more especially the gift of the doctor. The other half of the time allowed is to be taken up in raising of doctrines and observations from the text, and applying them in their several uses; which last part is called *adding*, and it requires more especially the gift, and necessarily the authority of the pastor. After the exercise is over, and the presbytery constitute, the censure of the exercise they have heard useth always to be their first work, which may be done before them who had the exercise. Beside this, the brethren of the presbytery, by the act of Assembly December 17. 18. 1638, are to have some common head of doctrine publicly disputed in the presbytery among the brethren, every first presbytery of the month, according to the act of Assembly holden at Dundee 1598, sess. 12.

§ 3. By the foresaid act 1638, presbyterial meetings are **Absents to be censured.** to be weekly, except in places far distant, who, between the 1st of October and 1st of April, are dispensed with for meeting once in the fourteen days. See § 1. tit. 12. Likewise that act appoints all absents to be censured, especially those that should exercise and add, according to the act of Assembly April 24. 1582.

§ 4. The presbytery treats of such matters as concern **Matters treated of in presbyteries.** the particular churches within their bounds, as the examination, admission, ordination, and censuring of ministers; the licensing of probationers, rebuking of gross or contumacious sinners; the directing of the censure of excommunication; the cognoscing upon references and appeals from kirk-sessions; the revising and rectifying what hath been ill done or negligently omitted by them, at their approving of the kirk-session books and records; the answering of questions, cases of conscience, and solving of difficulties in doctrine or discipline, with petitions from their own or those in other presbyteries; the examining and censuring according

cording to the word of God, any erroneous doctrine, which hath been publickly or more privately vented within their bounds, and the endeavouring the reducing and conversion of any that remain in error and schism; the appointing of visitation of churches by themselves as occasion offers, or the perambulation of parishes, in order to their uniting or disjoining; all which are either concluded or continued to further consideration, or referred to the synod.

Processes that begin, but cannot be determined by the session, but referred to the presbytery, as the judges competent.

§ 5. By chap. 6. act 11. of Assembly 1707, there are some processes which natively begin at the kirk-session, but for the atrocity of the scandal, or difficulty in the affair, or general concern, the session having frequent meetings of the presbytery to have recourse unto, do not determine of themselves; such as, scandals of incest, adultery, trilapse in fornication, murder, atheism, idolatry, witchcraft, charming, heresy and error vented and made public by any in the congregation, schism and separation from the public ordinances, processes in order to the highest censure, and continued contumacy. But processes for all such crimes and scandals, are to be referred to the presbytery, by an extract of their procedure thereanent. And when there is no confession of the scandals above-mentioned, the session is not so much as to proceed to lead probation by witnesses or presumptions, till they be authorized thereto by the presbytery's answer to their reference foresaid.

When the session may cite a person to the presbytery.

§ 6. When the process is so clear, as in the case of a judicial confession, then the kirk-session may summon the delinquent, when before them *apud acta*, to compear before the presbytery: but where there is any difficulty, they should first inform the presbytery, and get their allowance before the party be summoned before them.

Sessions cannot absolve from such scandals without the presbytery.

§ 7. When persons censured for these grosser scandals do apply to the kirk-session for relaxation, they may both be privately conferred with, and likewise their acknowledgements heard before the session, but they ought not to be brought before the congregation, in order to their absolution, nor absolved but by direction and order of the presbytery.

Correspondence of presbyteries.

§ 8. Presbyteries in some cases may send commissioners to other presbyteries, either to advise them, or to seek advice from them. By act of Assembly June 18. 1646, it

is

is recommended, that a correspondence be kept among presbyteries constantly by letters, whereby they may be mutually assisting to each other.

§ 9. In every presbytery, at least twice a year, on days for prayer, as should be done in sessions likewise, before each synod, there ought to be privy censures, whereby each minister is removed by course, and then inquiry is made at the pastors and elders, if there be any known scandal, fault, or negligence in him, that it may be in a brotherly manner censured; after the ministers, the presbytery clerk is to pass these censures likewise. By the 6th article of the 7th chapter of the French church discipline, at the end of the colloquies, amicable and brotherly censures shall be made, as well by the pastors as by the elders, which shall be there present, of all things which shall be thought fit to be represented unto them.

<small>Privycensures in presbyteries, their season upon days of prayer.</small>

TITLE XIII.

Of Parochial Visitations by the Presbytery.

§ 1. PArishes are visited by presbyteries, either occasionally, *pro re nata*, according to the weight of the emergent which doth require the visitation, or ordinarily and in course, whereby every congregational church is visited once a year, Assem. 1638. sess. 23. 24. art. 3. at least, this ordinary visitation should be going round all the parishes in order till they be visited, before others be revisited in ordinary; for by the 16th act of Assembly 1706, presbyterial visitations of parishes are to be frequent.

<small>Visitations occasional or ordinary.</small>

§ 2. The presbytery is to cause intimation to be made of their appointed day for the visitation of that parish, by a brother of another congregation, from the pulpit, immediately after the forenoon's sermon, on the Sabbath, ten days preceding the day for the visitation, requiring the minister of the parish to preach at that time and place on his ordinary text, and summoning the heritors, elders, and whole congregation, to be present that day, to hear sermon; and thereafter, that the minister, heritors, elders, and heads of families, do attend the presbytery, to acquaint them with the state of that kirk and congregation in every point; and if any of them have certain knowledge of any thing

<small>How the day for the visitation is to be intimated.</small>

thing amiss in their minister, elders, deacons, precenter, session-clerk, schoolmaster, or beddal, that they do then acquaint the presbytery therewith.

The minister's library, and session register, to be seen and revised.

§ 3. The session registers, together with a catalogue of the minister's books, are to be produced to the presbytery, before the visitation, and given to two of the fittest brethren, and best acquainted with that minister and people, to be seen and revised; and they to report at the visitation.

Preliminaries to the visitation; and how the elders are to be interrogate.

§ 4. Sermon being ended, and the presbytery constituted, the minister's doctrine he had in his sermon, is first to be considered, as in the presbyterial exercise, then the church Bible, Confession of Faith, Acts of the General Assemblies, acts and proclamations against profaneness, and other acts and papers relative to the church, are all to be called for and produced before the presbytery. The visitors of the session's registers, and minister's liberary, are to make their report. The presbytery, at the entry on the visitation, having removed the minister, are to cause read over their actings at the last visitation, and see if what was then recommended or ordered hath been made effectual, and take the excuses of absent elders and deacons therefrom; and, if need be, to call in any party for information. If nothing arise from that, to divert the presbytery from the orderly method, all parties being removed, the presbytery is to call in the session one by one, and to enquire them concerning their minister: yea further, by the act of Assembly June 13. 1646, at visitation of kirks, the elders, one by one, the rest being removed, are to be called in, and examined upon oath concerning the minister's behaviour.

Ministers families to be interrogate concerning their lives.

§ 5. By the act of Assembly 1596, ratified December 17. 18. 1638, at visitation of kirks, the families of ministers are to give an account, and to be tried concerning the good order and behaviour that they observe within their families; and such as are found neglecters of family-worship, or instructing of all in their families, or such as remove not those who are offensive therefrom, shall, after due admonition, be judged unfit to rule the house of God; for he ought to be one that ruleth well his own house, 1 Tim. iii. 4.

Kirk-sessions interrogate concerning their pastor.

§ 6. The questions to be inquired by a presbytery at the eldership concerning a minister may be these, and such like: 1. Hath your minister a gospel walk and conversation

tion before the people? And doth he keep family-worship? And is he one who rules well his own house? Is he a haunter of ale-houses and taverns? Is he a dancer, carder, or dicer? Is he proud or vain-glorious? Is he greedy, or worldly, or an usurer? Is he contentious, a brawler, fighter, or striker? Is he a swearer of small or minced oaths? Useth he to say, Before God it is so; or, in his common conference, I protest, or, I protest before God? Or, says he, Lord, what is that? All which are more than yea and nay? Is he a filthy speaker or jester? Bears he familiar company with disaffected, profane, or scandalous persons? Is he dissolute, prodigal, light, or loose in his carriage, apparel, or words? How spends he the Sabbath after sermon? Saw ye him ever drink healths? Is he at variance with any? Is there any that reproaches him? Or, is he well beloved of all? And upon what ground is it that the variance or good liking of the people is?—2. Keeps he much at home at his ministerial work? Or, doth he occasion to himself distractions and unnecessary diversions therefrom? Is he constant at his calling and studies, or takes he but pains at fits and starts, such as at fasts, communions, visitations, &c.? Is Saturday only his book-day, or is he constantly at his calling?—3. Doth he discountenance or discourage any that is seeking Christ? Doth he preach sound doctrine, so far as ye can understand? Doth he preach plainly, or is he hard to be understood for his scholastic terms, matter, or manner of preaching? Doth he faithfully reprove sin, especially such as most prevail in the parish? What time of day doth he ordinarily begin sermon on the Sabbath? And when doth he dismiss the people? Spends he too much time in his sermon, in repetition of what he said before? Doth he lecture and preach in the forenoon, and preach again in the afternoon on the Lord's day, and that both summer and winter? Doth he read a large portion of scripture in public, and expound the same? Doth he preach chatechetic doctrine ordinarily in the afternoon? Hath he a week day's sermon, and collections on these days? When the Lord in his providence is speaking extraordinary things, doth he tie himself to his ordinary text; or makes he choice of one more apposite and suitable to the dispensation? Seeks he to preach Christ his beauty and excellency, and to open up the power and life of godliness? Endeavours he to discuss cases of conscience, to let you know your spiritual state, what it is?—4. Doth he, according to the act of Assembly 1708, visit the people and families, at least once a year in a ministerial way, teaching and admonishing from house to house? And doth he visit the sick when needful, and pray over them? Doth he visit them who, through age or sickness, cannot come to the public worship? Doth he labour to speak to the sick suitably to their various inward conditions? Doth he not especially visit such as be exercised in conscience? Doth he visit such as are afflicted by death of children or other relations? Visits he the widows, orphans, and poor? If he be minister of a burgh, visits he the prisoners? Is he not careful when he visits families to confer with them in private, and pray with them, thereby learning the case of their souls, that so the doctrine in public may the better meet with their condition?—5. Doth he administer the sacrament of baptism in an orderly way, when the congregation is convened; or doth he it at any time privately? Doth he add any word to, or alter the words of institution?—6. Doth he frequently catechise his parishioners, and administer the sacrament of the Lord's supper to them? And is he careful in keeping from that holy ordinance all who are known to be scandalous, grossly ignorant, or erroneous? How often have ye the communion every year? Doth he not begin to catechise young ones about nine or ten years of age, and how censures he contemners of catechising? What course is taken with contemners of the Lord's supper upon frivolous pretences? At the Lord's supper doth he not cause cut the bread in large and fair shaves fit for mutual fraction and distribution, that as they give the cup to the nearest assident, so having broken off a part of the bread with their hand for themselves, they give the rest to the person sitting nearest them? Do your people all sit at the Lord's table? In the time of distribution, eating, and drinking, is there any reading, or singing of psalms, or is there silence, and so time for meditation, except it be a short, pertinent, and awakening word dropped by the pastor?—7. Hath he a competent number of elders? And hath he deacons in the parish distinct from elders? Doth he keep sessional meetings frequently? And is he impartial n the exercise of discipline against all offenders? Is there frequent meetings of the members of session, for fasting and prayer, according to the act of Assembly 1699? Doth he travel with public penitents in private, to make them sensible of their sin, according to its circumstances, and sensible of mercy, that the love of Christ may overcome the love of sin? And then doth he absolve them, when brought up to some ingenuous confession and resolution for the future? Doth he ever censure persons for living idle, breaking of promise, or for backbiting? Doth he censure keepers of superstitious days? How doth he restrain abuses at penny-bridals? Doth your session meet weekly? Doth your minister coolzie any whom another brother hath in process? Or doth he carry any way partially, that so he may become popular? Doth he in session assume to himself a negative voice? When he is necessitated to leave his flock, doth he not acquaint the session with it?—8. Is he careful to take away variances that fall out among families, and compose differences among particular persons in the congregation?

Pastor and heads of families interrogate concerning the kirk-session.

§ 7. After that the elders have answered to these or the like questions, then the heads of families are to be interrogate in general concerning the lives and manners of the members of the session; and the pastor is to answer more particularly to these or the like questions: 1. Is your session rightly constitute, and all the elders and deacons duly admitted according to the acts of the Assembly? 2. Do they all attend gospel-ordinances, and the diets of the session? 3. Are they grave, pious, and exemplary in their lives and conversations? Do they worship God in their families? Is any of your elders an ignorant man, a drinker of healths, a tipler, a drinker excessively to drunkenness, a swearer, an observer of Yule-days, &c? Is he one that observes not the Sabbath? Is he careful to keep his oath of admission taken before God in face of the congregation, not to delate or censure, but as edification requires? Do any of them work on solemn fast or thanksgiving days? Is any of them a mocker of piety? 4. Are they diligent, careful, and impartial in the exercise of their offices? Do the elders visit the families within the quarter and bounds assigned to each of them? Are they careful to have the worship of God set up in the families of their bounds?

Are they careful in calling for testimonials from persons who come to reside in the parish? Do the elders take all discipline upon themselves without the minister? Or do they labour to carry things factiously, or by plurality of voices, contrary to God's word, and the laudable acts of the presbytery, provincial, or General Assemblies? 5. Have the elders subscribed the Confession of Faith? And are they well affected to the government, worship, and discipline of this church? 6. Have the elders and deacons their distinct bounds assigned them for their particular inspection? 7. Does your session always appoint a ruling elder to attend presbyteries and synods? 8. Are the deacons faithful in their office, in collecting and distributing all the kirk-goods, and in having a care of the sick poor? After all these queries are over, the minister and elders are to be severally encouraged or admonished as the presbytery sees need.

The precentor, beadle, &c.

§ 8. Then the precentor, schoolmaster, and clerk of the session, who in country congregations are ordinarily one and the same, and after them the beadles, bell-men, and church servants, being removed, the presbytery is to inquire at the minister, session, and heads of families, concerning their conversation, fidelity, and diligence, in their offices; and the presbytery is thereupon to proceed as the matter requires.

Pastor and elders interrogate concerning the congregation

§ 9. After all these inquires, the presbytery removing the heads of families, the minister and elders are to be inquired concerning the congregation, 1. Doth the body of the people attend ordinances duly and timeously, and stay till the blessing be pronounced? Are they diligent in improving the means of knowledge, and are they growing therein? 2. Are they submissive to public and private exhortations, and to the discipline and censure of the church, by admonitions and reproofs, as need requires? And do they by their words and actions manifest a suitable respect to their minister and respective elders? 3. Are they careful to educate their children and servants in the knowledge of God? What success hath the gospel and labours of ministers and elders among them? What scandals, schisms, heresies, or divisions are among them, and if on the growing hand? How doth they observe the Lord's day?

§ 10. The

§. 10. Then the minister, heritors, session, and heads of families, being present, the presbytery is to inquire after the state of the church, as to its fabric, the seats therein, and division of the same, the church-yard dikes, the utensils of the church, communion cups, cloaths, the minister's manse, if it be in repair, the glebe and stipend, the salary of the schoolmaster, precentor, session-clerk, and beadles, and how the communion-elements are provided, whether they be paid for out of the poor's money, and that when the communion is but celebrated once a year? See lib. II. tit. 2. § 23. Inquiry is to be made how much the stipend is? of what nature? how paid? and if there be a decreet of locality for it? As also about the state of the poor, whether there be any mortifications and legacies for them, or other pious uses? and how these are secured, and their interest paid and applied, and how they have been managed and employed from time to time? sess. 18. Assemb 1700. After the visitation is over, all parties are to be called in, and the moderator is to conclude all with prayer.

Pastor, kirk-session, and heads of families, interrogate about things of common concern.

TITLE XIV.

Of Provincial Synods.

§ 1. THE synod or provincial assembly is immediately superior to the presbytery, and consists of several presbyteries met together for their mutual help and comfort, and for managing the affairs of public concern within their bounds. The number of presbyteries in each synod is determined by the national Assembly, and they meet ordinarily twice every year, and at such set times as the neighbouring synods may conveniently correspond one with another, which is done by sending a minister and ruling elder mutually from one to another, viz. the provincials of Lothian, Merse, &c.; the provincials of Dumfries, Galloway, Glasgow, and Argyle; the provincials of Perth, Fife, and Angus, &c.; the provincials of Aberdeen and Murray; the provincials of Ross, Caithness, and Orkney. See likewise the order of the provincial assemblies in Scotland, according to the presbytries therein contained in the act of Assembly, December 17. 18. 1638, act 24.

The constituents of a synod, their time of meeting, &c.

§ 2. The

Synod opened, rolls made up, moderator chosen, and correspondence inrolled.

§ 2. The moderator of the former synod doth, in the morning before the meeting, preach a sermon suited to the occasion, and after sermon doth intimate to the members, that they immediately repair to the synod-house; when they are met, he doth open the meeting with solemn prayer: then the clerk having made up the synod roll from the rolls of each presbytery presented to him by their respective moderators, he is to call the same over, and to mark the absents. In making up the synod roll, it is usual to change the order thereof every synod, so that the presbytery that was first called in the roll of the former synod is now called last. Then the synod proceeds to the choice of a new moderator, who first calls for the correspondents from the neighbouring synods: and their commissions being read, they are inrolled as correspondents.

Committees of synods, their work, use, and power.

§ 3. Committees are to prepare matters, and to lop off unnecessary work for gaining of time, and to hinder heats by public debates, and to facilitate their work, they may subcommit any part thereof to a few of their own number; and they may likewise advise one with another in weighty affairs, even before report to the synod, thereby the more to prevent debates. Any affair tabled before them, though by them rejected, may be brought in in full synod; yet so as the member or party who bringeth in the matter, be sure to have very much reason or necessity for so doing. All synods may have the following committees. 1. A committee for overtures; 2. Another for bills, references, and appeals; and, 3. For revising presbytery-books, who are to meet at such times and places as the synod appoints: each committee and sub-committee is to consist of ministers and ruling elders: the moderator and clerk of the synod is moderator and clerk to the committee of overtures. All other committees chuse their own moderator and clerk, who is to present their report to the synod in writing. Any member of a judicature may be present with the committee though none of the number, and may advise, but not vote there: as also, one of a committee may be present in sub-committees of their own appointment; all which committees are chosen by the synod only, as General Assemblies do theirs.

§ 4. The presbytery-books are called for and produced,

ced, and each book is committed to some members of other presbyteries to be revised and examined by them, that it may appear how each presbytery hath keep order, and performed what was recommended to them by synods or General Assemblies; and upon the revisers their report, they are censured or approved accordingly. What was obscure or difficult for the presbyteries, or might concern them all in common, is resolved and ordered; what hath been done amiss by presbyteries is redressed: and if any difficulty arise which doth not fall under some church-constitution, it is referred to the national Assembly. *Matters treated by synods.*

§ 5. Every presbytery is to get an extract of the acts of every synod, and to read such of them in the presbytery as are of general concern, or which particularly relate to any in their bounds, that they may be the better observed. *Presbyteries are to carry home and read synod acts.*

§ 6. At the privy censures, none ought to be present but members. Upon the revisers their report of the presbytery-books, each presbytery is removed *per vices*, in order to privy censure, in the same manner as was said of the ministers in presbyteries, and of elders in sessions. See tit. 15. § 1. *Privy censures by synods.*

§ 7. By article 12. chap. 8. of the French church-discipline, concerning provincial synods, the pastors in each province shall represent the widows and children of ministers which died in the service of the church, to be supported and maintained at the common charge of each province; and where the province shall be ingrateful, the national synod shall redress it. Our church proposeth the same persons as proper objects for the pastors in the synods their charity, and the *centesima* or hundredth part of each benefice to be the fund, and paid in to the collector thereof yearly, who is to be appointed by each synod, and is to distribute the same to the relicts, and children of deceased ministers within the bounds of the synod, conform to their order. *Centesima to ministers widows and children.*

TITLE XV.

Of Extraordinary Synods and General Assemblies.

Extraordinary synods only to be held in a disturbed state of the church.

§ 1. Extraordinary synods I call such as that of the Assembly at Westminster, which consisted of divines and gentlemen, many of whom were not elders, called and nominated by the civil power to consult about the doctrine, worship, and government of the church: or, when ministers, without delegation from the church, do of themselves meet by virtue of their office: Which synods this church doth not approve of in a settled and constitute condition, but only in such churches as are not yet constituted. It being always free to the magistrate to advise with synods of ministers and ruling elders, meeting upon delegation from their churches, either ordinarily, or being indicted by his authority occasionally. See the act of Assembly 1647, approving the Confession of Faith. Yet by act of Assembly December 19. 1638, ministers are obliged to give their advice and good counsel in matters concerning the kirk, or the conscience of any whatsoever, to his Majesty, to the parliament, to the council, or to any members thereof, for their resolutions from the word of God.

Members of a national assembly by the directory should be as many ministers at least as ruling elders.

§ 2. By the directory for church-government, as it was printed in the year 1647, to be examined by presbyteries, the Assembly was to consist of as many ruling elders as ministers, which doth agree with the chap. 9. art. 3. of the French church-discipline: but by the directions of the English parliament, August 19. 1645, it is provided, That there be in all Assemblies two ruling-elders to one minister. It seems indeed but reasonable, when presbyteries, the constituents of General Assemblies, do consist of ministers and ruling elders equally, that they should be equally represented there likewise.

The nature of our first General Assembly after the Reformation.

§ 3. At the beginning of our Reformation, the Assembly did consist of those of the reformed religion, delegated from some shires and burghs where the reformed dwelt. The number of pastors was then so small, that it did not exceed the fourth part of the meeting, as may be seen from their federunts in the copy of the M. S. acts of of Assemblies: and until the number of ministers did increase and multiply, it was at first a general meeting of them all; but thereafter they did impower and commission a few to represent them, who are thereupon only designed *the Commissioners of the General Assembly.*

§ 4. If an Assembly be indicted by the civil magistrate on so short an advertisement as twenty days, that presbyteries (especially the more remote) are not timeously advertised to chuse commissioners, and so the church not fully represented, an Assembly so meeting is declared null. All new Scots parliaments were called on forty days, and what prejudice can it do if presbyteries receive as fair an advertisement, unless it be to the service of some present design against the church? 2*do*, An Assembly is null where the members, or a great many of them, are not elected by presbyteries, but named by the magistrate; in which case, though they may act as advisers of the magistrate, yet they cannot act as these having authority from the church. 3*tio*, An Assembly is null, when presbyteries are represented by more ministers than the standing acts of Assemblies, regulating the representation, doth allow, or where no ruling elders are commissioned. 4*to*, An Assembly is null, when members do vote for these matters, to which they are threatened to give their vote, by the civil magistrate. 5*to*, An Assembly is null, when a moderator or clerk is imposed upon them without their suffrage: see at length acts of Assembly, December 4. 1638.

What may annul a General Assembly.

§ 5. The General Assembly December 20. 1638, declares, that by divine, ecclesiastical, and civil warrant, the Assembly of this national church hath power and liberty to assemble and convene in her yearly General Assemblies, and oftener, *pro re nata*, as occasion and necessity shall require: To this agrees the act of parliament 1690, ratifying the Confession of Faith, and settling Presbyterial church-government; so that the Sovereign, till these laws be altered, cannot, by his mere authority or proclamation, render the meetings of Assemblies precarious and uncertain, unless he run the risk of renewing the dispensing power.

Assemblies may meet yearly, and oftener, pro re nata.

§ 6. By the 5th act of Assembly 1694, the representation of the several presbyteries in this national church

The representation in General Assemblies, and the number of members.

in its General Assemblies, shall hold proportion to the number of parishes, whether vacant or planted, within each presbytery, in manner following: All presbyteries consisting of twelve parishes, or under that number, shall send two ministers and one ruling elder And all presbyteries consisting of eighteen parishes, or under that number, but above twelve, shall send three ministers and one ruling elder. And all presbyteries consisting of twenty-four parishes, or under that number, but above eighteen, shall send four ministers and two ruling elders. And, lastly, All presbyteries consisting of above twenty-four parishes, shall send five ministers and two ruling elders. And every collegiate church where there use to be two or more ministers, are, so far as concerns the design of this act, understood to be as many distinct parishes: So that presbyteries delegate not less than a sixth part, nor more than a fifth part of the ministry. Conform to the representation proportioned by this act, the number of ministers delegate from presbyteries are one hundred and eighty, and of ruling elders sixty-eight. But each royal burgh having the privilege (if they please to use it) to be represented there by a ruling elder, and the city of Edinburgh by two, this would add sixty-seven more ruling elders to that order, making in all of elders one hundred and thirty-five. By that same act, no persons shall be admitted members of Assemblies, but such as are either ministers or ruling elders. And by the 6th act of Assembly 1698, it is recommended to presbyteries to chuse only such ruling elders as may and will give attendance.

There should be no delegations but from presbyteries only.

§ 7. Commissioners from royal burghs, till the matter be further thought upon, by the act of Assembly July 15. 1648, are to observe the ordinary practice, viz that each burgh send one, and Edinburgh send two ruling elders, approven of and consented to by the ministry and session of the burgh: but yet each university may be represented by a minister or ruling elder Neither is that kind of approbation of the choice required, albeit there may be the same reason for it: For the members of a faculty, as such, are not obliged to be either ministers or ruling elders. But, upon the whole, our practice would be more easily accounted for, and a great deal more agreeable to that of foreign churches,

churches, if delegations were only from presbyteries, and the delegates equally both of ministers and elders.

§ 8. By the 6th act of Assembly 1704, no minister or elder can be commissioned to the General Assembly by any presbytery, burgh, or university, but such as usually reside in, or have a relation to the presbytery, burgh, or university they are commissioned from. This is enacted, that pragmatic and designing men may be kept out from being members of Assemblies, after their own presbyteries, &c. (perhaps from some such apprehension) had been pleased to neglect them in their choice. *All commissioners must reside, or have relation to the bounds they represent.*

§ 9. The Assembly, by their act the 5th of August 1641, considering, that if the Scots kirk at Campvere were joined as a member of the kirk of Scotland, it would be convenient for correspondence from foreign parts for the well of this kirk: therefore they desired the said kirk of Campvere to send their minister with a ruling elder, with their commission to the next General Assembly, at which time they should be inrolled as commissioners from that kirk. When that church is vacant, the convention of royal burrows have been in use to present a minister, and act as patrons. And by the act of Assembly 1704, some propositions concerning the said kirk, approved by the Assembly 1642, are of new enacted and authorised, viz (1) That the said kirk observe that order in the outward worship of God, and exercise of discipline, as is here received by law and practice. (2.) That, at least, every third year their commissioners be at the Assembly, whose expences are to be paid by their own kirk, till this church be in a better capacity to do it. (3.) That they advise with the presbytery of Edinburgh, or commission of Assembly, concerning emergent difficulties. *The Scots kirk at Campvere represented. Their instructions, &c.*

§ 10. By the act of Assembly 1638, December 17. 18. it is referred to particular presbyteries, and especially to the ruling elders therein, that commissioners to Assemblies their expences be borne conform to former acts of Assemblies, by the particular parishes in every presbytery, and proportionally, by all sorts of persons therein, able in land or money: which act is ratified by the Assembly 1639, August 29. and extended to the expences bearing of such as shall be sent in commission by General Assemblies: but it is referred to the parliament for making these *Commissioners to and from Assemblies. Their expences.*

who are stented to pay their proportions: by which it is clear that presbyteries may stent the people within their own bounds, for defraying the charges of those therein, who attend General Assemblies: but then it must not be exacted, but only received from a willing condescending people, which will certainly be very unserviceable, if otherwise received, unless the expences be most inconsiderable. And the practice might prove more serviceable in a disturbed state of the church, when ministers come to be deprived of their stipends. Since the year 1642, our sovereigns have bestowed four or five hundred pounds sterling yearly, to be employed by General Assemblies, which will do much to defray the expences of commissions from General Assemblies, sent to visit the remoter parts of the church; see Ass. 1642, August 5.

The stile of commissions to General Assemblies.

§ 11. The General Assembly, by their 8th act 1695, gives the form after insert for a directory to presbyteries in their giving commissions to their members for General Assemblies; which form is likewise observed by universities, each whereof sends one, as also royal burghs, *mutatis mutandis*. At   the   day of   years. The which day the presbytery of   did, and hereby does nominate and appoint Mr. A. B. minister at C. Mr D. E. minister at F. and   ruling elders, their commissioners to the next General Assembly of this church, indicted to meet at   the   day of   next to come, or when or where it shall happen to sit, willing them to repair thereto, and attend at all the diets of the same, and there to consult, vote, and determine in all matters that come before them, to the glory of God, and good of his church, according to the word of God, the Confession of Faith, and agreeable to the constitutions of this church, as they will be answerable, and that they report their diligence therein at their return therefrom. Extracted by me, &c. And by the 6th act of Assembly 1704, this clause must be insert and added to the said form of all commissions, viz. that they have subscribed the Confession of Faith of this church, according to the 11th act of the General Assembly anno 1700.

The reason for this uniformity.

§ 12 The reason for enacting this uniform method was, that all members might be alike free: for before this time several presbyteries did insert in their commissions particular

particular instructions and limitations, which did not a little muzzle and confuse the members, and might at some occasions have proved an advantageous handle for such as were not tender of the church's peace.

§ 13. By the 4th act of Assembly 1694, commissioners from presbyteries and others are appointed to give in their respective commissions to the clerk of the General Assembly, the night at least before the first diet or meeting thereof, to the effect the rolls may be timeously made up, and that the commissions may be considered by the Assembly without any interruption: and all commissions not so given in, shall be delivered in the intervals, betwixt and the after diets. *When commissions are to be given in.*

§ 14. By the 6th act of Assembly 1698, presbyteries are appointed to chuse their commissioners to General Assemblies at least forty days before the sitting thereof: that which gave rise to this act was, that the civil authority, for some time before that, had been pleased (though not agreeably to the act of parliament 1690, in favours of the church) to interpose a privative power in adjourning General Assemblies to a longer time than the appointment of the preceeding Assembly, whereby their meetings were rendered both unfrequent and uncertain: and with some view to obviate this, I think, the act hath been made, but yet especially that members might be in case to attend, being so long chosen before the time. *Commissioners are to be elected forty days before they meet, and why.*

§ 15. The General Assembly useth to be honoured with the Sovereign's presence, either by their royal person, or by their High Commissioner: for which the moderator, in the Assembly's name, doth use to express their thankfulness, and how great a mercy they do esteem it to have the countenance of civil authority. But there have been many General Assemblies begun, held, and continued in Scotland, without either the King or his Commissioner's presence: and that it was not, nor yet is contrary to law, is evident, if the first act of parliament 1592, ratified in parliament 1690, be duely considered. *The Sovereign, or his commissioner, honours the Assembly by their presence, which, though acceptable, yet is not essential to an Assembly.*

§ 16. The first commission that was granted, was by King James VI. anno 1580, as may be seen in an old M. S. of the acts of Assemblies, and was nothing else but a missive letter under the King's own hand, the tenor whereof follows: " Trusty and well beloved friends, we greet
" you *The first commission was the king's missive.*

"you well We have directed towards you our trusty
"friends the Prior of Pittenweem, and the Laird of Lun-
"die, intrusted with our power for that effect, for assist-
"ing you with their presence and counsel in all things
"that they may, tending to the glory of God, and pre-
"servation of us and our estate; desiring you heartily ac-
"cept them, and our good will committed to them for the
"present in good part. Sua we recommend you to God's
"blessed protection. From our palace at Falkland, the 22d
"day of July 1580. JAMES R"

The form now is more solemn. § 17. But now these commissions are more pompous and solemn, passing in Latin under the great seal. Sometimes they have been complex, cloathing the commissioners with somewhat of a viceroyship in the state, as well as commissioner to the Assembly: thus it is said the Marquis of Hamilton, and Earl of Traquair, their commissions were in the years 1638, and 1639. The commissions granted since the revolution, you may see in the printed acts of Assemblies. Though these commissioners be respected in the Assemblies, and about Assembly-affairs, as representing the Sovereign's person; yet I doubt if they could claim any place or precedency in meetings of state, meerly as commissioners to the Assembly. But this is still kept undecided, as appears by their disappearing at such meetings while the General Assembly is sitting.

Presbytery of Darien represented. § 18. The presbytery of Caledonia in Darien is authorised to send yearly two representatives to the General Assembly: they being a part of this national church, and subject to her Assemblies, as appears from the instructions given them by the commission of the General Assembly 1699.

The opening of the Assembly. § 19. The moderator of the former Assembly opens it with a sermon; but in case of his absence, his predecessor in that chair hath the sermon: and in absence of them both, the eldest minister of the town where they meet preacheth, and openeth the Assembly by prayer, and moderates till a new moderator be chosen. Thus it was done in the Assembly at Glasgow 1638. After sermon the members go into the Assembly-house, where, after prayer by him who preached, a new moderator is chosen in the manner before mentioned, their clerk continuing by commission, sometimes during life. It is to be remembred, that before the new moderator is chosen, the rolls must first

first be made up; and at the calling of each presbytery, burgh, and university, their commission is read. After the Assembly is thus constitute, the person representing the Sovereign, produceth the commission to him for that effect, and ordinarily a letter also from the Sovereign to the Assembly, both which are publicly read with great honour and respect, the members standing all the time that the letter directed to them is a reading; and by their appointment, both commission and letter are recorded in their books. And all the time of the commissioner's presence, the members sit uncovered. The commissioner ordinarily has a discourse to the Assembly, assuring them of their Majesty's protection, and continued favour; and he intreats them to unanimity and dispatch in their affairs; to which the new moderator useth, in name of the Assembly, to make a short and suitable return; both which are likewise recorded.

§ 20. By the act of Assembly July 29. 1640, it is appointed, that the commissioners sit together unmixed, and the places where they sit be divided from the seats of others. As also, that four persons of respect have warrant to injoin that there be no noise, no standing, nor disorderly behaviour; and if any shall disobey them, or direct his speech to any, except to the moderator, and that one at once, with leave first asked and given, he is to be rebuked by the moderator: and if he desist not, he is to be removed out of the Assembly for that session. As also, that the minutes of ilk session be read before their rising; and if the matter concern the whole kirk, let it be read in the beginning of the next session. This order is to be read the first session of each Assembly, and the act is ratified July 28. 1641, and August 6. 1642. *The order observed among the members, and in the Assembly-house.*

§ 21. The ordinary committees used in General Assemblies are, 1. The committee for overtures. 2. The committee for bills, references, and appeals. 3. The committee for elections and commissions. 4. Committees for revising synod-books and registers, and of commissions of General Assemblies. 5. A committee for censuring of absents, and nominating ministers to preach before the commissioner, if present. 6. When the King or Queen honours them with a letter, there is, in the first place, appointed a committee for drawing an answer thereto. There *Committees of Assemblies, their number and way of being chosen.*

are also other committees for particular matters, named as is found needful. All committees of Assemblies are to consist of ministers and ruling elders, members of several synods; and in more numerous committees, some out of every synod: all which commitees are ordinarily named by the moderator, in presence, and approved by tacit consent, only sometimes members propose the adding of some others, whose motion useth likewise to be acquiesced in: so that there hath never yet been any election of committees, either by synods giving in separate lists, or by members giving in lists, as hath been done in our late parliaments. Only for preventing the perplexing of Assembly business, it is fit that no member be put upon more committees than one.

Committee of overtures and others their power, how restricted.

§ 22. Albeit no business ought to come in to the Assembly directly, till it be proposed to, and prepared by some committee to whom it properly belongs; yet no committee hath a negative over the Assembly: and it was never their intention to confine and restrict themselves only to consider of these matters which their commitees were pleased to allow and transmit to their consideration: for, by act of Assembly, July 29. 1640, an overture (and from a parity of reason, a petition or any other thing) may be proposed in full Assembly, with the reasons thereof, after that the committee hath refused to transmit the same.

No ecclesiastical process to be printed without allowance.

§ 23. To avoid altercations and debates in open Assembly, which might prove dangerous, and are always very indecent, after matters have been prepared by committees, they are transmitted to the Assembly. Now this design and order may be much struck at and inverted, when members or particular persons do print their petitions or overtures to the General Assembly and nation, before they be orderly brought in: Therefore by the 17th act of Assembly 1700, all persons are discharged to presume to print any petition, appeal, reasons, or answers, or any part of any process to be brought in to the General Assembly, or any other church judicatory, without leave given by them, with certification, that the same shall not be read nor considered.

A diet for prayer.

§ 24. It is the laudable custom of Assemblies, before they begin close to their work, to appoint betwixt nine and twelve

twelve in the forenoon, to be set apart by the members for public prayer in the Assembly house, to the Almighty God, for his countenancing and directing them in the matters that shall come before them: where the commissioner is likewise pleased to attend and join in prayer: as may be seen in the first three printed acts of Assembly since the Revolution, and among the indices of unprinted acts thereafter

§ 25. Conform to ancient custom, by the 3d act of Assembly 1704, all synod books are appointed to be punctually brought in and presented to the General Assembly yearly, in the beginning thereof: which books, after hearing a report concerning them, from the committee appointed to revise them, the Assembly does approve or disallow thereof as they find ground. All references from synods, appeals, grievances, petitions and complaints, are here examined and answered: acts and constitutions for all the churches are agreed upon with common consent, conform to the 9th act of Assembly 1697, of which hereafter about preventing of innovations. Here course is taken for planting of churches with well qualified ministers: rules are set down, by which inferior judicatures shall be directed in all their proceedings. It is their business to see that the small part of the patrimony of the church yet remaining be preserved and rightly applied. They join or disjoin parishes from presbyteries, and presbyteries from synods: they indict national fasts and thanksgivings: they are concerned to appoint fit persons and methods for drawing up the history of the church: they also ought to take care that works of charity, for sustentation of the poor, be promoted. By the wisdom and authority of this Assembly, gangrenes of errors and divisions are prevented, that they spread not against truth and unity. But they decline to meddle in these matters they judge civil, as being incompetent to them, as may be seen by the index of unprinted acts of Assembly 1690. Church-judicatures ought not to meddle formally with civil matters, no more than the state ought to meddle formally with matters ecclesiastic; but the object materially considered may be the same, and fall under consideration, both of church and state, in different respects. By the 5th article of the 31st chapter of our Confession, synods or councils are to handle or

Matters treated in Assemblies.

conclude

conclude nothing but what is ecclesiastical, and are not to intermeddle with civil affairs which concern the commonwealth, unless by way of humble petition in cases extraordinary, or by way of advice for satisfaction of conscience, if they be thereunto required by the civil magistrate.

Commissions of General Assemblies their power.

§ 26 What matters General Assemblies cannot overtake themselves, they do refer to their commissions; in propriety of speech they do import the same thing with committees: yet, *de praxi*, a committee is appointed only to prepare matters, whereas a commission determines in matters committed to them, and from whose sentence therein there lieth no appeal to the ensuing General Assembly, though a complaint may be tabled before the next Assembly against the commission their proceedings. The power of the General Assembly is never lodged in them, as to making acts in any case: and it is both more expedient and decent that the Assembly determine in cases of appeals from synods, where they have been unanimous in their sentence, than to refer the final decision to a commission, who may be of a smaller number than the synod, and whose quorum is but about the eight part of some synods. Delegation, or commission to determine, seems inconsistent with the principles of Presbyterial government: for if the Assemblies of the church can give power to delegates to determine in one point, they may in more, and consequently in all, and thereby may introduce a Prelacy. General Assemblies should not give any other delegations but executive, except in extraordinary cases: for they being delegates themselves, ought least of any church-assembly to delegate: and if they can commit their power to twenty-one, certainly they may commit the same to fourteen. Commissions may have sub-committees for preparing and reporting, but not to determine, or so as to roll the commission upon them. The commission and the proceedings, and register of their actings are always subject to the censure of a General Assembly. If the Assembly do not appoint their moderator and clerk to attend them in those stations, they may then nominate their own moderator and clerk. Their quorum is twenty-one, whereof fifteen to be always ministers, and they continue till a new General Assembly meet, as may be seen in the printed commissions in the acts of Assemblies.

§ 27. The

§ 27. The General Assembly, by their 6th act 1705, does appoint that the whole presbyteries of this national church be equally represented in commissions, and that their representation be proportioned to the number of ministers that are in each presbytery; the old ministers which were ordained before the year 1661, being always supernumerary: and that two or three of the members of the General Assembly in each synod, be appointed as a committee to name the members of the commission, and that the whole representatives of presbyteries in the several synods at Assemblies, do meet by themselves, and name their respective members of the said committee. And the General Assembly by the same act. does appoint the expences of the said commissioners to be born and defrayed by the several presbyteries which they represent, according to the number of the days of their attendance; and that their presbyteries take care to supply their charges with preaching during their absence on the account foresaid. *The method of chusing members of the commission, their charges to be paid, and churches supplied.*

§ 28. The General Assembly, by their 6th act 1703, does require the members of the commission to give all due attendance thereon, as they will be answerable, which members are condescended upon by the 15th act of Assembly 1705, to be one at least of that number of the several presbyteries who are members of the commission, and they are to attend the meetings thereof by turns. And presbyteries are ordained to send in to the commission, the names of such as they have appointed to attend the several diets thereof. And by the forsaid act 1703, the clerks of the commission are ordained to record lists of the absents from each quarterly meeting, and from the meetings in time of parliament, or who shall go away therefrom without leave first obtained, and send an extract of their names to the respective synods, who are impartially to censure them, and make report thereof to the next General Assembly: and to this effect, the clerks of the commission are ordered to lay before that Assembly the lists of these absents. And in the instructions to the commission 1708, all presbyteries within twelve miles of Edinburgh are discharged to meet during sitting of the commission *Absents from the commission, how censured.*

§ 29. Some few years ago, the presbyteries of this church, conform to what had been before practised, did delegate

delegate one of their number, being a minister, to repair to the city where the parliament did sit, and during that time attend, and watch *ne quid detrimenti caperet ecclesia*. But the commission consisting of both ministers and elders, without which no ecclesiastical judicatory or committee thereof can be lawful, (see § 4 of this title), and also, that all the presbyteries are therein represented, and that the commission now is ordered to attend in the time of parliament, the former meeting of such delegates is now supplied more conveniently by the meeting of the commission; and I am sure, much more legally both by church and state constitutions: for neither do authorise any other ecclesiastical judicatory but Assemblies, synods, presbyteries and kirk sessions, or their committees, consisting of ministers and ruling-elders. And the act of parliament 1690, ratifying the Confession of Faith, and settling Presbyterian church-government, doth establish the exercise of that church-government in the hands of ministers and ruling elders. And it may be doubted if the state would correspond with such delegates, or regard addresses from them, their meetings wanting the stamp, both of civil and ecclesiastical authority.

Delegates from presbyteries to attend parliaments.

No lawful church court without elders.

§ 30. In the act of Assembly 29th July 1640, art. 2. concerning ordering the Assembly-house, the commissioners to General Assemblies are to receive tickets from the magistrates of the burgh where the Assembly sits, at the delivery of their commissions, whereby they may have ready access to the Assembly-house: and this act is renewed by the Assembly 1690, and is among the unprinted acts.

Members of Assembly should have tickets for access.

§ 31. By that same act, whatsoever presbytery, burgh, or university, shall not send commissioners, is to be summoned to the next General Assembly, to be censured by them as they find reasonable. And by the 6th act of Assembly 1699, such commissioners as do not attend duly from the beginning, and through the whole diets of the General Assembly, and the committees which they may be put upon, not having a relevant excuse, may be censured as the Assembly shall think fit.

Absents from Assemblies how censured.

§ 32. The stile of acts of the General Assembly runs thus: The General Assembly appoints and ordains, and sometimes recommends. Their acts should rather be like directions from the chair, than discourses from the pulpit. Though

The stile of acts of Assembly, and petitions thereto. They must not run in the magistrates name.

Though the Sovereign's perfon be therein fometimes reprefented, yet his name cannot be joined with the General Affembly in making of acts; becaufe the civil magiftrate, confidered as fuch, is neither head nor member of the church, nor of any of her judicatures; and it is the authority of the General Affembly of this national church that can alone bind her members: Which authority doth not fo properly confift in making of laws, as it doth in declaring what their Lord and Mafter hath already appointed And though ecclefiaftical conftitutions fhould be enacted in the foverei_n's name and authority, yet thefe could never bind the fubjects as fuch, becaufe the legiflative power is lodged in the Sovereign and eftates of parliament, and in them only. Hence all petitions to the General Affembly are only addreffed to the moderator and members thereof, and not to the Sovereign nor his commiffioner, though prefent; for petitions can be prefented to none but to fuch as thofe in whofe name and authority they are granted.

§ 33. By the act of Affembly December 20. 1638, they ordain prefbyteries, and provincial Affemblies, to convene before them fuch as will not acknowledge that Affembly, (and from a parity of reafon any other Affembly), nor acquiefce unto the acts thereof, and to cenfure them accordingly; and refractory prefbyteries are to be fummoned by the commiffion to compear before the next General Affembly to abide their trial; and by a claufe in the end of the 5th act, feffion 2. King William and Queen Mary's parliament, it is provided, that whatfoever minifter being convened before the General Affembly, or reprefentatives of this church, or their commiffions, or the vifitors to be by them appointed, fhall either prove contumacious in not appearing, or be found guilty, and therefore cenfured, whether by fufpenfion or depofition, they fhall *ipfo facto* be fufpended from, or deprived of their ftipends and benefices. And by the book of canons put in form for the government of the church of Scotland, by Englifh bifhops their counfel and influence, and approved by King Charles I. his proclamation, dated at Greenwich the 23d day of May 1635, it is appointed, that national fynods called by his Majefty's authority, for matters concerning the ftate of the church in general, fhall bind all perfons, as well abfent as prefent,

The authorities of Affemblies and their acts. The pain of difobeying and declining the fame.

present, to the obedience of the decrees thereof in matters ecclesiastical. And if any shall affirm or maintain, that a national synod so assembled ought not to be obeyed, he shall be excommunicated till he publicly repent and revoke his error.

Advocate or procurator, follicitor or agent for the kirk.

§ 34. Beside the clerk of the Assembly, there useth to be an advocate or procurator for the kirk chosen by them, who was to advise them in matters of civil right, and to plead what concerns the right of the church before civil courts; and in his name summonses are raised before the commission of parliament for plantation of kirks, or Lords of session. The agent or follicitor for the kirk is likewise elected by the Assembly and he acts and agents their business in such order as they appoint him. Their agent was priviledged to be present at all the meetings of that commission of parliament, even when they acted with close doors. In the late Prelatic times, the King's follicitor was, by his patent, constitute follicitor for the church too. But whether in this government her Majesty's advocate be also by his patent constitute advocate for the church, is a thing I cannot certainly assert. The agent has the care put upon him of sending dispatches to the several presbyteries.

The adjourning and disfolving of Assemblies and other church judicatures.

§ 35. All church judicatures at every rising appoint their next sitting, so that their meetings are not precarious and uncertain, but entirely and intrinsically, as to their time and frequency, lodged in the will and discretion of the plurality of the members of her respective judicatures. The kirk session, being properly the only radical church judicature, not consisting of delegate, but of perpetual and fixed members, cannot be at any time dissolved, but by themselves are adjourned from time to time: Albeit they use to begin and conclude the number of their sessions, at and after the presbytery hath approved of their proceedings. All church judicatures, but especially this, were called Consistories, where the judges did stand in administring justice (see Stair's Instit. p. 5¹⁴.) and even yet, their moderators, presidents, or prolocutors do stand, as the mouth of their meetings. Presbyteries are radical as to the pastors, and delegate as to the ruling elders, (see tit 12. § 1.) For the first presbytery after each ordinary meeting of the synod, when new elections of elders are returned, that presbytery doth begin the first session thereof, and so
other

other seffions of the same continue till the next synod in ordinary be over. And provincial synods confifting of presbyteries, they do in part diffolve twice a year, and fo the fynodical feffions are counted from one ordinary synod to the next ordinary meeting of another synod. But national Affemblies being annual, and confifting all of delegates, as hath been faid, the feffions thereof are counted from the firft meeting until they part and diffolve in the fame place, at leaft by the conftitutions and practice of this church, until, and no longer than the ordinary time for a new annual Affembly: for no doubt, an Affembly, if the affairs of the church fo require, may tranflate, and alfo continue their meeting, as was done anno 16.1; but it neceffarily diffolves before the year. At the clofing of every feffion of the Affembly, the moderator appoints the next diet, in prefence, and with confent of the members; then he turns to the commiffioner, and acquaints his Grace thereof, to which he ordinarily anfwers, Be it fo, or, I am fatisfied; whereupon the adjournment is intimated publicly at the door by the beddal, afterwards the moderator clofes with prayer.

§ 36. At clofing of the General Affembly, fome few of their number are nominated to affift the moderator and clerk, in revifing the minutes and proceedings of that Affembly, before the fame be recorded in their regifters, and to determine what of their acts are fit to be printed: but it were as proper for the Affembly to give orders therein, as the acts are paffed. *Committee for revifing the minutes and printing the acts.*

§ 37. All the affairs which the Affembly could overtake, being brought to a clofe, the moderator caufeth read the minutes of the laft federunt, thefe of former federunts being always read at the beginning of each feffion; which being done, he difcourfeth to the Affembly concerning the good providence of God that brought them together, and in allowing them the countenance and protection of the fupreme magiftrate; and exhorteth the members, to faithfulnefs, loyalty, and diligence in their ftations. The moderator having underftood the mind of the Affembly from previous communings with the members, as to the particular time and place of the next Affembly's meeting, which diet being concerted before, alfo with the commiffioner, he doth in their name reprefent the fame to the King or Queen, *The ordinary way of diffolving Affemblies.*

Queen, or their commissioner, if present, and upon their agreeing thereto, it is to be recorded and publicly intimate at the door of the Assembly-house by their order. The commissioner agrees ordinarily thereto in these or the like words (to many offensive enough) I do in my Master's name (or her Majesty's name) dissolve this Assembly; and, in the same name and authority, I appoint the next General Assembly to meet at such a time and place. which ordinarily is the same with that which the moderator in name of the Assembly did represent. Then the moderator closeth the Assembly with prayer, singing of psalms, and pronouncing of the blessing.

How two Assemblies were dissolved in an extraordinary manner, and their behaviour in these cases.

§ 38. Indeed when it happens that a commissioner doth rather cross than countenance the Assembly, either by an abrupt and interrupting dissolution, or by not appointing the next annual Assembly according to law; in these cases their behaviour is different, as may appear in the two following instances. The first was in the Assembly 1638. There the M. of H. his Majesty's commissioner, having dissolved them after some few days sitting, both in the Assembly-house and by public proclamation; they did notwithstanding (having protested against their dissolution) continue their sitting till they ended the work they met for, and appointed the time for their next General Assembly, for which you will find their apologetical vindication in their printed letter to the King. Another instance is this, the E. of Lothian, their Majesties commissioner to the General Assembly 1692, upon Saturday the 13th of February, (the Assembly being met and constitute by prayer) did immediately thereafter deliver himself as follows: Moderator, what I said last had so little success, that I intend to give you no more trouble of that nature; only this, you have now sat about a month, which was a competent time both to have done what was the principal design in calling this Assembly, (of uniting with your brethren) and to have done what else related unto the church; but his Majesty perceiving no great inclination among you to comply with his demands, hath commanded me to dissolve this present General Assembly; so I, in their Majesties name and authority, do dissolve this present General Assembly. Whereupon the moderator asked his Grace, if this Assembly was dissolved, without naming a diet for another? To this his Grace made return in thefe words: His Majefty will appoint another Affembly in due time, wherewith you will be timeoufly advertifed. Upon this, the moderator defiring of his Grace that he might be heard a few words, his Grace told him that he could not hear him as moderator, but only as a private perfon: the moderator anfwered, in whatever capacity your Grace pleafeth, I beg to be heard a few words. His Grace replied, That as a private man he might fpeak; whereupon the moderator delivered himfelf as follows: May it pleafe your Grace, this Affembly, and all the members of this national church, are under the greateft obligations poffible to his Majefty, and if his Majefty's commands to us had been in any or all our concerns in the world, we would have laid our hands on our mouths and been filent: but they being for a diffolution of this Affembly, without indicting another to a certain day; therefore, (having been moderator to this Affembly), in their name, they adhering to me, I humbly crave leave to declare, that the officebearers in the houfe of God, have a fpiritual intrinfic power from Jefus Chrift, the only head of his church to meet in affemblies about the affairs thereof, the neceffity of the fame being firft reprefented to the magiftrate. And further, I humbly crave, that the diffolution of this Affembly, without indicting a new one to a certain day, may not be to the prejudice of our yearly General Affemblies granted to us by the laws of this kingdom. Here the members rofe up, and with one voice, declared their adherence to what the moderator had faid; whereupon the moderator, turning himfelf to the Affembly, cried, Brethren, let us pray: but the members, by a general cry, preffed to name a diet for the next General Affembly. Whereupon the moderator faid, If they pleafed, the next General Affembly might meet here at Edinburgh upon the third Wednefday of Auguft 1693; and the members did again with one voice declare their approbation thereof. Then the moderator having ordered filence, concluded with prayer, and finging the 133d pfalm, and pronouncing of the bleffing.

The church's intrinfic power afferted.

§ 39. In the end of the act of Affembly 1647, approving the Confeffion of Faith, it is afferted, that it is always

The church's judgement about their right to meet fynodically.

ways free to the magistrate to advise with synods of ministers and ruling elders meeting upon delegation from their churches, either ordinarily, or being indicted by his authority occasionally, and *pro re nata*. It being also free to assemble together synodically, as well *pro re nata*, as at the ordinary times upon delegations from the churches, by the intrinsic power received from Christ, as often as it is necessary for the good of the church to assemble, in case the magistrate, to the detriment of the church, with hold or deny his consent, the necessity of occasional Assemblies being first remonstrate unto him by humble supplication; see §. 1. of this title.

TITLE XVI.

The Order of the Rolls of Church-Judicatures, and Ranking of Church Office-bearers. And of her Registers.

<small>Rolls of kirk-sessions, and ranking of elders.</small>

§ 1. RULING elders and deacons in church-sessions, should be regularly inrolled, and called to take place, according to the seniority of their ordination: but the poverty of the church being such, that there is no maintenance or benefice annexed to these offices therefore they use to be ranked according to their secular stations and employments; only seniority of ordination may be a rule whereby disputes for precedency among equals are to be decided.

<small>How ministers take place of one another.</small>

§ 2 All ministers are inrolled in presbyteries, and have place only according to the seniority of their ordination; a presbyter labouring in the word and doctrine, being the highest officer in the church, to be sure no office-bearer of an inferior order will ever compete with him: and therefore a minister of a later ordination, albeit he have the character and station of almoner or chaplain to the Royal Family, or of being historiographer, principal, or professor of theology or philosophy in any university, yet he will not presume thereupon to take place from one of a prior ordination; because all these stations and characters, ecclesiastically considered, are of an inferior order to t at of the pastor, unless he pretend unto it by virtue of civil

place

place and power, which is condemned in pastors as incompatible with their spiritual function, by Assembly 1638, Decem. 9. but the order in which ministers deliver the presbyterial exercises, is according to the seniority of erection of the parish churches where they officiate

§ 3. It is usual to change the order of the roll every synod, so that the presbytery that was first called in the roll of the former synod, is now called last (as was said above), and that which was in the second place is now called first: and the members are called according to the roll of each presbytery, presented to the clerk by the moderators thereof, with the ruling elders therein insert. And though a parish be vacant, or the minister thereof not present, yet the ruling elder for that church session is to be called for and inrolled. But those who are against ruling elders their being supernumerary to ministers in judicatures may dislike this: Yet if once a judicature fix on a quorum, whereof always so many are to be ministers, though double their number of elders should come and be present, there is nothing as yet to hinder them all from voting. *Rolls of synods, how ordered. No act to hinder elders to vote when they may be supernumerary to ministers.*

§ 4. The rolls of General Assemblies do begin with the synod which in the former Assembly was called in the second place, leaving the synod which was then first called now last; by which rotation the equality is better preserved. Commissioners from presbyteries are placed in their commissions according to the seniority of their ordination: next to them are inrolled the commissioners from the universities within the bounds; and next to them such as have commissions from royal burghs therein. In General Assemblies, ruling elders are called immediately after the ministers their colleague commissioners. *Rolls of General Assemblies.*

§ 5. The first thing to be done at every diet, after calling the rolls, is the hearing the minutes of the last federunt or session read; and till they be passed and allowed by the judicature, and also subscribed by the moderator, there ought no extracts thereof to be given; nor, till then, should it be warrantable for the clerk to enter them into the register. *Minutes revised and signed before extract, or recording.*

§ 6. In any thing wherein the moderator or clerk is particularly concerned, they ought in that case both to subscribe the minutes, as the privy seal used to be appended to *Clerk and moderator a check to one another. The attestation and title of the registers.*

to charters, or the like passing the great seal in favours of the keeper of the great seal. And at the close of the register of every General Assembly, and of each inferior church judicature, when they are given in to be approved by their next immediately superior judicature, they bear, "Here ends the register of the acts and proceedings " of   from   to   consisting of   pages." And this attestation is to be subscribed by the moderator and clerk: and every record at the beginning is to bear its own proper title, viz. The register of the acts and proceedings of such a judicature, begun at   the   day of   &c.

<small>Form of approving church-registers runs in a negative style.</small>

§ 7. By the ninth act of Assembly 1700, they appoint all provincial synods and presbyteries to be careful in revising the registers of the judicatures under their immediate inspection, and that they appoint a competent number of the most fit and experienced among them for that work; and when they find nothing to challenge in any register, they are to give it the attestation following: "The pro-
" vincial synod of   having heard the report of those
" appointed to revise the presbytery book of
" and having heard their remarks thereupon, and the said
" presbytery's answer thereto; and it having been inquired
" by the moderator, if any other had any complaints to
" make against the actings of the said presbytery, and no-
" thing appearing censurable, ordered the clerk to attest
" this in their presbytery book." And so for the registers of provincial synods and kirk-sessions, *mutatis mutandis*; and also for the registers of the commissions of Assemblies, by the 8th act of Assembly 1700. But if there be any thing truely censurable in the said books, with respect to discipline, that it be recorded as censured, both in the synod book and attestation.

<small>Order in filling up blanks, deletings, interlings, and omissions in registers.</small>

§ 8. All sentences and acts are to be filled up in the records, as all other things should be, according to the priority of their being voted or agreed unto, and that although no extract hath been, or perhaps ever may be called for. And when any thing is omitted in the body of a record, it may be written on the margin, which the moderator and clerk must subscribe again. When any thing is delete, let it be marked delete on the margin, and subscribed as the other, counting the lines or words blotted out. But

But interlinings are moſt improper, and derogatory to that credit which a record ſhould bear Further, when any blank is left in the record, and yet there is nothing wanting, it may be ſcored, or which is more proper, filled up with *nihil hic deeſt*; which words may be lengthened or ſhortened according to the bounds of the blank. See the 9th act of Aſſembly 1706.

§ 9. By the 11th act of Aſſembly 1703, for the better preſervation of their regiſters, they enact and appoint, that there be two authentic copies thereof, both ſubſcribed by the moderator and clerk; one copy whereof to lie in the clerk's cuſtody, and the other to be ſealed, and laid in ſome ſecure place, where the Aſſembly or Commiſſion ſhall appoint: As alſo, that a ſubſcribed extract of the proceedings of each General Aſſembly be ſent, a little after the riſing thereof, to the ſeveral ſynods within this church, to be by them recorded in a book *The regiſters how to be preſerved.*

§ 10 As to the ſtyle of the Aſſembly's addreſſes and letters to their Sovereigns, or foreign churches, and as to the ſtyle of their letters to the Aſſembly, both may be ſeen in their printed regiſters; as alſo, theſe, with the records of their commiſſions, will evidence what civilities the church pays in congratulating and attending on the miniſters of ſtate, and other great men: thus they court their favour, and return them their thanks, all done for the benefit and advantage of the preſent church-eſtabliſhment. *Civilities paid by the church.*

TITLE XVII.

Of Viſitation of Schools and Univerſities.

§ 1. ALL ſchools and colleges were to be reformed, and none admitted to inſtruct the youth privately or publicly, but ſuch as ſhould be tried by the viſitors of the kirk, James VI. parl. 1. cap. 11. and even under the late Prelacy, none were admitted to teach in any public ſchools, without licence from the ordinary, Charles II. parl. 1. ſeſſ. 2. cap. 4. *ſub fin.*; and alſo, by the act of Aſſembly, Dec. 17. 18. 1638, art. 4. they ratify the acts of Aſſembly 1565, 1567, and 1595, whereby viſitation of colleges is to be by way of commiſſion from the General Aſſembly; and the principal regents and profeſſors within *Viſitations of ſchools and colleges were appointed by authority of the Aſſembly.*

in colleges, and masters and doctors of schools, are to be tried by them concerning the soundness of their judgement in matters of religion, their ability for discharge of their calling, and the honesty of their conversation. It is no wonder the church think herself much concerned, that these seminaries of learning be duly regulated, considering how much it tends to the increase of Christian knowledge and learning, and the advantage of true piety and religion. By the General Assembly 1638, they grant commissions for visitation of the colleges of Aberdeen and Glasgow; and the Assembly 1649, appoints visitations of the universities of St Andrews and Glasgow. Again, the Assembly 1640, appoints visitations of Glasgow and Aberdeen colleges, as may be seen in the index of the unprinted acts of these and subsequent Assemblies.

Power of visitation claimed by the Sovereign. Visitors power and work distinguished.

§ 2 The power of visitations of universities, colleges, and schools, is now claimed by the Sovereigns to be their undoubted right and prerogative, as is evident from the narrative of the act of parliament 1690, for the visitation of universities The power granted to the visitors by that act is only executive or judicative, and not legislative, which neither can nor should be; for seeing the trust wherewith the legislators themselves are cloathed is only personal, it cannot be delegated to others, unless they receive power from their constituents for that effect and purpose: But though their power could be delegated, it should not be done; for some designing and disaffected members, in such commissions, might so manage the plurality of a quorum to plant and regulate these nurseries of church and state, as might pave the way, and dispose the nation more easily for some pernicious revolution. The visitors appointed in that commission are both members of parliament and ministers. The one sort I think, is appointed to remove disloyal teachers, and to consider the foundations of these seminaries, with the rents and revenues thereof, and how the same have been managed, and to set down good rules for the management thereof. And ministers, I think, are named to take trial if the teachers be erroneous, scandalous, negligent, or insufficient, and for ordering the manner of teaching; and thereupon present their humble advice to the statesmen; for authoritatively they cannot

cannot act without delegation from the church. See the title about extraordinary synods, § 1.

§ 3. There is none will grudge the church the exercise of this power of visiting colleges, so much as those masters who have ground to fear that their insufficiency and negligence may come to be exposed and discovered upon an exact and judicious trial. Again there are some factious masters that desire only statesmen to be visitors, among whom they think some of their *quondam* disciples may be found, who will be influenced to favour their ambitious or revengeful designs. *Who are ordinarily the greatest enemies to the church-visitations.*

§ 4. As to grammar schools, the power of visiting them remains with presbyteries; for by the 2d act, parl. 16 3, it is declared, that all schoolmasters and teachers of youth in schools, are, and shall be liable to the trial, judgement, and censure of the presbyteries of the bounds for their sufficiency, qualifications, and deportment in the said office. By the act of Assembly 7th Feb. 1645, they appoint that every grammar-school be visited twice in the year, by visitors to be appointed by presbyteries and kirk sessions in land-ward parishes and by the town-council in burghs, with their ministers; and where universities are, by the universities, with consent always of the patron of the schools, that both the fidelity and diligence of the masters and proficiency of the scholars in piety and learning, may appear. Inquiry is also to be made, if masters be diverted from due attendance by any other employment. By the 15th act, Assembly 706, somewhat of the same nature is injoined, viz. That presbyteries visit grammar schools twice a year, by some of their own number. *Presbyteries may yet visit grammar-schools twice a-year.*

§ 5. By the foresaid act 1645, they appoint, that no schoolmaster be admitted to teach a grammar school in burghs, or other considerable parishes, but such as, after examination by the ministers, deputies of the town and kirk session and parish (which is, I think the heritors), shall be found skillful in the Latin tongue, not only for prose, but also for verse, and shall be also approved by the presbytery therein. *Who examines schoolmasters at their admission.*

§ 6. By the foresaid act, they appoint, that at the time of every General Assembly, the commissioners directed thereto from universities, meet and consult together for the advancement of piety and learning, and keeping of an uniformity *Corresponding of universities.*

formity in doctrine, and good order among the universities. What they do this way, is not to bind the universities, till it be presented to the General Assembly, and receive their authority, as may be gathered from the Assembly's act, 18th June 1646. This of new is enacted by the 6th act of Assembly 1707.

TITLE XVIII.

Of a General Council of Protestants.

Corresponding with foreign churches, such as Magdeburg, 1577, and Westminster, 1643, the expences and safe conduct of correspondents.

§ 1. AS provincial Assemblies may, and do correspond with other provincial Assemblies, so may General Assemblies with the Assemblies of other churches. In a manuscript of the acts of Assemblies, Edinburgh October 26. 1577, you will find that Casimir having written to the Queen of England, of a council to be held at Magdeburg, for establishing the Augustine Confession, the Queen wrote thereof to the regent in Scotland, who communicated her letter to the Assembly, and desired they might send some of their number to assist thereat. Whereupon the Assembly named Mr Andrew Melvill and some others. And some ministers and elders were sent from the Assembly to the Assembly of Divines at Westminster, in order to carry on the unity and uniformity in religion and church-government. It belongs in these cases to the civil powers of these nations from which they go, to take care that their charges be honestly defrayed; and the states, in whose dominions the council is to be, use to grant a safe conduct to the foreign correspondents. See tit 15. § 9

General council, its authority.

§ 2. In the book of policy of the kirk, agreed unto anno 1581, they say, besides these Assemblies, there is another more general kind of Assembly, an universal Assembly of the Church of Christ in the world, which was commonly called an œcumenic council, representing the universal Church, which is the body of Christ. Their warrant to meet, and the authority of their meeting, must be as good and as great, with respect to national and general assemblies or convocations, as the authority of these are with respect to provincial assemblies or synods.

§ 3. If the Protestant Princes and Commonwealths would condescend and concert, that there should be a ge-
nerel

neral council at such a time and place; then the national or rather provincial Assemblies, at the appointment of their respective sovereigns, might meet and delegate one pastor and elder for each province, consisting of an hundred parishes: only from each distinct sovereignty, though consisting of less than fifty parishes, there might be at least a representation of the church therein by one pastor and ruling elder.

The manner of convocating and proportioning the representation.

§ 4. Most of the churches being already bound and obliged to own and maintain that Confession of Faith which they have by their canons authorised and approved: and there being an universal harmony in the doctrine contained in all the Confessions of the Reformed Churches, the work of a General Council, as to matters of faith, would, in all probability, be sweet and easy: and if, in what relateth to the worship, discipline, or government of the church, there should be some misunderstandings, God should even reveal this unto them. Nevertheless, whereto we have already attained, let us walk by the same rule, let us mind the same things, Phil. iii. 15. 16.

Matters of faith almost agreed to already.

§ 5. If this council were once met and constitute, and countenanced by the authority of their several sovereigns, then they might appoint the time and place of their next council, which might be every seventh year; and let one from different churches be chosen to the chair at every new council. To prepare the way for such a Catholic meeting, it were fit, in the mean time, to have a correspondence kept among all the churches. See § 1. of this title.

Time of meeting, and president of this council.

§ 6. In the subordination of these Assemblies, parochial, presbyterial, provincial and national, the lesser unto the greater, doth consist the external order, strength, and stedfastness of the Church of Scotland. And when it shall please the Lord to make ready and dispose the nations for a general council, then shall that beauty and strength appear more remarkably in the whole Catholic Church, which is the body of Christ. Then should the churches be established in the faith, increased in number daily; and as they went through the cities, delivering them the decrees to keep, that were ordained of the Apostles and Elders, which were at that general council, Acts xvi. 4. 5. they should give occasion to many to rejoice for the consolation. Such a time is rather to be wished than hoped for. See tit. 1. § 1. of this book.

The benefit of this subordination.

L   BOOK

BOOK II.

TITLE I.

Of Lecturing, Preaching, Catechising, Public Prayers before and after Sermon, Singing of Psalms, and Ministerial Benediction.

Nothing to be admitted in the worship of God, but what is prescribed in Scripture.

§ 1. BY the 15th act of Assembly 1707, they declare that there are some innovations set up of late by prelatists in their public Assemblies, which are dangerous to this church, and manifestly contrary to the constant practice and known principle thereof, which is, that nothing is to be admitted in the worship of God, but what is prescribed in the Holy Scriptures; therefore they discharge the practice of all such innovations in divine worship within this church; and ministers are required to inform their people of the evil thereof.

How the congregation doth assemble

§ 2. All are to enter the assembly in a grave and seemly manner, to take their seats or places without adoration, or bowing themselves towards one place or other. If any, through necessity, be hindered from being present at the beginning, they ought not, when they come into the congregation, to betake themselves to their private devotions, but reverently compose themselves to join with the Assembly in that ordinance of God, which is then in hand. Most of what is said on this title may be found in the Directory.

Their behaviour in the time of worship.

§ 3. The congregation being assembled, the minister, after solemn calling on them to the worshipping of the great name of God, is to begin with prayer. The public worship being begun, the people are wholly to attend on it; forbearing to read any thing, except what the minister is then reading or citing: Much more are they to abstain from all private whisperings, conferences, salutations, or doing reverence to any person present, or coming in; as also from all gazing, sleeping, or other indecent behaviour.

§ 4. Read-

§ 4. Reading of the Word in the congregation, being a part of the public worship of God, (wherein we acknowledge our dependence upon him, and subjection to him) and one mean sanctified by him for the edifying of his people, is to be performed by the pastors and teachers, and preachers licensed by the presbytery thereunto, who should (as Ezra and his companions did, Neh viii. 8) read in the book in the law of God distinctly, and give the sense, and cause them to understand the reading.

Why the Word is to be publicly read, and by whom.

§ 5. How large a portion is to be read at once is left to the wisdom and discretion of the minister: But it is convenient that ordinarily one chapter of each Testament be read at every meeting, and sometimes more, where the chapters be short, or the coherence of the matter requireth it. It is also requisite that all the canonical books be read over in order, that the people may be the better acquainted with the whole body of the scriptures, and where the reading in either Testament endeth on one Lord's day, it is to begin the next. The more frequent reading of such scriptures is also commended, as he that readeth shall think best for edification of his hearers, as the book of Psalms, and such like; and when he shall judge it necessary to expound any part of what is read, that work is not to begin until the reading of the whole chapter or psalm be ended.

How much is to be read at a time, and the order of reading and expounding.

§ 6. Regard is always to be had to the time, that neither preaching nor other ordinance be straitened or rendered tedious: Which rule is to be observed in all other public performances; and therefore, by the act of Assembly, Feb. 7. 1645, for regulating of that exercise of reading and expounding the scriptures upon the Lord's day, mentioned in the Directory, they ordain the minister and people to repair to the church half an hour before that time, at which ordinarily the minister now entereth to the public worship; and that that exercise of reading and expounding, together with the ordinary exercise of preaching, be perfected and ended at the time, which formerly closed the exercise of public worship. And for recovering the old custom established by the Directory, the General Assembly 1694, sess. 9. appoints ministers to read and open to the people some large and considerable portion of God's word. And the diligence of ministers in this is to be inquired into by presbyteries,

When lecturing begins, and how long to continue, according to the old and later acts.

byteries, at their privy censures, Assembly 1704, sess. 8. and also at parochial visitations Assembly 1706, act 10.

Preaching, its excellency and subject-matter.

§ 7. Preaching of the Word, being the power of God unto salvation, and one of the greatest and most excellent works belonging to the ministry of the gospel, should be so performed, that the workmen need not be ashamed, but may save himself and those that hear him. Ordinarily the subject of his sermon is to be some text of the scripture, holding forth some principle or head of religion, or suitable to the special occasion emergent: Or he may go on in some chapter, psalm, or book of the scripture, as he shall see fit. By the 8th art. cap. 3. of our Confession of Faith, the doctrine of the high mystery of predestination is to be handled with special prudence and care; and albeit Mr Turrentine in his Instit. Theol. l. c. 4. quest 6. maintains, very warrantably, that it should be publicly taught, yet he thinks it a subject more proper for the schools than the pulpits.

Introduction, sum, and division of the text.

§ 8. The introduction to the text is to be brief and perspicuous, drawn from the text itself, or context, or some parallel place of scripture. If the text be long, (as in histories and parables sometimes it must be), he is to give a brief sum of it; if short, a paraphrase thereof, if need be. In both, looking diligently to the scope of the text, and pointing at the chief heads and grounds of doctrines which he is to raise from it. In analysing and dividing his text, he is to regard more the order of matter than of words, and neither to burden the memory of the hearers in the beginning with too many members of division, nor to trouble their minds with obscure terms of art.

How doctrines are to be raised, explained, illustrated, and confirmed.

§ 9. In raising doctrines from the text, his care ought to be, 1st, That the matter be the truth of God. 2dly, That it be a truth grounded on, or contained in that text, that the hearers may discern how God teacheth it from thence. 3dly, That he chiefly insist upon these doctrines which are principally intended, and make most for the edification of the hearers. The doctrine is to be expressed in plain terms: or if any thing in it need explication, it is to be opened, and the consequence also from the text cleared. The parallel places of scripture confirming the doctrine are rather to be plain and pertinent than many; and, if need be, somewhat insisted upon, and applied to the purpose in hand.

hand. The reasons or arguments are to be solid, and, as much as may be, convincing. The illustrations, of what kind soever, ought to be full of light, and such as may convey the truth into the hearers hearts with spiritual delight.

§ 10. If any doubt, obvious from scripture or reason, or prejudice of the hearers, seem to arise, it is very requisite to remove it, by reconciling the seeming differences, answering the reasons, and discovering and taking away the causes of prejudice and mistakes: otherwise it is not fit to detain the hearers with propounding or answering vain or wicked cavils; which, as they are endless, so the propounding and answering of them, doth more hinder than promote edification. *What kind of doubts and controversies are to be raised and solved*

§ 11. The doctrine is to be brought home to special use by application to the hearers, that they may feel the word of God to be quick and powerful, and a discerner of the thoughts and intents of the heart. In the use of instruction or information in the knowledge of some truth, which is a consequence from his doctrine, he may, when convenient, confirm it by a few firm arguments, from the text in hand, and other places of scripture, or from the nature of that common place of divinity, whereof that truth is a branch. In confutation of false doctrines, he is neither to raise an old heresy from the grave, nor to mention a blasphemous opinion unnecessarily; but if the people be in danger of an error, he is to confute it soundly, and endeavour to satisfy their judgements and consciences against all objection. In exhortation to duties, he is, as he seeth cause, to teach also the means that help to the performance of them. In dehortation, reprehension, and admonition, which requireth special wisdom, he is, as need requires, not only to discover the nature and greatness of the sin, with the misery attending it, but also to shew the danger the hearers are in to be overtaken and surprised by it, together with the remedies and best way to avoid it. In applying comfort, whether general against all temptations, or particular against some special troubles and terrors, he is carefully to answer such objections as a troubled heart and afflicted spirit may suggest to the contrary. It is also sometimes requisite to give some notes of trial, which is very profitable, especially when performed by able and experienced ministers, with circumspection *Doctrines are to be applied in uses of instruction, confutation, exhortation, reproof, consolation, and and trial; and how.*

and

and prudence, and the signs clearly grounded on the holy scripture, whereby the hearers may be able to examine themselves, whether they have attained those graces, and performed those duties to which he exhorteth, or be guilty of the sin reprehended, and in danger of the judgement threatened, or are such to whom the consolations propounded do belong.

The design of this method. § 12 This method is not prescribed in the Directory as necessary for every man, or upon every text: nor is it necessary to prosecute every doctrine which lies in the text, and such uses as are wisely to be made choice of, as by the minister's residence and conversing with his flock he findeth most needful and seasonable for them: but only it is recommended as a method which hath in experience been found much blessed of God, and very helpful for the peoples understandings and memories.

Catechetical doctrine to be preached, and the nature of catechising. § 13. Ministers are to preach catechetical doctrine, besides their ordinary work of catechising, in such manner as they find most conducive to the edification of their flocks, by act of Assembly 1695, sess. 12. This work of catechising, is a familiar way of instruction or teaching, when the scholar answers the question asked. It is in a plain way to instruct those of their charge in the first principles of the Christian religion. This was the apostolical way of teaching the churches at their first plantation, Heb. v. 12. and vi. 1. 2. 1 Cor. iii. 1, 2. This is the periphrasis of pastor and people, which the Holy Ghost useth, setting forth the reciprocal relation and office betwixt them, Gal. vi 6. "Let him that is taught," or catechised, "in the word, communicate unto him that teacheth," or catechiseth, "in all good things." CATECHUMENI, was a word used by the primitive church, to signify such as learned the principles of religion, and were not yet baptised, and since, such as are catechised, but who have not received the Lord's Supper. These Catechumeni, were of two sorts: one sort was, of those who had not access to baptism till they made public profession of their faith in Jesus Christ, because their parents were Heathens, and themselves strangers to the Christian doctrine; such were catechised before baptism. The other sort of Catechumeni was, the children of professed believers, who were baptised when infants, having a right to
that

that seal by virtue of that promise made to believers and to their children; these, after their infancy was over, and they had been privately instructed in the principles of the Christian religion, offered themselves to public catechising. Both these sorts, after they had made such proficiency in the knowledge of religion, as thereupon they were admitted to the Lord's Table, they got the name of PERFECTI.

§ 14. By the 26th article cap. 1. French church-discipline, the minister of one parish cannot preach in another, without first obtaining leave of the minister of that, unless in case of his absence. In which case it must be the consistory that invites him: and if the flock be dispersed by reason of persecution or other trouble, the stranger shall endeavour to assemble the deacons and elders, which if he cannot do, he shall nevertheless be permitted to preach to re-unite the flock. And by the 20th canon *Concilii sexti, in Trullo:* " Ne liceat episcopo in alia, quæ ad se non " pertinet, civitate publice docere; si quis autem hoc fa- " cere deprehensus fuerit, ab episcopatu desistat, presby- " teri autem munere fungatur." *None to teach publicly out of their own bounds without leave.*

§ 15. Every minister is ordained to have weekly catechising of some part of the parish, and masters of families are to catechise their children and servants at home, whereof account shall be taken by the minister and elders assisting him in the visitation of every family; see act of Assembly, August 30. 1639. And by the act of Assembly, July 30. 1649, the foresaid act is renewed. I know no act for weekly sermons, yet weekly preaching there is; ministers it is true are appointed to preach every Lord's day, both before and after noon, Assem. 1648. sess. 38. But there is none for week-days sermons; yet the one is observed, and the other too much in desuetude. By that act 1649, ministers are so to order their catechetic questions, as thereby the people present may at every diet have the chief heads of saving knowledge presented unto them. And by the same act, every presbytery is ordained to take trial twice in the year, whether all the ministers be careful to keep weekly diets for catechising: and if any be found negligent therein, they shall be admonished for the first fault; and if after such admonition, they shall not amend, the presbytery then shall rebuke them sharply; and if after such rebuke, they shall not yet amend, they *Parochial catechising is appointed to be weekly, not so week-days sermons.*

shall

shall be suspended. Ministers of landward congregations are certainly to be exempted from this in seedtime and harvest; and the act is to be so understood.

Who are to be examined; how often, and from what age; with the use of examination-rolls.

§ 16. All of every quality are to be examined of whose knowledge ministers are not certain, (which clearly supposeth that a minister being once satisfied with a person's knowledge, is not obliged again to examine him), and young persons from the time they are capable of instruction, which it seems hath been thought to be about nine years of age, by the M. S. acts of Assembly at Edinburgh 1570. But see Assembly 1648. sess. 38. among remedies ecclesiastical, in particular against ignorance. And Assem. 1646, sess. 10. remed. 9. ministers are to have rolls of their parish, not only for examination, but for considering the several dispositions of the people, that accordingly they may be admonished and prayed for by them in secret.

Catechisms, larger and shorter, their use in catechising.

§ 17. The larger and shorter Catechisms agreed upon by the Assembly of divines at Westminster, with assistance of commissioners from this church, are by the Assembly 1648, July 28. and August 20. approved and appointed directories, the larger for catechising proficients in religion, and the shorter for catechising such as are of weaker capacity. By the act of Assembly 1649, sess. 30. sessions are to take care that in every family, there be at least one copy of these Catechisms, Confession of Faith, and Directory for worship.

A, B, C, Catechism condemned.

§ 18. By the act of Assembly July 28. 1648, they having found in a little catechism printed at Edinburgh 1647, intitled, "The A, B, C, with the Catechism," that is to say, "An instruction to be taught and learned of young children," very gross errors in the point of universal redemption, and in the number of the sacraments, they do discharge the selling, using, and reprinting thereof.

When a rebuke is to be given at catechising.

§ 19. Some persons may be rebuked at the time of catechising, who deserve more than a private rebuke, and yet need not be brought to public repentence, Assem. 1648, sess. 48.

Of public prayers, and the mind of the directory about them.

§ 20. The intention of the composers of our Directory for public prayer is expressed towards the end of their preface Their own words are, " our meaning therein be-
" ing only that the general heads, the sense and scope of
" the prayers and other parts of public worship being
" known

" known to all, there may be a consent of all the church-
" es in these things that contain the substance of the ser-
" vice and worship of God, and the ministers may be
" hereby directed in their administrations, to keep like
" soundness of doctrine and prayer, and may, if need be,
" have some help and furniture: yet so as they become
" not hereby slothful and negligent in stirring up the
" gifts of Christ in them; but that each one by medita-
" tion, by taking heed to himself, and the flock of God
" committed to him, and by wise observing the ways of
" divine Providence, may be careful to furnish his heart
" and tongue, with further or other materials for prayer,
" as shall be needful on all occasions."

§ 1. The Directory for public prayer doth recommend that prayer which Christ taught his disciples, to be also used in the prayers of the church: because it is not only a pattern of prayer, but is itself a most comprehensive prayer. I do think there are no public prayers used in our church, wherein the petitions in the Lord's prayer, are not expressed throughout their prayers; though perhaps neither at the beginning, or conclusion, or all at once, by way of form. But if any, notwithstanding, think fit to say it likewise all at once, the most proper time for that, some think, would be immediately before the other form used for the ministerial benediction. See § 29 of this title. *The present custom of using the Lord's prayer.*

§ 22. After reading of the word, and singing of the psalm, the Lord is to be called upon to this effect, viz. To acknowledge our great sinfulness, first, by reason of original sin, which, besides the guilt that makes us liable to everlasting damnation, is the seed of all other sins that hath depraved and poisoned all the faculties and powers of soul and body, doth defile our best actions; and were it not restrained, or our hearts renewed by grace, would break forth into innumerable transgressions, and greatest rebellions against the Lord, that ever were committed by the vilest of the sons of men. And next, by reason of actual sins, our own sins, the sins of magistrates, of ministers, and of the whole nation, unto which we are many ways accessory: which sins of ours, receive many fearful aggravations, we having broken all the commandments of the holy, just, and good law of God, doing that which *Of public prayers before sermon, taken out of the Directory for public worship, agreed unto by the Assembly 1645.*

is forbidden, and leaving undone that which is injoined, and that not only out of ignorance and infirmity, but also more presumptuously against the light of our minds, checks of our consciences, and motions of his own Holy Spirit to the contrary. So that we have no cloak for our sin, yea, not only despising the riches of God's goodness, forbearance, and long-suffering, but standing out against many invitations and offers of grace in the gospel. To bewail our blindness of mind, hardness of heart, unbelief, impenitency, security, backwardness, barrenness, our not endeavouring after mortification, and newness of life, nor after the exercise of godliness in the power thereof, and that the best of us have not walked so stedfastly with God, kept our garments so unspotted, nor been so zealous of his glory, and the good of others as we ought, and to mourn over such other sins as the congregation is particularly guilty of, notwithstanding the manifold and great mercies of our God, the love of Christ, the light of the gospel, and reformation of religion, our own purposes, promises, vows, solemn covenants and other obligations to the contrary. To acknowledge and confess, that as we are convinced of our guilt, so, out of a deep sense thereof, we judge ourselves unworthy of the smallest benefits, most worthy of God's fiercest wrath inflicted upon the most rebellious sinners, and that he might justly take his kingdom and gospel from us, plague us with all sorts of spiritual and temporal judgements in this life: and after cast us into utter darkness. Notwithstanding all which, to draw near to the throne of grace, encouraging ourselves with hopes of a gracious answer of our prayers in the riches and allsufficiency of that only one oblation, the satisfaction and intercession of the Lord Jesus Christ, at the right hand of his Father and our Father, and in confidence of the exceeding great and precious promises of mercy and grace in the New Covenant, through the same Mediator thereof, to deprecate the heavy wrath and curse of God, which we are not able to avoid or bear, and humbly and earnestly to supplicate for mercy in the free and full remission of our sins, and that only for the bitter sufferings and precious merits of that of our only Saviour Jesus Christ. That the Lord would vouchsafe to shed abroad his love in our hears by the Holy Ghost; seal unto us by the

the same spirit of adoption, the full assurance of our pardon and reconciliation; comfort all that mourn in Zion, speak peace to the wounded and troubled in spirit, and bind up the broken hearted: and as for secure and presumptuous sinners, that he would open their eyes, convince their consciences, and turn them from darkness unto light. To pray for sanctification by his spirit, the mortification of sin dwelling in, and many times tyrannising over us, the quickning of our dead spirits, with the life of God in Christ, grace to enable us for all duties of our conversation and callings towards God and men, strength against temptations, the sanctified use of blessings and crosses, and perseverance in faith and obedience unto the end. To pray for the propagation of the gospel and kingdom of Christ to all nations, for the conversion of the Jews, and the fullness of the Gentiles, the fall of Antichrist, and the hastening of the second coming of our Lord: for the deliverance of the distressed churches abroad, from the tyranny of the Antichristian faction, and from the cruel oppressions and blasphemies of the Turk; for the blessing of God upon all reformed churches, especially upon the churches and kingdoms of Scotland, England and Ireland, more particularly for that church and kingdom whereof we are members, that therein God would establish peace and truth, the purity of all his ordinances, and the power of godliness, prevent and remove heresy, schism, profaneness, superstition, security, and unfruitfulness under the means of grace, heal all our rents and divisions, preserve us from breach of our solemn covenant. Prayers are to be put up for all in supreme authority, and those in subordinate authority to them, 1 Tim. ii. 1. 2. 4. which prayers are to be directed by their circumstances. We are to pray for all pastors and teachers, that God would fill them with his Spirit, and make them powerful in their ministry, and give unto all his people pastors according to his own heart; for the universities and schools, and religious seminaries for church and common-wealth, that they may flourish more in learning and piety; for the particular city or congregation, that God would pour out a blessing upon the ministry of the word, sacraments, and discipline, upon the civil government, and all the families and persons therein; for mercy to the afflicted in any inward or outward distress; for seasonable weather, and fruitful seasons, as time may require; for averting judgements that we either feel or fear, or are liable unto, as famine, sword, pestilence, and such like. To pray earnestly for his grace and effectual assistance to the sanctification of his holy Sabbath, the Lord's day, in all the duties thereof; that the Lord, who teacheth to profit, would graciously please to pour out the spirit of grace, together with the outward means thereof, causing us to attain such a measure of the excellency of the knowledge of Christ Jesus our Lord, that we may account all things but as dross, in comparison of him; and that we, tasting the first fruits of the glory to come, may long for a more full and perfect communion with him. That God would in a special manner furnish his servant now called to dispense the bread of life unto his household, with wisdom, fidelity, zeal, and utterance, that he may divide the word of God aright, to every one his portion, in evidence and demonstration of the Spirit and Power, and that the Lord would circumcise the ears and hearts of the hearers to hear in love, and receive with meekness the ingrafted word, strengthen them against the temptations of Satan, the cares of the world, the hardness of their own hearts, and whatsoever else may hinder their profitable and saving hearing.

Public prayer after sermon.

§ 23. The sermon being ended, the minister is to give thanks for the great love of God, in sending of his Son Jesus Christ unto us, for the communication of his Holy Spirit, for the light and liberty of the glorious gospel, for the admirable goodness of God, in freeing the land from Antichristian darkness and tyranny, for the reformation of religion, and many temporal blessings: and to pray for the continuance of the gospel, and all ordinances thereof in their purity, power, and liberty: and to turn some of the most useful heads of the sermon into some few petitions, and to pray that it may abide in the heart, and bring forth fruit in the life and conversation. To pray for preparation for death and judgement, and a watching for the coming of our Lord Jesus Christ; to intreat of God the forgiveness of the iniquity of our holy things, and the acceptation of our spiritual sacrifice, through the merit and mediation of our great High Priest and Saviour, the Lord Jesus Christ.

§ 24. Notwithstanding of the above Directory for public prayers, the minister may (as in prudence he shall see meet) make use of some part of these petitions after the sermon, or he may offer up to God some of the thanksgivings in his prayer before sermon. *The meaning of the Directory.*

§ 25. By the act of Assembly, August 6. 1649, their commission being impowered to emit the paraphrase of the psalms, and establish the same for public use, they did accordingly conclude and establish the paraphrase of the psalms in metre, now used in this church, after the presbyteries had sent their animadversions thereupon. *Of singing of psalms, and the authority of the present paraphrase.*

§ 26. It was the ancient practice of the church, as it is yet of some reformed churches abroad, for the minister or precentor to read over as much of the psalm in metre together, as was intended to be sung at once, and then the harmony and melody followed without interruption, and people did either learn to read, or get most of the psalms by heart; but afterwards, it being found, that when a new paraphrase of the psalms was appointed, it could not at first be so easy for the people to follow, then it became customary that each line was read by itself, and then sung: But now, having for so long time made use of this paraphrase, and the number of those who can read being increased, it is but reasonable that the ancient custom should be revived, according to what is insinuated by the Directory on this subject. And that such who cannot read may know what psalms to get by heart, let such be affixed on some conspicuous part of the pulpit as are to be sung in public at next meeting of the congregation. It were to be wished that masters of families would path the way for the more easy introducing of our former practice, by reviving and observing the same in their family-worship. *Singing is not to be interrupted by reading of the line.*

§ 27. In the 8th sess. of Assembly 1648, there is an act for examining the labours of Mr Zachary Boyd, upon the other scripture-songs; and by Assembly 1706, sess. + the scripture-songs by Mr Patrick Sympson, minister at Renfrew, are recommended to be used in private families; and in order to prepare them for the public use of the church, this was renewed in Assembly 1707; and by the 15th act of Assembly 1708, their commission is instructed and appointed to consider the printed version of the scripture-songs, with the remarks of presbyteries thereupon; and after *Scripture-songs to be used in families, and prepared for public use.*

after examination thereof, they are authorised and impowered to conclude and emit the same, for the public use of the church. The present version of the psalms having been ordered in the same manner in the year 1649.

The design and intention of the soul in singing.

§ 28. Though a believer be afflicted, yet he is to sing, since it is such a duty as prayer is, as it tendeth to cheer the soul's disposition, and to sweeten and mitigate the cross under it. Complaints of our sin and failings may be mournful songs; and because God hath redeemed, pardoned, and comforted others, therefore we are to rejoice in the hope and desires of the same to ourselves. Though the subject of a song doth not always quadrate with our case, yet, unto a judicious attentive person, there is always some attribute of God, some providence, or word of his, in that very subject to be praised. In the imprecatory psalms, we sing to the praise of divine justice, against the malicious enemies of his church, like unto these that the Psalmist did aim against.

Ministerial benediction.

§ 29. The minister useth to dismiss the congregation with a solemn blessing, or prayer to God for them, which ordinarily is in these or the like words: " 2 Cor. xiii 14. " The grace of the Lord Jesus Christ, the love of God the " Father, and the communion of the Holy Ghost, be with " you all, *Amen*:" But when probationers for the ministry are preaching, they use to pronounce the blessing with this variation: Instead of " be with you," they say, " be " with us." And the moderators of General Assemblies observe the same stile in pronouncing of the blessing at their dissolution: Yet, seeing no minister of a congregation doth put up that public prayer alone, it would therefore seem, it should always run in the ordinary stile of other congregational petitions. viz. " be with us."

Bowing in the pulpit to be laid aside.

§ 30. Ministers their bowing in the pulpit, though a lawful custom, is hereafter to be laid aside, for satisfaction of the desires of the synod of England, February 7. 1645.

TITLE

TITLE II.

Of Family Worship.

§ 1. BY act of Assembly August 24. 1647, revived Assembly 1694, they approve of the following rules and directions for private and secret worship, and mutual edification, for cherishing piety, maintaining unity, and avoiding schism and division; and ministers and ruling elders are required to make diligent search in the congregation, whether there be among them any family which neglects to perform family worship; and if any such be found, the head of the family is first to be admonished privately to amend his fault; and in case of his continuance therein, he is to be gravely reproved by the session; after which reproof, if he be found still to neglect family-worship, let him be suspended from the Lord's Supper. *Habitual neglectors of family-worship censurable by suspension from the Lord's table.*

§ 2. The head of every family is to have a care, that both themselves, and all within their charge, be daily diligent in performing of secret worship, and be given to prayer and meditation. *Secret worship to be performed.*

§ 3. The ordinary duties of families convened for the exercise of piety are these, 1st, Prayer and praises; next, reading of the scriptures, with catechising in a plain way together, with godly conferences; as also admonitions and rebukes upon just reasons. *What family worship is.*

§ 4. The master of a family, though of the best qualifications, is not to take on him to interpret the scriptures; yet it is commendible, that, by way of conference, they make some good use of what hath been read and heard. As for example, if any sin be reproved in the word read, use may be made thereof, to make all the family circumspect and watchful against the same; or, if any judgement be threatened, or mentioned to have been inflicted in that portion of scripture which is read, use may be made, to make all the family fear, least the same or a worse judgement befal them, unless they beware of the sins that procured it. And finally, if any duty be required, or comfort held forth in a promise, use may be made to stir up themselves to implore Christ for strength to enable them for doing commanded duty, and to apply the offered comfort. *Reading of the scriptures to be improved in family conference.*

fort. In all which the master of the family is to have the chief hand, and any member of the family may propound a question or doubt for resolution.

Chaplains, their use and abuse.

§ 5. Persons of quality are allowed to entertain one approved by the presbytery, for performing the worship of God in their families. And in other families where the head is unfit, one constantly residing in the family, and approved by the minister and session may be employed in that service: yet it was never the mind of the church, that persons of quality should lay their family-worship entirely upon their chaplains, and never perform it in their own persons, as appears from the solemn acknowledgement of sins, where they confess, the ignorance of God and of his Son prevails exceedingly in the land; the greatest part of matters of families amongst noblemen, barons, gentlemen, burgesses, and commons, neglect to seek God in their families, and to endeavour the reformation thereof; and albeit it hath been much pressed, yet few of our nobles and great ones ever to this day could be persuaded to perform family-duties themselves, and in their own persons, which makes so necessary and useful a duty to be misregarded by others of inferior rank; nay, many of the nobility, gentry, and barons, who should have been examples of godliness and sober walking unto others, have been ring-leaders of excess and rioting.

No mere stranger to perform family worship.

§ 6. Considering that persons aiming at division may be ready to creep into houses, and lead captive silly and unstable souls; for preventing whereof, no idler who hath no particular calling, or vagrant person, under pretence of a calling, is to be suffered to perform worship in families. The not observing of this direction hath been of sad consequence to some families in this land in late times. Neither are persons from divers families to be invited or admitted into family-worship, unless it be these who are lodged with them or at meat, or otherways with them upon some lawful occasion.

Set forms for prayer, in cases of necessity, allowed.

§ 7. So many as can conceive prayer ought to make use of that gift of God, albeit those who are rude and weaker may begin with a set form of prayer, but so as they be not sluggish in stirring up in themselves the spirit of prayer, which is given to all the children of God in some measure.

§ 8. Let

§ 8. Let them confess to God how unworthy they are to come in his presence, and how unfit to worship his Majesty, and therefore earnestly ask of God the spirit of prayer. They are to confess their sins, and the sins of the family, accusing, judging, and condemning themselves for them, till they bring their souls to some measure of true humiliation; they are to pour out their souls to God, in the name of Christ, by the Spirit, for forgiveness of sins, for grace to repent, to believe, and to live soberly, righteously, and godly, and that they may serve God with joy and delight, walking before him; they are to give thanks to God for his many mercies to his people and to themselves, and especially for his love in Christ, and for the light of the gospel; they are to pray for such particular benefits, spiritual and temporal, as they stand in need of for the time; they ought to pray for the church of Christ in general, for all the reformed churches, and for this church in particular, and for all that suffer for the name of Christ, for all superiors, for the Queen's majesty, and inferior magistrates; for the magistrates, ministers, and whole body of the congregation; and for their neighbours absent about their lawful affairs, and for these that are at home. The prayer may be closed with an earnest desire that God may be glorified in the coming of the kingdom of his Son, and that what they have asked according to his will may be done.

Materials for family prayer

§ 9. Extraordinary duties both of humiliation and thanksgiving are to be carefully performed in families, when the Lord, by extraordinary occasions, private or public, calleth for them.

Fasts and thanksgiving days in families.

§ 10. Persons of divers families being abroad upon their particular vocations, or any necessary occasions, are to take care that the duties of prayer and thanksgiving be performed by such as the company shall judge fittest.

Travellers are to worship together

§ 11. By an act of Assembly 1697, sess. 5. such elders and deacons as obstinately refuse or neglect family-worship by themselves, or others appointed for that end, are to be removed from their office.

Church office bearers to be deposed who neglect family-worship.

TITLE III.

Of Baptism.

What baptism is.

§ 1. Baptism is a sacrament of the New Testament, wherein Christ hath ordained the washing with water in the name of the Father, Son, and Holy Ghost, to be a sign and seal of ingrafting into himself, and of partaking of the benefits of the covenant of grace, and whereby the parties baptised are solemnly admitted into the visible church, and enter into an open and professed engagement to be only and wholly the Lord's.

And to whom to be administered.

§ 2. The visible church, which is catholic or universal under the gospel, consists of all those throughout the world that profess the true religion, together with their children: and baptism is not to be administered to any that are out of the same, they being strangers to the covenant of promise, till they profess their faith in Christ, and obedience to him: But infants descending from parents, either both, or but one of them, professing faith in Christ, and obedience to him, are in that respect within the covenant, and to be baptised. The Directory for worship says, that children of professing parents are Christians, and federally holy before baptism, and therefore are they baptised; for their baptism supposeth them to be church-members, and doth not make or constitute them such: And therefore the practice of denying burial among Christians unto children unbaptised is unagreeable to this doctrine, and is most unwarrantable: If we consider, that the sacraments are ordinances to be administered in the church, and to the church, they necessarily suppose the pre-existence of a church, and the child's previous right of that seal.

The engagement of parents in baptism binds their children.

§ 3. By that covenant, whereof baptism is a seal, the Lord promiseth to be our God, and we are in his promised strength to engage to be his people; which engagement, though Christian infants be not capable to come under of themselves formally; yet, by their parents vowing in their name and stead, they do thereby become absolutely bound to the performance thereof, because their obligation and duty to be the Lord's were supposed, and previous unto their being baptised.

§ 4. When

§ 4. When both parents are dead, or necessarily absent, another sponsor is to be taken; or, when they are scandalous and erroneous, and thereby give ground to think they are none of Christ's, and for which they may merit the highest censures of the church, if not prevented by evidences of their sincere repentance: In that case, to testify that it doth not appear that the children have any right unto the privilege of that sealing ordinance through their immediate parents; and that they may, notwithstanding, have a right thereto by their more remote parents, it is necessary that a sponsor present the children, and engage for them. The parent is to be required to provide some fit person, and, if it can be, one related as a parent to the child should be sponsor. Yet it seems ignorant parents are to be admitted to present their children; for, by act of Assembly 1648, sess. 38. art. 3. of domestic remedies of the sins of the land, this is one, that persons to be married, and who have children to be baptised, who are very rude and ignorant, be stirred up and exhorted, as at all times, so especially at that time, to attain some measure of Christian knowledge in the grounds of religion, that they may give to the minister, before the elder of the bounds where they live, some account of their knowledge, that so they may the better teach their family, and train up their children. *When another sponsor than the parent is necessary.*

§ 5. In case of children exposed, whose baptism, after inquiry, cannot be known, the session is to order the presenting of the child to baptism, and the session itself is to see to the Christian education of the child: As also, when scandalous parents cannot prevail with any fit person, or rather relation, to present the child in their name, or when the relations of deceased parents refuse to become their sponsors, the session then is to order as is said. The magistrate is to take care that exposed infants be maintained, by laying the expences thereof upon the parish proportionally. By the 84th canon. con. 6. In Trullo, " Canonicas " patrum leges sequentes, de infantibus quoque decerni- " mus, quoties non inveniuntur firmi testes qui eos absque " ulla dubitatione baptisatos esse dicant, nec ipsi, propter " ætatem de sibi tradito mysterio aptè respondere possint, " debere absque ulla offensione baptisari." *When the session should be sponsor.*

§ 6. By the 4th article, cap. 11. of the French church-discipline, the children of fathers and mothers of the Romish church, and of excommunicated persons, cannot be admitted into the church, though they were presented by believing sponsors, unless their fathers and mothers consent to it, and desire it, in quiting and yielding up to the sponsors their right as to instructing them; for baptism being a privilege and benefit, it is not to be imposed, nor children baptised against their parents will, into a communion whereof they are not members: hence the custom of the church, at administering of baptism, is to ask the parent or sponsor, if they present that child to be baptised? to which they declare their willingness, by their answering affirmatively. By the 10th act of the said 11th chapter, these who present children to be baptised, must be, at least, fourteen years of age, having received the sacrament of the Lord's Supper; and if they have not, that they promise faithfully to use their endeavours to prepare for it.

baptism not to be imposed. The age and qualifications of a sponsor.

§ 7. When single persons or families remove unto other congregations, they cannot regularly there be admitted unto the benefit of the sacraments for themselves or children, till they produce a declaration of the church from which they came, testifying them to be free of any known scandal, otherways these holy things may be profaned, contrary unto that church practice and precept *sacra sacris*; of which testimonials there should a register be kept, and they run in this form: " These are to testify, that the
" bearer hereof   hath lived in this parish of
"   preceeding   last bypast; during
" which space he behaved himself civilly and honestly,
" free of all church-censure, or public scandal known to
" us. This given by command of the kirk-session of the
" said parish. At   the   day of
" years, by A. B. session-clerk."

The use, end, and form of testimonials.

§ 8. This testimonial imports, that the person attested is not *per famam clamosam*, or notourly scandalous, through error or immorality; but it doth not suppose him to have a competent measure of knowledge, for that is left to the trial and inquiry of the church, to which he seeks to be added as a member, therefore their judgement is never anticipate by any such clause, unless in testimonials for persons desiring the benefit of the Lord's Supper in another parish, where the pastor thereof cannot then get time to examine all strangers. It is true, when mens lives and measure

Their import, and how and why different from testimonials, in order to the Lord's Supper.

sure of knowledge are generally believed to be good and competent, this order, as to such, may be dispensed with; yet it were to be wished, that even those would observe it, and not give occasion to others, not so good or knowing, to be angry, when they are restricted or obliged unto it.

§ 9. In the baptismal engagement, the parent, or sponsor, is, in name of the child, to renounce the devil and all his works, the vain pomp and glory of this wicked world, and all the sinful lusts of the flesh. He is to promise to bring up the child in the knowledge of the grounds of the Christian religion, as they are contained in the holy scriptures of the Old and New Testament; and, lastly, he is to bring up the child in that holy life and practice which God hath commanded in his word. The engagements to be given in name of children at baptism, should be exprest in these or the like general terms, conform to the Directory for worship, approven by the General Assembly, 7th Feb. 1645. The due observation whereof is seriously recommended by the 10th act of Assembly 1705. *Form of baptismal engagement.*

§ 10. The sacrament of baptism is to be administrate in the face of the congregation after sermon, and before pronouncing of the blessing, (see act of Assem. Feb. 7. 1645.) The child to be baptised, after notice given to the minister the day before, is to be presented, the pastor remaining in the same place where he hath preached, and having water provided in a large bason; he is before baptism to use some words of instruction, touching the author, institution, nature, use, and end of this sacrament: he is also to admonish all that are present to repent of their sins against their covenant with God, and to improve and make the right use of their baptism: next, the parent, or sponsor, is to be exhorted to order his conversation aright, and walk circumspectly; when he is to be engaged in the words of the form above. This being done, prayer is also to be joined with the word of institution, for sanctifying the water to this spiritual use. The prayer is to this or the like effect, that the Lord, who hath not left us as strangers without the covenant of promise, but called us to the priviledges of his ordinances, would graciously vouchsafe to sanctify and bless his own ordinance of baptism at this time: that he would join the inward bap- *The form of ministration of baptism and the prayer.*

tism

tifm of his fpirit with the outward baptifm of water; make this baptifm to this infant a feal of adoption, regeneration, and eternal life, and of all other promifes of the Covenant of Grace; that the child may be planted in the likenefs of the death and refurrection of Chrift, and that the body of fin being deftroyed in him, he may ferve God in newnefs of life all his days. Then the minifter is to demand the name of the child, which being told him, he is to fay (calling the child by his name) "I baptife "thee in the name of the Father, of the Son, and of the "Holy Ghoft." As he pronounceth thefe words, he is to baptife the child with water, which, for the manner of doing, it is not only lawful but fufficient, and moft expedient, to be by pouring or fprinkling of the water on the face of the child, without adding any other ceremony. This done, he is to give thanks and pray to this or the like purpofe; acknowledging, with all thankfulnefs, that the Lord is true and faithful in keeping covenant and mercy; that he is good and gracious, not only that he numbereth us among his faints, but is pleafed alfo to beftow upon our children this fingular token and badge of his love in Chrift; that in his truth and fpecial Providence, he daily bringeth fome into the bofom of his church, to be partakers of his ineftimable benefits purchafed by the blood of his dear Son, for the continuance and increafe of his church; and praying, that the Lord would ftill continue and daily confirm more and more this his unfpeakable favour; that he would receive the infant now baptifed, and folemnly entered into the houfehold of faith, into his fatherly tuition and defence, and remember him with the favour he fheweth unto his people; that if he fhall be taken out of this life in his infancy, the Lord, who is rich in mercy, would be pleafed to receive him up into glory, and if he live and attain the years of difcretion, that the Lord would fo teach him by his Word and Spirit, and make his baptifm effectual to him, and fo uphold him by his divine power and grace, that by faith he may prevail againft the devil, the world, and the flefh; till in the end he obtain a full and final victory, and fo be kept by the power of God through faith unto falvation, through Jefus Chrift our Lord.

§ 11. By

§ 11. By the 14th article, chap. 11. of the French church difcipline, minifters fhall reject names given to children, that favour of ancient Paganifm, fuch as Diana, and the like; and the names attributed to God, fuch as Emmanual, and the like, but the names of holy men and women in fcripture are to be chofen. *Minifters are to reject indecent names to children.*

§ 12. By the 10th act of Affembly 1690, they confidering, that the parties receiving the facraments are folemnly devoted and engaged to God before angels and men, and are folemnly received as members of the church, and do entertain communion with her; and that by former acts, viz. December 10. 1638, and Feb. 7. 1645, the private ufe of them hath been condemned: as alfo, that by allowing the private ufe of the fame in pretended cafes of neceffity, the fuperftitious opinion is nourifhed, that they are neceffary unto falvation, not only as commanded duties, but as means without which falvation cannot be attained, therefore they difcharge the adminiftration of the Lord's Supper to fick perfons in their houfes, and all other ufe of the fame, except in the public Affemblies of the church; and alfo, they difcharge the adminiftration of baptifm in private, that is, in any place, or at any time, when the congregation is not orderly called together to wait on the difpenfing of the word, which is agreeable to the 6th article, chap. 11. of the French church-difcipline, and not to be difpenfed with, except in times of perfecution; and when a child is baptifed in a private houfe, as is ufed in England, in that cafe the minifter is to certify the congregation to which the child belongs, that the fame was baptifed by him, at fuch a time, and in fuch a place, before divers witneffes. By the 31ft can. conc. 6. in Trullo: "Clericos qui in oratoriis quæ " funt intra domos facra faciunt vel baptizant hoc illius " loci epifcopi fententia facere debere, decernimus. Qua- " re fi quis clericus hoc non fic fervaverit, deponatur." *Private ufe of facraments condemned.*

§ 13. There is a regifter to be kept of the names of all baptifed, and of their parents names and defignations, and of the time of their baptifm, and of the names of the witneffes thereto; and of all illegitimate children their names, and thofe of their parents fhall be likewife infert: But of fuch it is only faid, that they are not born in lawful marriage. When it is an inceftuous child, it fhall fuffice *Regifter of baptifm.*

suffice to name the mother, with the presenter of the child, that the remembrance of so heinous a sin may be extinguished This is conform to the 19th article of the foresaid 11th chapter.

Baptism to be but once administered.

§ 14. Baptism is not to be administered but once unto any person. It is not the practice of the reformed churches to re-baptise those who were baptised by the Popish clergy; for they baptise with water in the name of the Father, Son, and Holy Ghost, as we do. But Quakers, and others, who want this external seal of the Covenant of Grace, though such should make profession of the true faith, that sacrament of baptism doth remain to be administered unto them, before they or their children can enjoy the privileges of church-members.

He who baptiseth must be ordained and lawfully called.

§ 15. Neither of the sacraments may be dispensed by any but a minister of the word, lawfully ordained, saith our Confession of Faith, cap. 27. art. 4; and persons are to be baptised by a minister of the gospel lawfully called thereunto, according to art. 2. cap. 28. Our law makes infeftments void and null, where they are not given by such as it appoints and authoriseth to give them: thus are all infeftments in royal burghs, not given by some of the magistrates or clerks thereof Yet baptism, when it is administered by a person, whose ordination and call is not agreeable to the principles, constitutions, and practice of this church, the essentials of the sacrament being observed, that baptism is esteemed as valid, though not as lawful. And although the reformed churches, (so far as I can learn) would inflict the highest censure upon women or laicks, as profaners and mockers of the holy sacraments, if they presumed to dispense them, and would not have the least scruple to baptise those on whom they had wickedly usurped a power to impose a mock of it; yet I find they have declined to determine so clearly in the case of re-baptising of these who were baptised by deposed ministers; which, I think, doth not proceed so much from the want of a parity of reason, as it doth from the offence, which may sometimes be taken by a great part of a church, who do not understand, or are not satisfied with the grounds of their deposition, or perhaps may be altogether ignorant of their being deposed: but when a deposed minister hath so little interest,

est, and so few followers, that he is esteemed by most, yea, by a vast majority, to be lawfully deposed: in that case it might give offence not to re-baptise a child who was so unlawfully baptised.

TITLE IV.

Of the Lord's Supper.

§ 1. THE Lord's Supper, so called from the time of its institution and first celebration, is a sacrament of the New Testament, wherein, by giving and receiving bread and wine, according to the appointment of Jesus Christ, his death is shewed forth, and they that worthily communicate, not after a corporal and carnal manner, but by faith feed upon his body and blood, to their spiritual nourishment and growth in grace, have their union and communion with him confirmed, testify and renew their thankfulness and engagements to God, and their mutual love and fellowship each with another, as members of the same mystical body. *What the Lord's Supper is.*

§ 2. These who are to be admitted to this sacrament, must be found to have a competent knowledge of the fundamentals of the Christian religion, and to be of such an inoffensive walk and conversation, both towards God and their neighbours, that they are not known to be guilty of any scandal that meriteth church-censure. By the 12th chap. of the French-church discipline, art. 2. persons shall not be admitted to the Lord's Supper, till they be above twelve years of age. But I am sure, if children at nine years of age can express themselves piously and knowingly, shewing that they have the grace signified and promised, the seal of the promise cannot warrantably be denied unto them By the 6th art. of that chapter, a man that is deaf and dumb, shewing his piety and religion what he can, by evident signs, tokens, and gestures, may be admitted to partake, when by a long experience of the holiness of his life, the church shall perceive he has faith. By the 7th art. thereof, the bread of the sacrament is to be administered to those who cannot drink wine, they protesting that it is not through contempt, and they doing what they can towards it, by putting the cup as near *Who may be admitted thereto, and who not.*

their

their mouth as they may do, to avoid giving any manner of offence. And by the 10th art. of the same 12th chapter, they say, in as much as several sick persons come to receive this sacrament, which gives occasion that severals make scruple of drinking the wine after them, the pastors and elders shall be warned to take good heed that care and prudence be used in this matter; they may communicate last.

The ordinary elements to be used in the Lord's Supper.

§ 3. Ordinary bread is to be used; and it is most decent it be leavened wheat bread. Any kind of wine may be used in the Lord's Supper, yet wine of a red colour seemeth most suitable. In case a society of Christians should want the fruits of the vine of all sorts, I cannot think but it might be supplied by some composure as like unto it as could be made: and if any church laboured under that invincible necessity, were it not safer for them to interpret that as a call and warrant to communicate, though wanting the fruit of the vine, than to construct it an authorising them in a perpetual neglect of that sacrament?

Communicants to be recorded by the session's order, and admitted by their sentence after trial.

§ 4. When the admission of those who are allowed to partake of the Lord's Supper, is once recorded by a sentence of the church session, which is to proceed either upon the minister's examining of the parties in their presence, or at least of two or three of the elders, that so the rest may pass their sentence on their testimony and report; in that case there will never be any necessity of coming afterwards to ministers and elders for re-admission, unless by after-scandal they be judicially suspended from that privilege. See the vindication of presbyterial government, printed at London 1659, page 143. See § 6. and 16. of this title.

How strangers are admitted with, and how without testimonials.

§ 5. When the sacrament of the Lords Supper is to be celebrated in a neighbouring congregation, who have not leisure, and whose work is not to examine strangers, (as above) the minister, or any two elders in his absence, may give testimonials, yea, should give to any of their parish who communicate ordinarily at their own parish church, and are without scandal in their life for the time, who are thereupon to be admitted *ex debito*, and by reason of the communion of saints. But this is not to prejudge the admission of any honest person, who occasionally is in the place

place where the communion is celebrate, or such as by death or absence of their own minister or elders, could not have a testimonial. Act of Assembly Feb. 7. 1645, art. 12. about uniformity of worship.

§ 6. By the 11th act of Assembly 1706, it is recommended to all ministers, to take as strict a trial as can be of such as they admit to the Lord's Supper, especially before their first admission thereto, and that they diligently instruct them, particularly as to the Covenant of Grace, and the nature and end of that ordinance as a seal thereof, and charge upon their consciences the obligations they lie under from their baptismal covenant, and seriously exhort them to renew the same. This fully answers the end that any Protestant bishop can have in ministering of confirmation, or laying on of hands upon those that are baptised and come to years of discretion: neither doth it favour of any superstition, or any scandalous-like approach to the Papists their confirmation (by chrism on infants) for the receiving of the Holy Ghost, which is nothing else but an audacious and appish imitation of conveying miraculous operations by the apostles hands. *Ministers behaviour, especially with persons when first admitted.*

§ 7. It is agreeable to the law of nature to seek and promote the good of others, according to our ability and opportunity, by admonishing them to forbear sin, and repent for it, Lev. xix. 17. "Thou shalt not hate thy brother in thy heart; thou shalt in any wise rebuke thy neighbour, and not suffer sin upon him." See Matth. xviii. 15. I suppose that the sovereigns on earth did publish their intentions of pardoning all traitors, who should express their sorrow and hatred at former treasons; and as a mean to reduce them to that happy temper, had strictly commanded and required all their good subjects, to put them in mind of the ingratitude, folly, and danger of their treason: would not we conclude, that a neighbour seeing his fellow commit treason, and not reproving him therefor, did neither regard his sovereign's honour and authority, nor yet valued his neighbour's happiness? how much more justly may our Lord and Saviour load and charge church-rulers with this sin, if they fail to perform that duty, seeing he hath laid his special commands upon them to do it? and therefore, if any elder or minister, shall suffer one whom they know to be guilty of some *Persons guilty of more private scandals, how to be admitted.*

O 2 scandalous

scandalous or heinous sin though not public, to approach unto the Lord's table, without satisfying acknowledgements made in private for it, they do thereby, for ought they know, suffer him to partake of that holy Supper with unrepented sin upon him.

Persons who converse not together, how to be admitted.

§ 8. As there are divers kinds of good gifts, so there are divers degrees of them, according to which we may and ought to love our neighbour, more or less, because we are commanded to do good unto all men, both with our spiritual advice, and with our worldly goods, ministering to their necessities, but especially unto them who are of the household of faith, Gal. vi. 10. We are bound to shew our love to our enemies, by overcoming evil with good, Rom. xii. 21; which is the way, not only to be even with them that wrong us, but to be above them. Every man is called to provide for his own, especially for those of his own house, 1 Tim v. 8. We are to have a natural affection for such as be near to us in blood, and the want thereof is discovered by their want of converse. The apostle, 1 Cor. v. 11. forbids to keep company with some scandalous persons, and admitting that precept to be prohibitive of a civil intimacy, it holds as a stronger argument against religious communion with, or at least admission of them to such a distinguishing ordinance. Solomon, Prov. xxii. 24 forbids us to go into the company of a furious man, and to converse frequently and familiarly with an angry man, as friends use to do. So that, though there are common offices due to all men, yet that distinguishing practice of friends in frequent conversing together, is free and optional, as the bestowing of gifts is. Indeed, when notour scandalous breaches and differences do happen, in that case, the parties should be obliged to a formal agreement, by conversing in presence of those whose work it is to compose such differences; but even then, they can be obliged to continue in no more friendship than a common converse imports, especially the lesed party. They may be indeed both obliged to profess a sincere reconciliation, though not unto a familiar conversation. But as to the usual converse with those of our household and blood-relations, as husband with wife, and father with children, or the like, it is agreable both to the laws of nature and interest,

interest, firmly to preserve and persevere in that. Wherefore, upon the whole, where such near relations refuse usual converse with one another, or neighbours at variance, shall refuse to renew or continue a common converse, in that case neither of the guilty parties ought to be admitted to the Lord's table.

§ 9. *Fama clamosa, publica & frequens*, doth supply the part of an accuser, so that any who lie under the lash of such reports, must be so far from being admitted to the Lord's table, or yet attested of, as free of scandal, that they should be processed thereupon, and have the benefit of neither, till they justify themselves; see tit. of visitation of families. *(Persons scandalous per famam clamosam, how to be admitted or attested.)*

§ 10. When one church government is established, if the church shall even then be so unhappy as to be afflicted, with schism from those who own the same; in that case, there ought to be union and communion sought and admitted, notwithstanding failings and defects of several kinds, providing union and communion may be had without accession to the guilt or defects of others: that is, without being obliged to approve of them, or condemn in our own practice what we judged right, or that we be not by any engagement restrained from a duty. Indeed where there is no union in church government, Mr Durham on Scandal, chap. 13. says, he cannot, nor dares not offer any directions for making up an union here. As for allowing these who in their judgement differ about church-government to communicate with us, it is safer to allow them to communicate with us, than for us to communicate with them; for by this way, they may be brought unto us, and we out of hazard of being led away by them. But for all this, such persons are not to be admitted, if they be in their practice culpable of any thing which would justly keep back those of our own communion; that would be truly a contracting of too much guilt, for gaining of any occasional proselyte or communicant. *(How to admit those who take some different methods from the church.)*

§ 11. When there hath been a great and general defection by a church and kingdom, then the national Assembly useth to appoint a national fast and humiliation for these causes. See the act for a fast November 12. 1690. And whoever had been guilty or accessory to the sins and evils therein acknowledged, if they joined in the public fasting, they *(How these who are guilty of national sins should be admitted.)*

they did thereby acknowledge the causes thereof to be just and true, and professed their sorrow and humiliation therefor: wherewith the session ought to be satisfied, if they signify their meaning to have been so, or that they judge the causes of the fast true and relevant.

How non-communicants should be treated.

§ 12 By the act of Assembly 3d August 1642, every presbytery is enjoined to proceed against non-communicants; and by the 11th art. cap. 12. of the French church-discipline, these who have been a long time in the church, and will not communicate of the Lord's Supper, if they do it through contempt, or for fear of being obliged to forsake all manner of idolatry, after several admonitions, they shall be cut off from the body of the church; but if it be through infirmity, they shall be borne with for some time, until they can be established. And by the act of parliament 16th James VI. cap. 17. which is never yet rescinded, but rather included in the acts made and ratified against profaneness: By it all men are to communicate once a year, without respect to the excuse of deadly feuds, under pecunial pains, according to the quality of the transgressors. This act is ratified by the parliament 1641. Though people ought not, nor cannot, be compelled to communicate, yet non-communicating, not being a matter indifferent, but a palpable disobedience to God's voice in the gospel, (Luke xxii. 19.) they ought to account for that scandalous neglect and intermission, before they be of new admitted.

The design and distribution of tickets.

§ 13. None must presume to sit down at the Lord's table but such are admitted according to order, except those whose fitness is unquestioned and notour. Each person, before communicating, doth deliver the parish lead ticket, when sought for, to one of the elders or deacons when sitting at the table: but it were safer to demand these warrants or tokens at their entry to the tables; for a person unwarily or designedly approaching to the table without a token, may, with less observation or offence, be thus kept from it, than raised from it. These tickets are distributed by the session, or members thereof, by their allowance, to such as they have admitted, or know to be lawfully attested from other parishes.

Fencing and opening of the tables. Its use and end.

§ 14. The minister and session having, according to the rules of discipline, admitted unto, or debarred persons from the Lord's table, the pastor doth now, immediately before he

he read the words of inftitution, doctrinally debar from, and inviteth all unto the Lord's table, according to the ftate and condition they really are in. If there has been an unexactnefs or omiffion in the exercife of difcipline, through which fome are admitted whom the word of God forbids to approach on their peril, this doctrinal debarring may fcar fuch from partaking: but if there hath been an imprudent and uncharitable exercife of difcipline, in debaring of fome wrongoufly, then the paftor's doctrinal opening of the tables and inviting fuch from the word of God to approach, although debared by the key of difcipline, may neverthelefs comfort themfelves in the Lord, who will be a little fanctuary unto them who are thus roughly and indifcreetly treated by the watchmen. From all which we may gather, that it is fafer to err on the right hand of charity, than on the left hand of ftrictnefs and feverity: The civil law gives this rule, "Semper in dubiis benig-
" niora præferenda funt."

§ 15. It is fo far from being a warrant, and fatisfying Secret prepato a man's confcience, for approaching the Lord's table, ration. becaufe the difcipline of the church admits him, that even a man habitually gracious and prepared, will not for ordinary adventure to approach it, except he hath made confcience of getting himfelf actually prepared, and his graces put in exercife, and fet apart fome confiderable time for that purpofe.

§ 16. By the act of Affembly 7th February 1545, about Public prepathe obfervation of the Directory in fome points of public ration. worfhip, congregations are ftill to be tried and examined before the communion. Item, That when the communion is to be celebrate, one minifter may be employed for affifting the minifter of the parifh, or at the moft two. Item, That there be one fermon of preparation delivered in the ordinary place of public worfhip, upon the day immediately preceding. Item, That the minifter who cometh to affift, have a fpecial care to provide his own parifh. Item, That before ferving of the tables, there be only one fermon delivered to thefe who are to communicate, and that there be one fermon of thankfgiving after the communion is ended. Item, When the parifhioners are fo numerous, that many of them cannot conveniently have place, in that cafe, the brother who affifts the minifter of the parifh is to
preach

preach to them who are not to communicate that day, which is not to begin until the sermon in the kirk be ended, to wit, sermon in the forenoon.

The present practice.

§ 17. But by the present practice, the Thursday, or some other day of the week, preceding the communion, is kept as a fast day, on which there are three sermons, delivered by so many neighbouring ministers, which yet to some seems not very proper; for the design of that day being a congregational fast, on which the sins of that parish are to be mourned over before the Lord, no other minister can have such particular knowledge thereof, as he who labours and travels among them. Upon Saturday there are two preparation sermons, and upon the Lord's day there in some churches two action sermons, besides the thanksgiving in the afternoon; and on the Monday there are two thanksgiving sermons. There will be at these occasions, three, five, or perhaps more ministers assisting the pastor of the congregation, because of the great confluence of people that resort thereto. Intimation of the celebration of the Supper, is made two or three Sabbaths before: (the Directory speaks but of one) and on the Sabbath immediately preceding public intimation is made of the fast.

What intervenes betwixt the action-sermon and the action itself.

§ 18. Upon the day of the communion, a large table being so placed as the communicants may best sit, and the congregation may both see and hear, the public worship is begun as on other Sabbaths: and immediately after sermon, the minister prays and sings a part of some psalm; then, having had an exhortation, he desires the elders and deacons to bring forward the elements, while he cometh from the pulpit, and sitteth down at the table, and the congregation again sing; thereafter he fenceth and openeth the the tables, as before was said. The bread now standing before him in large dishes, fitly prepared for breaking and distribution, and the wine in large cups, he reads, and may shortly expound the words of institution, 1 Corinth. xi. 23.—27. Next, He useth a prayer, wherein he both giveth thanks for the inestimable benefit of redemption, and prays to God to sanctify the elements, and accompany his own ordinance with the effectual working of his Spirit.

The minister's behaviour at the action.

§ 19. The elements being thus sanctified by word and prayer, the minister is to take the bread, and say, according to the holy institution, command, and example of our
blessed

blessed Lord and Saviour Jesus Christ, I take this bread, and having given thanks, I break it, and give it unto you, Take ye, Eat ye, this is the body of Christ which is broken for you, do this in remembrance of him. In like manner, the minister is to take the cup, and say, according to the institution, command, and example of our Lord Jesus Christ, I take this cup, and give it unto you. This cup is the New Testament, in the blood of Christ, which is shed for the remission of the sins of many, drink ye all of it; for as oft as ye eat this bread, and drink this cup, ye do shew the Lord's death till he come. If the minister have no other brethren assisting him in the administration, from whom he is rather to take the communion at the next table, he is to communicate himself at the first breaking of the bread, and distributing the cup.

§ 20. All the while the elders and deacons in a competent number, and in a grave and reverend manner, do attend about the table, to see that none be admitted without tokens, as in the 13th sect. of this title, and that all who are admitted, may have the bread and wine in their own place and order of sitting, which is without difference of degrees, or respect of persons. *Service of tables by elders and deacons.*

§ 21. By the last-mentioned act of Assembly, there is to be no reading in the time of communicating, but the minister maketh a short exhortation at every table; that there be silence during the time of the communicants receiving, only the minister may drop a short and suitable sentence. By that same act, the distribution of the elements among the communicants is to be universally used, after the minister hath broken and delivered it to the nearest. Item, That while the tables are dissolving, and filling, there be always singing of some portion of a psalm. Item, That the communicants, both before their going to, and after their coming from the table, shall only join themselves to the present public exercise then in hand. Item, That none of those who are present in the kirk, where the communion is celebrate, be permitted to go forth till the whole tables be served, and the blessing pronounced, unless it be for more commodious order, and in other cases of necessity. *The behaviour of ministers and communicants during the service.*

§ 22. The last table, after they have received, ordinarily sitteth still, to avoid any trouble by going to their own *Exhortation and thanksgiving after all have communicate, and the conclusion.*

own places. Then the minister goes to the pulpit, where, in a few words, he putteth them in mind of the grace of God in Jesus Christ, held forth in this sacrament, and exhorts them to walk worthy of it. Then he gives solemn thanks to God for his rich mercy in Jesus Christ, begs his pardon for the defects of the whole service, and intreats his assistance to walk as becometh those who have received so great pledges of salvation, and then concludes with the usual petitions in the public prayers of the church. After prayer, all join in singing a part of a psalm suitable to the occasion, and are dismissed with the blessing.

The frequent celebration of the Lord's Supper recommended.

§ 23. In the manuscript acts of Assembly, there is an act, December 1562, appointing the communion to be celebrate four times a-year in towns, and twice a year in country parishes; yea, it was administered then once a month, as may be seen by the old discipline bound in with the old psalms, and forms for prayer in Mr Knox's time. And by the 14th article, cap. 12. of the French church-discipline, it is recommended to their national synod, to give directions about the more frequent celebration of the Lord's Supper, and their custom then was four times a-year: but our acts of Assembly 1638, sess. 23. act 12. act 19. of Assembly 1701, and Directory for worship, do only recommend the frequent celebration of the Lord's Supper; but how often is to be determined by the kirk-sessions, as they shall find most convenient for the people, their comfort and edification. These recommendations seem to be treated with little or no regard among us; for as yet, so far as I know, not one parish hath celebrate it once more than ordinary upon their account. I am sure, if they would have it but once a-year, yet parishes in the neighbourhood may so correspond, as to have it in that bounds all the months of the year, which will supply the want of its frequency in one parish, at least unto such as may well travel unto their neighbour churches.

How communion elements are paid, and applied when the communion is not celebrate.

§ 24. By the act James VI. parl. 3 cap. 24. *sub. fin.* the parsons of all parish-kirks are to furnish bread and wine to the communion so oft as it shall be administrate, And by the act of Assembly 1638, sess. 23. art. 12. where the minister of a parish has only allowance for furnishing communion elements once a year, it is declared, that the charges should rather be paid out of that day's collection, than

than that the congregation want the more frequent use of the sacrament. Spanhemius, in his introduction to sacred history, tells us, that in the second century, the Lord's Supper was then expressed by several names, and among others, it was called the OBLATION, from the people's offering the bread and wine: And truly, if the people were desired to contribute money for that end, it were but reasonable, and not to be grudged, even though it were but once a year celebrated, where the minister has no allowance even for that once, and wants likewise a legal maintenance allocated and secured unto him: but where the communion is but once a year, and the minister hath a legal stipend secured to him, he ought to be discharged to take or defray the expences of the elements out of the money given and mortified for the use of the poor; and this practice is rendered yet the more scandalous and inexcusable in parishes where this sacrament is but once a year celebrate, and where there be colleagues, who have both legal stipends. The sum ordinarily modified for communion elements doth not exceed fifty merks Scots, which the heritors are liable yearly to pay, although the communion be not administrate in the parish, providing the minister offer to apply it for the use of the poor.

TITLE V.

Of the Solemnization of Marriage.

§ 1. MAtrimonium is defined by Modestinus to be "Maris et faminæ conjunctio, et omnis vitæ consortium, divini et humani juris communicatio," i. e. the conjunction of man and woman to be comforts for all their life, with a communication of rights divine and human. By the laws of the church of England, as they are reformed by Henry VIII. and Edward VI. in the latter edition printed at London 1641, marriage is defined "Legitimus contractus mutuam et perpetuam viri cum "fœmina conjunctionem, Dei jussu inducens et perficiens; "in quo tradit uterque alteri potestatem sui corporis, vel "ad prolem suscipiendam, vel ad scortationem evitandam." Nuptiæ are sometimes taken pro ritu nuptiali, for wedding ceremonies.

Marriage described.

Sponsalia, or espousals, what.

§ 2. The sponsalia or espousals, sunt mentio et repromissio futurarum nuptiarum, or, de futuro matrimonio. It is only a consent de presenti that makes marriage; but the consent de futuro, which is given at the contract of marriage, or proclamation of banns, is only the espousals, which are premised to marriage; it being so solemn an act, should be performed with due deliberation. By the civil law and custom of this nation, there is place, rebus integris, for either party to repent and renounce the espousals. See Stair's Instit. p. 25.; and by the 9th article, cap. 13. of the French church-discipline, though it be prohibited to marry the sister of the deceased, yet it doth not condemn marrying the sister of one contracted that is dead, because it supposes that an alliance is not consummated but by commixion of blood or sex. See the commentary on that article.

Forbidden degrees.

§ 3. Marriage ought not to be within the degrees of consanguinity or affinity, forbidden by the 18th chapter of Leviticus. The man may not marry any of his wife's kindred nearer in blood than he may of his own, nor the woman of the husband's kindred nearer in blood than of her own, (see the Confession of Faith) otherwise the marriage may be declared to have been null. A man may marry any of his wife's allies, or a woman any of her husband's allies, "nam non datur affinitas affinitatis."

Marriage may be declared null upon impotency, and when not.

§ 4. Marriage being ordained for the increase of mankind, and for preventing of uncleanness, persons naturally impotent are therefore incapable to marry; yet by the laws of the church of England, as reformed by King Henry VIII. and King Edward VI. de Matrimonio, cap. 7. their canon runs thus: " Verum si nota sit utrique perver-
" sitas, et tamen mutus perducet de matrimonio consen-
" sus, nuptiæ procedant; quoniam volentibus nulla inju-
" ria potest fieri."

Who cannot consent cannot marry.

§ 5. These who cannot consent, cannot marry, such as ideots and furious persons, durante furore; neither they who have not the use of their reason, as infants and those under age, who are not come to the use of discretion, that is when the person is within the years of pupillarity, commonly established in law to be fourteen in males, and twelve in females, nisi malitia suppleat ætatem, which without further probation declares them to be arrived at that discretion which fits them for marriage.

§ 6. If it be asked, whether the consent of parents, curators, or nearest friends in their place be essential to marriage? The common sentence will resolve it, "Multa impediunt matrionium contrahendum, quæ non dirimunt contractum:" so that their consent becomes necessary, as it were, "necessitate præcepti, sed non necessitate medii." And by an overture of Assembly, June 4. 1644, it is proposed to be considered on, and reported by the presbyteries, that promises of marriage made by minors, to women with whom they have committed fornication, be declared null and of no effect; especially when the youth is not willing to observe the same, because his parents threaten him with the loss of their blessing and of his birth-right. This is proposed as being agreeable to the word of God. *Consent of parents, and of promises of marriage made by minors.*

§ 7. Errors in the substantials make void the consent, unless future consent supervene, as it did in Jacob, who supposed that he had married and received Rachel, but by mistake got Leah; yet was content to retain her, and to serve for the other also: but errors in qualities or circumstantials vitiate not, as if one supposing he had married a maid or chaste woman, had married a whore, according to Stair's Institutions, page 26. Yet by Deuteronomy xxii. 21. that error seemeth to be accounted substantial; for, by that text, a woman so deceiving a man was to be put to death; and by the 38th art. cap. 13. French church-discipline, if it should happen, that after contracts and promises made, and before the accomplishment of marriage, the bride is found to have committed fornication, before or after the said promises, and that it was unknown to him who had promised her marriage, the consistory may proceed to a new marriage; and the bride shall have the same liberty, if it be found that the bridegroom has been guilty of fornication before the said promise. By the 5th art. cap. 24. of our Confession of Faith, that case is only determined thus far, viz. adultery or fornication committed after a contract, being detected before marriage, giveth just occasion to the innocent party to dissolve that contract, and they support this from that scripture, Matth. i. 18. 19. 20. *Errors that annul the consent in marriage.*

§ 8. Parties

Testimonials for marriage. § 8. Parties cannot be married without they be known to be single persons, either by the minister's own proper knowledge, or by a testimonial from some minister, elders, or session, bearing the same: but albeit they cannot procure a testimonial in common form, through their being scandalous, yet the benefit of marriage cannot be denied them after the proclamation of banns. But by the 21st art. cap. 23. of the French church-discipline, if one of the parties who desire to be married is excommunicated, the marriage shall not be admitted in the church, unless the excommunicate person make confession of his faults; but those that are suspended from the Lord's Supper they allow to be married.

Marriage with Papists. § 9. By the 3d article, chap. 24. of our Confession of Faith, such as profess the true reformed religion, should not marry with Infidels, Papists, or with other idolaters, or with such as maintain damnable heresies. And in pursuance of that, by an overture of the Assembly 1701, the transgressors were to be excommunicated. But our statesmen disliking the same, this overture in the Assembly 1704. act 22. issued only in a recommendation. By the 72d canon concilii sexti in Trullo, it is determined thus; "Non licere virum orthodoxum cum muliere hæretica conjungi, neque vero orthodoxum cum viro hæretico copulari, sed & si quid ejusmodi ab ullo ex omnibus factum apparueret, irritas nuptias existimare & nefarium conjugium dissolvi." But if two infidels marry, and one of them becometh Christian, the person converted is not thereupon warranted to desert or put away the other party who continues blind, 1 Cor. vii. 13. 14.; and by can. 31. Concilii Laodiceni, "Quod non oportet cum omni hæretico matrimonium contrahere, vel dare filios aut filias, sed potius accipere si se Christanos futuros profiteantur." And by the 20th article, cap. 13. of the French church-discipline, when one of the parties is of a contrary religion, the purposes of marriage shall not be published in the church, until the party doth publicly profess in the church, that with full resolution he renounceth all idolatry and superstition, particularly the Mass; and if any pastor or consistory do otherwise, they may be suspended or turned out of their office: thus difference in religion justly impedes but doth not annul marriage.

§ 10. If

§ 10. If parties delay their marriage forty days after proclamation, they are to be put to the renewing of the same before they be married; and the French discipline, cap. 13th art. 26. doth recommend not to delay the celebration, after proclamation of banns, above six weeks, to prevent inconveniencies and ill consequences. The resiling of parties after proclamation, is commonly called among us, a scorning of the kirk, though the injury or affront redounds mostly against themselves, and not so much upon the congregation. Indeed, if it could be known that parties never had a serious purpose for marriage, but only from a profane, making, and vain temper, had desired themselves to be proclaimed; in this case, they deserve to be treated as mockers of God and his people. There are other ways whereby God and his church may be mocked, when persons, who be found in body and mind, are given up to be minded in the public prayers of the church, when they are truely distressed in neither, the authors of which mocking and forgery deserve to be proceeded against with the censures of the church.

Marriage delayed forty days after proclamation and scorning the kirk.

§ 11. Adultray and willful desertion do not annul the marriage on any absolute necessity, but they are just occasions upon which the persons injured may annul it, and be free; otherwise, if they please to continue, the marriage remains valid, excepting when the adultery is committed or accompanyed with incest, as if a man should ly with his wife's sister, in which case the wife cannot free herself from the scandal of incest, if she, after knowledge thereof, continue to co-habit with him as her husband. And by the parl. 1573. cap. 55. it is ordered, that the deserter, after four years wilful desertion without a reasonable cause, must be first pursued, and decerned to adhere, and being thereupon denounced, and also after private and public admonitions by the church, excommunicate, the commissaries are warranted to proceed to divorce. But simple absence will not be accounted wilful desertion, if he be following any lawful employment abroad. In case then, a party be out of the country, I see not how this order can be used and proceeded in, unless it were sufficiently verified and made appear, that he knew of his being cited before their consistorial courts, and that his absence was wilful and not necessary.

When adultery and wilful desertion annul marriage.

Re-marrying in case of divorce or proven adultery.

§ 12. A party divorced for adultery n so it be not to those with whom the adult the divorce proceeded, was committed: tween such is declared null, and the issue ceed to their parents as heirs, parl. 160 it seems agreeable to equity and reason, tery was proven, albeit no divorce ensu the adulterers cannot marry together. W the Civilians, that, "Dolus malus facit "que privilegium, fraus enim nemini "imo punienda."

Force annulls marriage.

§ 13. Marriage contracted with a w violently taken away and still reclaiming, the beginning; see Mackenzie & Math and to this agrees that forecited book of laws of England, cap. 12. *de matrim* sure it is unjust to treat their children as See lib. 3. tit. Ravishers of women.

Time and place of marriage.

§ 14. After banns have been lawfully none found objecting against the marriag thereafter be celebrate in private houses, as the custom is now become, upon an being a fast-day. Albeit by the Direct it is publicly to be solemnized in the pla authority for public worship, before a co of credible witnesses, and they advise tha Lord's day. I am sure, seamen who are to sea on Monday, may marry on the Sa on the Sabbath before

No marriage without proclamation of banns, unless the presbytery dispense therewith.

§ 15. Marriage without proclamation having dangerous effects, excepting wher in some necessary exigences, dispense th bly 1638. sess. 23. art. 21. Assem. 169 fore any proclamation of banns be mad parties, and there parents, tutors, or cu given up to the minister, that the consen be known, and the proclamation is to be nine service begin, for three several Sabb named being designed as fully as they us or contracts of marriage, and in collegia proclamation is to be in every church of 1699. sess. 5. By the 18th art. 13th ca church-discipline, these who live in places where the usual exercises of religion is not established, may cause their banns to be published in Romish churches, in as much as the matter is partly of a political nature. And by the 22d article of that chapter, the banns of widows who remarry shall not be published in the church, till seven months and two weeks, at least, after the decease of their former husbands, to avoid the scandals and inconveniencies that may happen by it, unless it so happen, that the magistrates order may interpose to the contrary.

§ 16. One may be clandestinely married, either when banns are not proclaimed, or when the marriage is celebrated by one not ordained and admitted by the church, nor authorized by the state. By our acts of parliament William's parl. sess. 5. cap. 12. the persons clandestinely married, may now be prosecuted by every procurator fiscal. And by cap. 6. sess. 7. parl. K. William, persons clandestinely married, are obliged, when required, to declare the name of the celebrator, and witnesses, under the pains following, viz. each nobleman 2000 l. the landed gentleman 2000 merks, any other gentlemen or burgess 1000 l. and any other person 200 merks, and to be imprisoned till they declare and pay. The celebrator is punishable by the council, not only with banishment, but in such pecunial or corporal pains as they shall think fit; the witnesses are made liable in the sum of 100 l. None of the parties (if both be residing in Scotland) shall get themselves married in England, or Ireland, without proclamation of banns in Scotland, and against the order of the kirk, under the pains as aforesaid, which are always without prejudice of kirk-censure. And there is no doubt they should be rebuked as unnecessary transgressors of a very comely and rational church-order. *Clandestine marriage, what; its punishment and censure.*

§ 17. By the form of solemnization of matrimony, prescribed by the church of England, in the book of Common Prayer, if any man upon the day of marriage, do alledge and declare any impediment, why the parties may not be coupled together in matrimony, by God's laws, and the laws of the realm, and will be bound, and sufficient sureties with him, to the parties, or else put in a caution (to the full value of such charges as the persons to be married do thereby sustain) to prove his allegation; then the solemnization must be deferred until such time as the truth be tried. *Objectors against the marriage on that day ought to find caution.*

§ 18. After

Form of solemnization of the marriage covenant.

§ 18. After the purpose of marriage hath been orderly published, the minister is first to pray for a blessing upon the parties appearing to be married: which being ended, he is briefly to declare unto them out of the scripture the institution, use, and ends of marriage, with the conjugal duties Then he is solemnly to charge the persons to be married, that they would answer as in the sight of God, to whom they must give a strict account at the last day, that if either of them know any cause, by pre-contract or otherwise, why they may not lawfully proceed to marriage, that they now discover it. The minister, if no impediment be acknowledged, shall cause first the man take the woman by the right hand, saying these words. " I, N. do take thee N to be my married wife, and do, " in the presence of God, and before these witnesses, " promise and covenant to be a loving and faithful husband " unto thee, until God shall separate us by death." Then the woman shall take the man by the right hand, saying these words. " I, N. do take thee N. to be my married " husband, and I do, in the presence of God, and before " these witnesses, promise and covenant, to be a loving, " faithful, and obedient wife unto thee, until God shall " separate us by death." Then without further ceremony, the minister shall pronounce them to be husband and wife, according to God's ordinance, and so conclude the action with prayer

Register of marriage and baptisms; how to bear faith.

§ 19. By the Directory for worship on this head, a register is to be carefully kept, wherein the names of the parties so married, with the time of their marriage, are forthwith to be fairly recorded, for the perusal of all whom it may concern. And that the registers of baptisms and marriages may bear the greater faith, it is fit they be subscribed on each page by the minister; or, in a vacancy, by two elders, and the clerk of the session.

TITLE VI.

Of Visitation of the Sick.

Ministers, elders, or deacons, should be cautious in

§ 1. WE are admonished by the Apostle Paul, 1 Cor. x. 32 to give offence neither to the Jews, nor to the Gentles, nor to the church of God. By the

4:ſt canon *Concil. Carthagin* "Clerici ad viduas vel vir- *being alone*
"gines non ingrediantur, ſed cum con-clericis, vel ubi *with unmar-*
"adſunt clerici, vel aliqui bonæ exiſtimationis Chriſtiani," *ried women*
And by the act of Aſſembly Auguſt 24. 1647. ſeſſ. 19. *in trouble.*
art. 13. ſometimes the perſon troubled may be of that condition, or that ſex, that diſcretion, modeſty, or fear of
ſcandal, requireth a godly grave friend to be preſent,
when the paſtor is viſiting the troubled perſon.

§ 2. It is the miniſter's duty to admoniſh, exhort, re- *Miniſters and*
prove, and comfort theſe committed to his charge, upon *people are*
all ſeaſonable occaſions, ſo far as his time, ſtrength, and *frequently to*
perſonal ſafety will permit. The people are often to *converſe a-*
confer with their miniſter about the ſtate of their ſouls, *ſoul-matters.*
and in times of ſickneſs to deſire his advice and help, before their ſtrength and underſtanding fail them: for this
and what follows of this title, ſee the Directory.

§ 3. The miniſter being ſent for, is to repair to the *The matter*
ſick, and to apply himſelf with all tenderneſs and love to *of his confer-*
his ſoul, inſtructing him out of the ſcripture, that diſea- *ence when*
ſes come not by chance, or by diſtempers of body only, *the ſick.*
but by the wiſe hand of God; and whether it be laid upon one out of diſpleaſure for ſin, for his correction or a-
mendment, or for trial and exerciſe of his graces, or for
other ſpecial and excellent ends, all his ſufferings ſhall
turn to his profit, if he ſincerely labour to make a ſancti-
fied uſe of God's viſitation, neither deſpiſing his chaſten-
ing, nor waxing weary of his correction.

§ 4. If the miniſter ſuſpect him of ignorance, he ſhall *How to deal*
examine and inſtruct him in the principles of religion, and *with the ig-*
in the nature, uſe, excellency and neceſſity of the graces *norant,*
of the ſpirit of God. He ſhall ſtir up the ſick perſon to *ſecure.*
examine himſelf, to ſearch and try his former ways, and
his ſtate towards God. If the ſick perſon ſhall declare
any ſcruple, doubt, or temptation, that is upon him, in-
ſtructions and reſolutions ſhall be given to ſettle him. But
if it appear that he hath not a due ſenſe of his ſins, endeavours ought to be uſed to convince him, of the guilt,
pollution and deſert of them; and withal, to make known
the danger of delaying repentance, and to rouſe him out
of a ſtupid ſecure condition, to apprehend the juſtice and
wrath of God, before whom none who are out of Chriſt
can ſtand: care muſt be taken that the ſick perſon be not
caſt

cast down into despair, by such a severe representation of the wrath of God due to him for his sins, as is not molified by a seasonable propounding of Christ and his merits, for a door of hope to every penitent believer.

How to deal with those of whose well-being there is ground of hope.

§ 5. If the sick person have endeavoured to walk in the ways of holiness, and to serve God in uprightness, although not without many failings and infirmities; or, if his spirit be broken with the sense of sin, or cast down through the sense of the want of God's favour, then it will be fit to raise him up, by setting before him the freeness and fulness of God's grace, the sufficiency of Christ's righteousness, and the gracious offers in the gospel: it may be also useful to shew him, that death hath no spiritual evil to be feared by those who are in Christ, because sin, the sting of death, is taken away by him who hath delivered all that are his from the bondage of the fear of death. Let advice also be given, as to beware of an ill-grounded persuasion on mercy, or on the goodness of his condition for heaven, so to disclaim all merit in himself, and to cast himself wholly upon God for mercy, in the sole merits and mediation of Jesus Christ.

The minister is to pray if desired, and for what.

§ 6. When the sick person is best composed, may be least disturbed, and other necessary offices about him least hindred, the minister, if desired, shall pray with and for him, confessing and bewailing original and actual sin, acknowledging it to be the cause of all misery; imploring God's mercy for the sick person through the blood of Christ, beseeching that God would open his eyes, cause him to see himself lost in himself, make known to him the cause why God smitteth him, reveal Jesus Christ to his soul for righteousness and life, give unto him his holy spirit to create and strengthen faith, to work in him comfortable evidences of his love, to arm him against temptations, to take off his heart from the world, to furnish him with patience and strength to bear his present visitation, and to give him perseverance in faith to the end; that if God shall please to add to his days, he would vouchsafe to bless all means of his recovery, renew his strength, and enable him to walk worthy of God by a faithful rememberance and diligent observing of his vows and promises of holiness and obedience: and if God hath determined to finish his days, by the present visitation, he may find

find such evidence of his interest in Christ, as may cause his inward man to be renewed, while his outward man decayeth

§ 7. The minister shall admonish him also, as there shall be cause, to set his house in order, thereby to prevent inconveniencies, to take care for the payment of his debts, and to make restitution or satisfaction where he hath done any wrong, to be reconciled to those with whom he hath been at variance, and fully to forgive, as he expects forgiveness. He may also improve the present occasion, to exhort those about the sick person to consider their own mortality; and in health, so to prepare for sickness, death, and judgement, that when Christ, who is our life, shall appear, they may appear with him in glory. When sick persons desire the prayers of the congregation, it is like an intimation and suit to those who have any moyen with God to pray for them in secret, and continue so to do, as well as in public. *Peculiar admonitions to the sick, and exhortations to such as are present. Why the sick roll is read in public.*

TITLE VII.

Of Burial of the Dead, Lyke-wakes, and Dirgies.

§ 1. BY the Directory for worship, upon the day of burial, the dead body is to be attended decently, suitable to the rank of the deceased party, to the burial-place, and there immediately interred, without any ceremony. It is most convenient that at such occasions, we have meditations and conferences suited thereto, and that the minister, as upon other occasions, so at this time, if he be present, may put them in remembrance of their duty. *The manner of burial.*

§ 2. By the old book of discipline, in Mr Knox's time, annexed to the old paraphrase of the Psalms, after burial, the minister, if present, and desired, goeth to the church, if it be not far off, and maketh some comfortable exhortation to the people, touching death and the resurrection; but by the act of Assembly 1638, sess. 23. 24. art. 22. all funeral sermons are discharged. *No funeral sermons.*

§ 3. By the act of Assembly 1643, sess. 9. they discharge burials, and hanging of honours, broads, and arms of persons, of whatsoever quality, within the kirk where the people meet for public worship; for perhaps at some times the *No burial in the body of the church.*

the people would be incommoded with open graves. Bishop Hall of Norwich was of opinion, that God's house was not a mere repository for the bodies of the greatest saints.

Lyke-wakes and dirgies difcharged. § 4. By the acts of Affembly 1645, feff. 8. Affembly 1701. feff. ult. all lyke-wakes are difcharged, as foftering fuperftition and profanity through the land. No doubt, dirgies have likewife had as bad effects; and from the fame reafon may be alfo underftood to be difcharged.

TITLE VIII.

Of Minifterial Vifitation of Families.

Annual vifitations of families, the cuftom of this church. § 1. IT hath been the laudable practice of this church, at leaft once a year, (if the largenefs of the parifh, or bodily inability, or other fuch like do not hinder) for minifters to vifit all the families in their parifh, and oftner, if the bounds be fmall, and they able to perform it. Among other reafons for thefe annnal vifitations of families, this may be one, that becaufe, by the order prefcribed by our Lord, Matth. xviii there may be feveral offences known to minifters, elders, or neighbours, which may juftly keep back offenders from partaking of the Lord's Supper; and yet it were diforderly and unedifying to remove thefe offences in a public way. Thefe vifitations may ferve to purge a congregation of fuch private fcandals.

The defign of the following overtures. § 2. Although in regard of the different circumftances of fome parifhes, families, and perfons, much of the management of the work muft be left to the prudence and difcretion of minifters, in their refpective overfights; yet thefe following directions are offered by Affembly 1708, April 27. as helps for the more uniform and fuccefsful management thereof, that it be not done in a flight and overly manner, which fuppofeth the univerfal practice thereof through this church, and that the total neglectors may be cenfured therefor as fupinely negligent.

Time of vifitation, its intimation, &c. § 3. Such a time of year is to be chofen for minifterial vifitation, as the families which he vifits may be beft at leifure to meet with him; and if that time fhould happen immediately after the communion, then it is feafonable, as it were, to beat the iron while it is hot. Timeous intimation

tion is to be made to them of the visitation; and the elder of that bounds of the parish which is to be visited, is to accompany the minister, and they should previously confer together concerning the condition and state of the persons and families of those bounds.

§ 4. When they enter a house, they are to express their wishes and desires for the blessing of God upon it, and that above all, that their souls may prosper: Then let them take an account of the names of the family, inquire for testimonials from them who are lately come to the parish, and mark them in the roll for catechising, and let them take notice who can read, and of the age of children capable to be catechised; then the minister is to speak to them all in general, of the necessity and advantage of godliness, of justice and charity towards man. *First work to salute the family, inquire for their names, testimonials, &c.*

§ 5. He is next, more particularly, to speak to servants of their duty, to serve and fear God; to be dutiful, faithful, and obedient servants, and of the promises made to such, commending to them the reading of the scriptures, and secret worship, and love and concord among themselves, and in particular, a holy care of sanctifying the Lord's day. *Servants spoken to in particular.*

§ 6. The minister is to show the children and young servants the advantage of knowing, seeking, and loving God, and remembering their Creator and Redeemer in the days of their youth, and to mind them how they are dedicated to God in baptism; and when of age, and after due instruction in the nature of the covenant of grace, to excite them to engage themselves personally to the Lord, and to design and prepare for the first opportunity they can have of partaking of the Lord's Supper, to be especially careful how they at first communicate. *Children to be spoken to.*

§ 7. Then he is to speak privately to the heads of the family about their personal duties towards God, and the care of their own souls; and their obligation to promote religion and the worship of God in their family, and to restrain and get vice punished, and piety encouraged, and to be careful that they, and all in their house serve the Lord, and sanctify his day. He is more particularly to inquire, 1. Whether God be worshiped in the family, by prayers, praises, and reading of the scripture? 2. Concerning the behaviour of servants towards God and towards man; *Heads of families spoken to.*

man, if they attend family and public worship? How they sanctify the Lord's day? And if they be given to secret prayer and reading the scriptures? 3. If there be catechising in the family? If their children be trained up in reading, according to the act of Assembly, Aug. 10. 1648. in all which the minister may intermix suitable directions, encouragements, and admonitions as may be most edifying.

General questions and exhortations. § 8. The minister is to inquire who want bibles; and if they be not able to buy them, let the poors box be at the expences: and recommend to the heads of the family to get the Confession of Faith, Catechisms, and other good books, for instructing in life and faith, according to their ability. 2*do*. Those who are tainted with error or vice are to be admonished secretly, or in the family, as may most edify: and all are to be exhorted to carry toward such as walk orderly according to the rule, Matth. xviii. 15. 3*tio*. The minister is to endeavour to remove divisions in the family, or with their neighbours, and exhort them to follow peace with all men, as far as is possible. 4*to*. Let it be inquired who have communicated, that they may be called to an account privately how they have profited, and put in mind to pay their vows to the Lord. Confer also with others about the causes of their not communicating.

How to visit such as keep not communion with us. § 9. As for those who pretend conscience for not keeping communion with us, or whatever their motives be, ministers ought to deal with God for them, and with themselves, in such a way as may be most proper to gain them, and exoner their consciences, waiting if peradventure God will prevail with him. Who can tell if their making them sensible of their tender love and affection to their persons, especially to their souls, giving them all due respect, and doing them all the good they can, yet still discountenancing their sin, may in the end be blessed of God for their good, Jud. v. 22. 23. 2 Tim. ii. 24, 25.

Visitation a difficult work. § 10. Seeing in the whole of this work, there is great need of much prudence, zeal for God, and love to souls, visitation of families should be carried on with dependence on God, and fervent prayer to him, both before the minister set forth to such a work, and with the visited, as there can be access to, and opportunity for it.

TITLE IX.

Of Sanctification of the Lord's Day; and observing Fast and Thanksgiving Days.

§ 1. THE Sabbath is to be sanctified by an holy resting all that day, even from such worldly employments and recreations as are lawful on other days, and spending the whole time in the public and private exercises of God's worship, except so much as is to be taken up in the works of necessity and mercy, as our Shorter Catechism beareth, authorized by Assembly, Aug. 28. 1648; from which we may gather what the church understands by sanctifying or profaning of the Lord's day, and so will either approve or censure. *How the Sabbath is to be sanctified.*

§ 2. By the act of Assembly 1647, concerning family-worship, direct 4. the master of the family ought to take care, that all within his charge repair to the public worship, which being finished, he is to see the rest of that day spent in the private and secret exercises of piety. Care is also to be taken that the diet on that day be so ordered, that neither servants be unnecessarily detained from the public worship of God, nor any other persons hindered from sanctifying that day. Private preparation is likewise to be made for the Sabbath, by prayer and such holy exercises, as may dispose to a more comfortable communion with God in his public ordinances. See the Directory. *How to be sanctified in private families.*

§ 3. When some great and notable judgements are either inflicted or imminent, or by some extraordinary provocation notoriously deserved; as also, when some special blessing is to be sought or obtained; when great duties are called for, or when sins are extraordinary for their number or nature, then it is that a church may injoin fasting: which is observed by a total abstinence, not only from all food, (unless bodily weakness do manifestly disable from holding out till the fast be ended, in which case somewhat may be taken, yet very sparingly, to support nature when ready to faint), but also from all worldly labour, discourses and thoughts, and from all bodily delights though at other times lawful, rich apparel, ornaments, and such like, *Times for fasting, and how observed.*

during

during the fast; and much more from whatever is in its nature or use scandalous or offensive, as gadish attire, lascivious habits and gestures, and other vanities of either sex: which the composers of the Directory recommend to all ministers in their places diligently and zealously to reprove, as at other times, so especially at a fast.

Intimation of the fast. Materials for public prayer.

§ 4. The Sabbath before the fast, the causes thereof are publicly read from the pulpit, and the day of the week intimated upon which it is to be kept. The people are then to be earnestly exhorted to prepare themselves for afflicting their souls upon that day of extraordinary humiliation. So large a portion of that day, as conveniently may be, is to be spent in public reading, and preaching of the word, with singing of psalms, fit to quicken affections suitable to such a duty, but especially in prayer, to this or the like effect; giving glory to the great majesty of God, the Creator, Preserver, and Supreme Ruler of all the world, acknowledging his manifold great and tender mercies, especially to the church and nation, humbly confessing sins of all sorts, with their several aggravations, justifying God's righteous judgements, as being far less than our sins do deserve, yet humbly and earnestly imploring his mercy and grace for ourselves, the church and nation, the Queen, and all in authority, and for all others for whom we are bound to pray, (according as the present exigency requireth) with more special importunity and enlargement than at other times; applying by faith the promises and goodness of God for pardon, help, and deliverance from the evils felt, feared, or deserved; and for obtaining the blessings which we need and expect, together with a giving up of ourselves wholly, and for ever unto the Lord.

Several fasts, general and particular.

§ 5. Besides solemn and general fasts appointed by the Assemblies or their Commissions, or by civil authority, upon application from some church judicature unto them, provincial synods, presbyteries, and kirk-sessions, may appoint fast days to be kept within their respective bounds, as Divine Providence shall administer unto them special occasions. Likewise families and particular persons may do the same, providing their fasts be not on those days on which the congregation is to meet for public worship.

§ 6. Our

§ 6. Our fasting days must be indicted for such causes as are both clear and just, and when it will be most for edification; for that, as other positive duties, doth not always bind: therefore the church is to take heed of appointing fasts through insinuations or solicitations from statesmen, lest they be branded as tools, to some who would fast for strife and debate, that others who differ from them about state-matters may be exposed to the odium of the people, as ill country-men. *When the church should be most cautious in appointing fasts.*

§ 7. The causes of the fast enumerate in the act of Assembly 1690, November 12. were these and the like. 1. Perjury; dealing treacherously with the Lord, and being unstedfast in his covenant. 2. Unfruitfulness under the purity of doctrine, worship and government, having a form of godliness, but denying the power thereof. 3. Abuse of God's great goodness and deliverance, evidenced by a course of manifest wickedness, and shameful debauchery, such as drunkenness, cursing, swearing, adultery, and uncleanness of all sorts. 4. The supremacy, which was advanced in such a way, and to such a height, as never any Christian church acknowledged, and whereby the interest of our Lord Jesus Christ was entirely sacrificed to the lawless lusts and wills of men. 5. Abjured Prelacy was introduced, and the government of the church was overturned, without the church's consent, and contrary to the standing acts of our national Assemblies. 6. Compliance with that defection, both in ministers and others, some from a principle of pride and covetousness, or man-pleasing, and others through infirmity and weakness, or fear of man, and want of courage and zeal for God. 7. Persecution of the godly for non-compliance with that sinful course: many faithful ministers were cast out, and many insufficient and scandalous men thrust in on their charges, and many families ruined because they would not own them as their pastors. 8. Decay of piety under the late Prelacy, so that it was enough to make a man be nick-nam'd a Phanatic, if he did not run to the same excess of riot with others. 9. Atheism, which discovered itself in some by their dreadful boldness against God, in disputing his being, and providence, the divine authority of the scriptures, the life to come, and immortality of the soul; yea, and scoffed at those things. 10. Imposing and taking unlawful oaths and bonds: lawful *Causes of a fast in this national church.*

oaths have been broken, ungodly and conscience-polluting oaths have been imposed and taken, whereby the consciences of many through the land are become so debauched, that they scruple at no oath, though many have been oppressed and ruined for refusing them. 11. Neglect of the worship of God, both in public, in private families, and in secret. 12. Profanation of the Lord's day, succeeded in place of that wonted care of strict and religious sanctifying of it. 13. The shedding of innocent blood. 14. Pride and vanity, yea, Sodom's sins have abounded among us, idleness, fulness of bread, vanity of apparel, and shameful sensuality filled the land. 15. As also, great perverting of justice, by making and executing unrighteous statutes. 16. Silence of ministers in the time of such a great defection, as well as too general a fainting among professors: and as some shewed no zeal in giving seasonable and necessary testimony against the defections and evils of the time, nor keeped a due distance from them; so on the other hand, some managed their zeal with too little discretion and meekness. 17. The abominable idolatry of the Mass was set up in many places, and Popish schools erected, whereby shameful advances were made towards Popery. 18. Great ignorance of the way of salvation through the Lord Jesus Christ. Though we profess to acknowledge there can be no pardon of sins, no peace and reconciliation with God but by his blood, yet few know him, or see the necessity and excellency of him, and few esteem, desire, or receive him as he is offered in the gospel: and as few are acquainted with faith in him, and living by faith on him, so few walk as becometh the gospel, and imitate our holy Lord in humility, meekness, self-denial, heavenly mindedness, zeal for God, and charity towards men. 19. Great contempt of the gospel, barrenness under it, and a deep security under our sin and danger 20 Though the Lord, by calling us into the furnace of affliction, hath been giving us a sight of the vanity of all things beside himself, yet, to this day, there is a woeful selfishness among us, every one seeking his own things, few or none the things of Jesus Christ, the public good, or one another's welfare. 21. A bitter spirit of censoriousness, whereby the most part are more ready to carp at the sins and defections of others, than to repent

pent and mourn for their own. These, and the like, were the causes of the fast in the year 1690, and to them the fasts appointed since do ordinarily refer. See also how the land expressed the sense it had of the guilt of all ranks in the solemn acknowledgement of public sins, and breaches of the covenant; and a solemn engagement to all the duties contained therein; namely, those who did in a more special way relate unto the dangers of that time. Act of the commission of Assembly October 6. 1648. for renewing the solemn league and covenant, ratified by the Assembly thereafter.

§ 8. Albeit by the treatise of fasting, emitted by the Assembly 25th December 1565, the Sundays were appointed for some fasts, as being for the greater ease of the people; and since, by the last act of Assembly 1646, a fast is appointed on the Sabbath next except one, preceding the then following General Assembly; yet seeing the work to be performed on the first day of the week is by divine institution already determined, we ought to set about it exactly, which we all acknowledge to be a thanksgiving and not a fast. Extraordinary duties are not to interfere with the ordinary, nor is one duty to shuffle out another. If either should be allowed, it would look somewhat like the reverse of redeeming the time, for thereby diligence is rather diminished, than doubled in the service of God. *No fast to be on the Lord's day.*

§ 9 Days of thanksgiving being intimate on the preceding Sabbath, for some deliverance obtained, or mercy received, are wholly to be spent in the public and private exercises of divine worship and praises: the people are to rejoice with trembling, and to beware of all excess in eating or drinking. And demonstrations of civil mirth, such as ringing of bells, firing of guns, bonefires, and illuminating of windows, should not be intermixed with the religious duties of that day: but as upon fasts, so upon those days, there should be liberal collections for the poor, that their bowels may bless us, and rejoice the more with us. In the 6th section, the church was cautioned against appointing fasts for strife and debate, so I hope they shall be directed to avoid injoining of thanksgiving days from any false or unjust ends. *Thanksgiving days how observed.*

TITLE X.

Of Collections and Recommendations for the Poor.

When collections for the poor are made.

§ 1. BY the act of Assembly 11th August 1648, collections for the poor, in time of divine service, (which is practised in some churches abroad) are discharged, as being a very great and unseemly disturbance thereof. And kirk-sessions are ordained to appoint some other way for receiving these collections. The method now ordinarily taken is this: the elders or deacons do collect at the church-door from the people as they enter in, or else from them when within the church, immediately before pronouncing the blessing, and after divine service is ended.

Extraordinary collections.

§ 2. Beside these ordinary collections for the poor, there are frequently extraordinary collections made for charitable and pious uses; particularly, by session 10. Assembly 1704, there is an act for a voluntary contribution, by way of subscription, in each presbytery, for gathering from noblemen, gentlemen, and other charitably disposed people, for erecting English schools, and educating youth in the Highlands and Isles.

Recommendations are for a definite time.

§ 3. For preventing unnecessary begging, or imposing upon charitable people, no church-judicature is to give recommendations for charity to any without their own bounds; and these recommendations are to be only for a definite time. Assembly 1695, sess. 17.

TITLE XI.

Of Provision for Schools and Universities.

How salaries for school-masters are established.

§ 1. BY King William's parl. sess. 6. cap. 26. it is appointed that there be a schoolmaster and school in every parish, his fee not under one hundred merks, nor above two, to be paid by the heritors and liferenters of the parish, who are to have relief for the half of it off their tenants; and that letters of horning be therefor directed at the instance of the schoolmaster, conform to the proportions due by the heritors, laid on by the major part of them; (I suppose, convened by public intimation from the minister in the pulpit, by order or advice of the session)

sion) or, failing of whom, by any five commissioners of supply within the shire, upon the presbytery's application to them; and the heritors for the salary are to be stinted conform to their valued rent. Item, Provision for schools and schoolmasters are declared to be a pious use, to which patrons may employ vacant stipends, at the sight of the sheriff of the bounds. Excepting from this act the stipends vacant in the synod of Argyle, because of the act, parl. William and Mary, sess. 2. cap. 24. in their favours. And by the 10th act, Assembly 1699, it is recommended to the several presbyteries, to use their endeavours, that schools be erected in every parish, conform to the acts of parliament, and acts of Assembly, and it is recommended to synods to see this observed.

§ 2. By the foresaid 26th act, and likewise by the 14th act of the same session of parliament, the privileges granted to ministers for their stipends, viz. That there be no suspension, except on consignation, are extended to universities, schools, and hospitals, for the ingathering of their rents and debts. See more of this on the title of mortifications and ministers stipends. *School-revenues privileged.*

§ 3. When the Directory was established, by which public reading of the scriptures was committed to the preachers; and fearing left the maintenance on that pretence might be withdrawn from the readers, the Assembly did, August 6. 1649, require the presbyteries, to see that none of the maintenance given to such readers, precentors, and schoolmasters, be taken from them, notwithstanding that recommended alteration in the Directory. *The maintenance for school-masters and precentors to continue, though they read not.*

§ 4. A tack or lease of teinds, set by an university for a definite time, with an obligement to renew the same in all time thereafter, was found not effectual after the definite time was expired; though the same rent was received for some years after, that was not sustained as an homologation, but as a tacit relocation. See Stair's Instit. p. 301. so that after the definite time is expired, they might increase the tack-duty. *How far universities may set tacks of their teinds.*

§ 5. So careful have our sovereigns and parliaments been for the flourishing of these seminaries of church and state, that for their provision and bettering of their stocks, they have sometimes, upon the offer made by the clergy, ordained forty pounds, or 6 *per cent.* out of every thousand merks *Extraordinary supply for universities and schools.*

merks of ministers rents, to be paid yearly for five years, Car. II. par. 1. sess. 3. cap. 21. and at other times vacant stipends are assigned for their better provision for a time, Car. II. parl. 2. sess. 3. cap. 20. Ja. VII. parl. 1. cap. 18. They have likewise imposed a cess upon the kingdom for preserving of some universities, Car. II. par 3. cap. 23. Now the universities, by gift under the great seal, do share liberally of the bishops rents, and some of them have lucrative and easy tacks of certain bishopricks, and large allowances too, even out of these tack-duties, sometimes for salaries to new proffessions.

TITLE XII.

Of the Immunity and Union of Churches.

<small>Local privileges within church-walls and yards what, and how far extended.</small>

§ 1. BY the canon law, there are certain immunities or privileges granted within church-walls and church yards, called local, so as that secular judges within that bounds can cognosce upon no civil or criminal action: also, that no incorporations, councils, or fairs, meet or hold there: that there be no university discourses there: that secular affairs be not the subject of any conversation there: moreover, that there be no feastings there, and that these bounds be sanctuaries to the guilty flying there for refuge, and they are not to be pulled thence to punishment, unless the attrocity of the crime be such as may induce the church to surrender them. This privilege is also extended to the houses and palaces of bishops. The temple of Jerusalem was built by God's direction, it was dedicated by man, and God's acceptation of it was testified. It appears by John ii. 19. that it was an illustrious type of Christ's body, and by the 16th ver. we find that our Lord resented the profanation of that holy place. Yet, notwithstanding of all that, God doth so abhor proud and malicious sinners, that he commands them to be taken from his altar that they may die, Ex. xxi. 14. and Joab was slain in the tabernacle of the Lord, 1 Kings ii. 31. But that special kind of respect which was due to that hallowed and typical temple, is not communicate, extended, or confined to the places of worship under the New Testament, John iv. 21.

§ 2. Like-

§ 2. Likewise by the canon law, there is another immunity or privilege, called personal, granted to the clergy, such as, that they are excused from accepting to be tutors or curators, and that none in sacred orders shall be liable to the payment of public burdens. I acknowledge, ministers ought not to be so imposed upon as to be perplexed with secular affairs, and far less should they ever do it of choice: And albeit the vocation of a pastor, his commission and instructions relating thereto, be all of a spiritual nature, and of divine original, yet their persons, estates, and behaviour, considered in a civil capacity, are, according to scripture and reason, subject to the civil government. Their persons are accounted so sacred among our people, and they judge themselves so secure from that venerable impression, they very well know, is generally received of their character, that they rarely make ordinary journies with arms, as gentlemen and other travellers do. They are by law still exeemed from attending the king's host, except the nation become so miserable, that necessity or their own security oblige them: And even in that extraordinary case, they may, if they please, only act in the army as ministers or chaplains. Since the year 1689, both poll and hearth money have been imposed upon ministers by authority of parliament. *Personal immunity, how far allowed to ministers.*

§ 3. By the canon law on this title, two churches may be made one, when the maintenance is so inconsiderable, that two pastors can have no comfortable living upon them, or when one of them is become desolate by the sword of an enemy, or the number of parishioners small or very much diminished. In which case it would be for the greater good of the church, if two such small charges were reduced into one, providing the benefice of the small charge, now united, be not condemned to any secular or other use, but only applied to maintain a pastor in a new erection, or else a collegue in some numerous congregation; for two competent stipends are not to be united, till there be no need for any new erection or augmentation in the church. *When churches and stipends are to be united.*

§ 4. If the heritors and elders of two kirk-sessions shall agree to the uniting of some parts or skirts of one of the parishes to another, or to transplant the church from one part of the same parish to another part therein, for the peoples greater ease and convenience, in that case, the presbytery, *When presbyteries may authorise partial union, or transplantation of churches.*

ry, upon application of the parties concerned, may, for any of these ends, interpose their authority to their agreement, providing they find it may tend to the greater ease and edification of the people; and providing there be still two distinct parishes, and the quantity and quality of both stipends preserved undiminished and unaltered. What I here propose is conform to the 5th art. cap. 7. of the French church discipline, in these words: "The colloquies and synods shall deliberate of limiting the extent of places wherein each minister shall exercise his ministry."

TITLE XIII.

Of Churches, Church-dikes, Manses, Yards, Glebes, Bells, Utensils, Ornaments, Books, and High-roads to Churches.

What a church is, and by whom to be repaired.

§ 1. CHURCHES are public houses erected for public divine worship, and for hearing the preaching of the word of God; they are to be repaired out of the vacant stipend; for that 18th act, Jam. VII. par. 1. is never yet in so far rescinded: and when the vacant stipends fail, the burden of building and repairing the church doth lie upon the heritors, whether residing in the parish or not. The majority of these that meet, must stent themselves for that effect, according to their rents. But if the heritors refuse, being required thereto by the minister from the kirk-session, the Lords of session, by a bill given in by the minister, will grant warrant to him and his session to convene at a certain day, for trying what sum will repair the church, and to stent the heritors in that sum conform to their valued rents, and to appoint a collector to uplift the same. But before the making up of that stent-roll, the heritors ought again to be publicly advertised to meet, and then to make the same. If, after this order is used, they fail, the session then concludes the stent, and letters will be directed at their collector's instance, against the heritors for paying the proportions they are stented in Stair's Instit. p. 192. and act ult. par. 3. Jam. VI.

Kirk-yards, and yard-dikes.

§ 2. Church-yards are dormitories for human bodies, and ordinarily that spot of ground within which the church stands. Our law allows to church-yards equal privileges
with

with churches, in many things; particularly, that the raising of tumults or frays in time of divine service in churches, or church-yards, is punished with loss of moveables, act 7. par. 11. Jam. VI. The church-yard is fenced with dikes, partly for ornament, and partly as a preservative to the dead bodies from being digged up or torn by beasts. The only right that ministers have to the grass growing in the church-yards, is, that they may cause their servants cut it, and hinder others from doing so; the heritors are obliged to repair the church-yard dikes with stone and morter, two ells high, with sufficient stiles and entries; and the Lords of session are obliged to direct letters of horning against them for that effect, cap. 232. par. 15. Jam. VI.

§ 3. The minister, at the sight of the presbytery, or such of their number as they shall appoint, with two or three discreet men of the parish, may build or repair his own manse upon the expences of the heritors and liferenters, who are respectively liable to reimburse him of what he truely and profitably hath bestowed that way, unless they offered to contribute their own materials, and he refused them: See Mackenzie's observations on the 48 act, par. 3. Jam. VI. Where there is a competent manse already, the heritors must repair it once sufficiently at the ministers entry, who is thereafter to uphold the same during his incumbency, and they out of the vacant stipend, in time of the vacancy. act 21. par. 1. sess. 3, Car II. As the minister is obliged to leave the manse in as good condition as he entred to it, so before he can be made liable so to do, the heritors ought to move the presbytery to pass an act in their favours, to declare it a free manse; but before they can pass any such act, a committee of their number must visit it, after it is built or repaired, and find, upon the depositions of four discreet workmen, who understand that work, but have not been employed therein, two whereof to be chosen by the heritors, and other two by the minister, that the building or reparation is sufficiently finished. And if there be any materials left, or money remaining not expended, after that is declared, the superplus belongs to the heritors. If the minister be not able or willing to advance that money, which has been declared to be necessary for materials and workman-ship, or if heritors refuse to

Who are liable to build and repair manses.

meet and stent themselves for that effect, then what should hinder the minister to take the same course, and obtain the same redress that is granted against refusers to build or repair churches, as in § 1. &ʒ 2.

How much expence and ground for manse, yard, and glebe.

§ 4. It is usual to allow half an acre of ground for manse and yard. The manse is not to exceed 1000 pounds, nor to be under 500 merks of value. Ministers hold their manses and glebes of none but the King. Glebes are to consist of four acres of arable ground; failing of which, sixteen soums grass of the best and most commodious pasturage of any kirklands within the parish, Jam VI. par 18. cap. 7. and by the 21 act par. 1. sess. 3. Car. II. ministers (excepting ministers of burghs royal where there is no landward parish, and who have no right to glebes) are to have grass for one horse and two kine, or else, that the heritors pay to the minister twenty pounds yearly.

Designation of ground for manses and glebes.

§ 5 Manses and glebes, where they have not been designed, or not the full quantity, are now designed by the presbytery, or their committee, with two or three discreet men of the parish. The minister, or a procurator in his name, receives infeaftment therein from the moderator, upon which he takes instruments in the hands of a notary, or of the clerk of the presbytery. And upon a petition given in by the minister to the Lords of session, with the act of designation and instrument, they will interpose their authority for removing the heritors and possessors of the lands designed, in terms of the 48. act, par. 3. Jam. VI. by granting letters of horning, to charge them to remove within ten days. And glebes are designed with freedom of foggage, feuel, feal, divot, loaning, free ish and entry, and other privileges, according to use and wont. Jam. VI. par. 13. cap 161.

How the heritor of the lands designed obtains relief.

§ 6. The proprietors of the lands designed must get relief pro rata, off the rest of the heritors of kirk-lands, within the parish, if the designation was out of kirk-lands, and they not being the glebes and manses of old pertaining to persons or vicars; for there is no relief competent to the feuers or tacksmen of such lands, except only against such as have feus of other parts of the said old glebe or manse, act 199. par. 18. Jam. VI. When the designation is out of temporal lands, the rest of the heritors of the like lands are to contribute proportionally for relief thereof.

§ 7. It

§ 7. It would look more impartial like, and resemble more that humility, love, and simplicity recommended to Christians by the apostle (Jam. ii. 1.) and would look liker the subjects of Christ's kingdom, which is not of this world, if church members would take their seats in the church without respect of their civil character, as they do at the Lord's table. Some seats are built and repaired at the general charge of the parish, in which all have a common interest; and there are others, which particular heritors have built for their own use, with consent of the kirk-session, or which they have prescribed a right unto by forty years possession. In several burghs royal within this kingdom, the disposal of all the church seats, at least upon the bounds at first allotted to them for their inhabitants by the kirk-session, is thereafter ordered and parceled out by the town council, and burdened with certain yearly sums for a minister's stipend, and where the seats are disposed upon to burgesses without that burden; and it be found that without it there cannot be a competent stipend to the ministers. The dispositions and rights so made, may, no doubt, be reduced on that head; for it was never the intention of the kirk-session, who gave these rights, to authorise an absolute alienation of seats, to the obstructing and preventing funds, for maintaining the public preaching of God's word. *Seats common and particular, how acquired, and how burdened.*

§ 8. The keys of seats are to be kept by beddals, that when the proprietors are absent, such as want seats, or throng the seats of others, may be accommodated for the time; but in case the owners be so little concerned with religion, as not to countenance the public worship of God, or averse to serve such as attend upon it with their empty seats, the people that want accommodation cannot be blamed to possess and occupy that void in their absence; and if the owners, or others by their order, shall offer to dispossess them violently, especially in time of divine service, they should be prosecuted as disturbers of public worship, both before the civil magistrate and church judicatures. *Beddals should keep the keys of seats, and why.*

§ 9. The heritors are bound to pay for, and are stated in the property of the bells, books, utensils, and ornaments of the church; but the minister and kirk-session, to whose custody they are committed, may pursue for any of them that are abstracted. A charge for a stent imposed *Who are the proprietors of bells, books, &c.*

sed for buying of bells to a church within a burgh royal, hath been sustained against the landward heritors, albeit the burgesses and indwellers would have more advantage by them. See the new treatise on church lands, p 212.

Kirk-roads.

§ 10. Every one must have some way to the church, but cannot pretend to any special way, as the nearest, through another man's land, without proving immemorial possession, which is reckoned forty years, of such a gate or passage; and to make up this immemorial possession, a person will be allowed to conjoin his predecessors possession of that road with his own. See the forecited book, p. 212.

TITLE XIV.

Of Tithes, Stipends, and Mortifications.

What is meant by stipend, benefice, and the church's patrimony.

§ 1. THE maintenance belonging to ministers for their labours we call stipends; but more commonly, and by the canon law, they are named benefices. Calvin, in his Lexicon Juridicum, tells us, that the rewards and privileges given and granted of old to soldiers for their service, were called benefices and stipends. The canonists define a stipend or benefice thus: "Est jus per-"petuum percipiendi fructus ex bonis ecclesiasticis, prop-"ter aliquod officium spirituale, auctoritate ecclesiæ con-"stitutum." Whatever belongs to church-men is likewise called the patrimony of the church, the word signifying an inheritance left by a father; because, when legislators or private persons do authorise or destinate suitable encouragement for the comfortable life of church-guides and pastors, they do, in so far, act the part of nursing fathers unto the church. In the 9th chapter of the Policy of the Kirk, they comprehend, under the churches patrimony, all things given, or to be given to the kirk, and service of God, as lands, buildings, possessions, annualrents, and all such like wherewith the kirk is doted, either by donations, mortifications, or any other lawful titles, together with the continual oblations of the faithful; as also teinds, manses, glebes, and such like; which, by the common and municipal laws, and universal-customs, are possessed by the kirk. And to take any of this patrimony,

mony, and convert it to the particular and private use of any person, is reputed a detestable sacrilege before God by our church.

§ 2. The work of the ministry is a warfare, and it is not ordinary for soldiers to maintain themselves without pay, 1 Cor. ix. 7. and the light of nature teacheth, that the labourer is worthy of his hire. By the 42d article of cap. 1. French church-discipline, it is found, that ministers who are rich, and have of their own, should, nevertheless, take wages of their flocks, lest their example do prejudice to other pastors and churches. And Mackenzie and Stair, in their Institutions, do maintain, that some part of our goods is due, by divine right, towards the maintenance of the clergy; but that the proportion may be determined by human laws, according to circumstances. By the 19th act of parliament 1633, all ministers are appointed to be provided with sufficient stipends, being eight chalders of victual, or eight hundred merks at least, beside manse and glebe, except in singular cases referred to the commission for plantation of kirks. In some places of Scotland, ministers may maintain their families for less than the half, which must be allowed to maintain the same families in other parts of the kingdom. Seeing ministers do deny themselves to the gain of civil employments, whereby they might have a more unlimited prospect, not only of maintaining their families, but of purchasing stocks for their posterity, therefore the Dutch custom is not unreasonable, which alloweth to ministers so much for every son, in order to his better education and breeding.

That stipends are due, and how much is competent.

§ 3. The canon law defines tithes thus: " Est quota " honorum mobilium, licite quæsitorum, pro sacerdotibus " Dei, ipsius locum in terris tenentibus, tam divina quam " humana constitutione debita." Ministers stipends, and augmentations thereof, are legal burdens, and the main one to which teinds are liable; against which no title or right whatsoever can secure: and the truth is, till once the parish minister is sufficiently provided, no person can safely buy his own teinds; for they are always subject to be evicted for that end, by the common law and our custom, even after the heritor has bought him. See that new treatise on tithes, p. 340. By William and Mary's parl. sess.

Tithes the fund for stipends.

4.

4. cap. 24. it is appointed, that teinds belonging to their Majesties, by the abolishing of Prelacy, so long as they remain undisponed, as likewise teinds belonging to colleges and hospitals, or destined to pious uses, are not to be sold, but may only be valued, and made liable thereafter for payment of the valued duties.

Some tithes cannot be sold, but only valued.

§ 4. Former parliaments referred to their commissions the plantation of kirks and valuation of teinds; but now, the last session of the last parliament, have, in place of all further commissions for such matters, impowered and appointed the Lords of session to judge in all affairs and causes, which by former laws did pertain to the cognizance and jurisdiction of commissions of parliament: only they are restricted from transporting of a kirk without consent of most of the heritors of the parish. Every Wednesday afternoon in time of session, the Lords meet to call and discuss such causes.

Plantation of kirks remitted to the Lords of Session.

§ 5. By the 4th act, parl. 22. Jam. VI. bishops are discharged to set in tack longer than nineteen years, and inferior beneficed persons for longer space than their own lifetime, and five years thereafter (except the commission authorise it) under the pain of deprivation; and further, the contraveners declared infamous, and incapable of any church office. Longer tacks were ordained to be registrate within forty days, in a particular book to be kept by the clerk-register for that effect, otherwise to be null. And where it is said, that the inferior clergy can set tacks to run five years after their decease, that is always to be understood with consent of the patron, obtained either before or after the setting of the tacks: for without that they can set but three years tacks, act 15. par. 23. Jam. VI. and that the ecclesiastical rents may suffice to their uses, all alienations, setting of feus, or tacks of the rents of the kirk, as well lands as teinds, in hurt and diminution of the old rentals, ought to be reduced and annulled. And likewise, that in all times coming, the teinds be set to none but to the labourers of the ground, or else not set at all. See cap. 12. of the Policy of the Kirk.

How long church-men may set tacks.

§ 6. The legal terms of paying or vaiking of benefices and stipends are Whitsunday, at which time the fruits are held to be fully sown, and Michaelmas, when they are presumed to be fully separated. If the incumbent's entry be

The term of payment and vaiking of stipends.

be after Michaelmas, and before Whitfunday, he hath that whole year; if after Whitfunday, the half of that year: or if he die, be depofed, or tranfported before Whitfunday, he hath no part of that year; if after Whitfunday, and before Michaelmas, he hath the half of that year.

§ 7. Although a benefice be vaik when a minifter is depofed, yet till the fame be intimate, the parifhioners may pay their ftipends in to him, and his difcharges will defend them. But after intimation is made, no payment will be fuftained. See Stair's Inft. p. 151. *Benefices vaik upon intimation of the fentences.*

§ 8. The annat due to the executors of deceafed minifters, is declared to be half a year's rent, over what is due to the defunct for his incumbency, to wit, if he furvive Whitfunday, the half of that year is due for his incumbency, and the other half for the annat: and if he furvive Michaelmas, the whole year is due for his incumbency, and the half of the next year for the annat, and the executors need not to confirm it, parl. 2. feff. 3. cap. 13. Car. II. neither can it be difponed to ftrangers by the defunct, nor affected by his creditors, for it did never belong unto him, it being only a gratuity which the law indulgeth, upon the account that minifters are fuppofed not to die rich. The annat divides betwixt the relict and the nearest of kin, if there be no children, and is extended to the profit of the glebe, if there be no new intrant: But where there is an intrant, the glebe belongs to him, and is no part of the annat, nor did belong to the former minifter, unlefs it was fown by him, and the crop upon it at the entry of the intrant. See Stair's Inft. p. 306. *Annat, what it is, and to whom it falls.*

§ 9. General letters of horning (fo called, becaufe they do not exprefs *nominatim* the perfons to be charged) are allowed upon decreets of locality, act 13. feff. 2. parl. Will. and Mary; and thefe letters are effectual, not only againft the perfons decerned in the decreets, but alfo againft their heirs and fingular fucceffors poffeffing the lands affected with the locality. But fummar horning was not fuftained at the inftance of a minifter's executor for his ftipend. Minifters poinding for their ftipends need not to carry the goods to the market-crofs of the head-burgh of the proper jurifdiction, but may comprife them on the ground where they are, by honeft fworn men, act 21. feff. 3. parl. 1. Car. II. No fufpenfions of fpecial decreets for minifters ftipends can pafs, except upon production of difcharges, *The privileges of procefses for ftipends.*

charges, or upon consignation of the sums charged for; and if victual be the subject of the charge, one hundred merks must be consigned for each chalder, and proportionally where less than a chalder is charged, without prejudice to the Lords of session to modify more or less at the discussing act 6. sess 1. parl. 2. Car. II. Actions for ministers stipends commenced in inferior courts cannot be advocated. Suspensions of and actions for them before the session are discussed summarily, without abiding the course of the roll; and suspenders, against whom letters are found orderly proceeded should be decerned in a fifth part more at least than the sums charged for, to pay the minister's expences and damage, act 27. sess. 5. of K. William's parl.

Who dispose on vacant local stipends; and for what uses.

§ 10. Although the power of presenting ministers by patrons to vacant churches be discharged, yet that is but prejudice to them of their right to employ the vacant stipends on pious uses within the respective parishes, except where the patron is popish; in which case he is to employ the same on pious uses, by the advice, and at appointment of the presbytery; and in case the patron shall fail in applying the vacant stipends for the uses foresaid, that he shall lose his right of administration of the vacant stipend for that and the next vacancy, and the same shall be disposed upon by the presbytery to the uses foresaid. Excepting always the vacant stipends within the bounds of the synod of Argyle; which synod is impowered to dispose thereof for training up of youth at schools and colleges, and for other pious uses, with consent of the heritors, Will. and Mary's parl. sess 2, acts 23. 24.

Stipends quoad modum probandi, prescribe in five years.

§ 11. Ministers stipends prescribe, *quoad modum probandi*, if not pursued within five years after the same are due; so that after that time they cannot be proven to be resting unpaid, except by the defenders their oaths, or by a special writ under their hands, acknowledging what is resting.

How bygone victual bolls are liquidate.

§ 12. A minister having charged for the payment of the bolls contained in his decreet of locality, the debtor was ordained by the Lords to depone upon the prices he got; although he had offered the fiars by way of instrument within seven days after the charge, and produced receipts of the charger and his predecessors, for instructing that they were not in use to uplift the bolls *in ipsis corporibus*. It seems as unreasonable to oblige a minister to accept the fiars from the heritors, as it were to oblige the heritors to accept

accept the fiars from their tenants. Yet I think the liquid price of vacant stipends, according to custom, is the fiar of the respective shires: see that forecited treatise on tithes, pag. 427.

§ 13. The bolls contained in a minister's decreet, if no measure be therein specified, should be paid according to the Linlithgow measure: unless the minister hath been thirteen years in possession of uplifting according to another measure, or the modified stipend would fall short of the quantity in the act of parliament by Linlithgow measure; for in that case the minister ought to be paid conform to the measure of the shire in which the parish lies; see that treatise on church-lands, p. 408. *According to what measure stipends are to be paid.*

§ 14. An ecclesiastical pension is a certain portion of yearly rent payable for a time out of another's benefice. Ecclesiastical pensions seem to have been introduced at first, as a mean of subsistance to incumbents, who, through sickness or infirmity of old age, were turned unable to officiate: for such were allowed to resign their benefices, reserving to themselves pensions out of them, as they might live upon, suitable to their former character. As church-men turned afterwards more degenerate, and benefices became merchandise, resignations and pensions upon trivial reasons were sustained; see book foresaid, page 160. *Ecclesiastical pensions, what.*

§ 15. The pastoral charge, or the office of professor of theology in schools, is of that weight and consequence, that to discharge any one of them satisfyingly, will be exercise enough to any honest man, however sufficient, all the days of his life. By the canons of the synod of London, October 25. 1597, in Bishop Sparrow's collections. the extraordinary parts and merits of some is pretended for a ground to dispense with a plurality. This were relevant to be practised for some time in ecclesia constituenda, where gifted men are rare: but to continue that custom in ecclesia constituta, where gifts do abound, it were to neglect both the maintenance, and likewise the gifts of God that he hath bestowed on some, and to overvalue the gifts he hath given to others, and hinder them from discharging of the duties belonging to one office eminently. There were in Christ's time abundance of idle Pharisees, Scribes, and priests, that spent their time in teaching *Plurality of benefices not to be tolerated in a constitute church and why.*

teaching the people their rites, ceremonies and traditions: but there were always but a few labourers in God's harvest; hence Chrysostome thought that but few ministers will be saved. What man or angel is sufficient for the ministerial work! But their sufficiency is of God.

Mortifications under the presbyteries inspection.

§ 16. By the 2?d act, Assembly 1700, presbyteries are to take notice, how sums of money mortified, or otherwise belonging to the poor of the parish, have been managed and applied from time to time, and if they shall find dilapidations of any such sums, that those guilty thereof be pursued according to law, and the synods are to see to the presbyteries diligence herein.

Pious donations must be applied as they were destinate by the disponer.

§ 17. By cap. 6 parl. 1. Car. I. gifts, legacies, or donations for pious uses, must not be inverted from the specific use destinate by the disponer, and the persons intrusted are made countable for the same, and ordinary profits thereof to the kirks, colleges, and others to whom they are disponed; and this is extended to all such dispositions as have been made since the majority of King James VI. and that letters be thereon direct.

Mortifications ought not to be accepted in prejudice of blood relations.

§ 18. That forecited book on church-lands, p. 107. tells us, that Charles the Great discharged ecclesiastics to accept of mortifications, whereby children would in effect be disinherited. So good Augustine refused universal legacies in favours of his church, when the testator left children or parents who might be prejudged and suffer thereby. Nor was this generosity of his singular, for a certain man having no children, nor hopes of any, having gifted his estate to the church of Carthage, only with the reservation of his own liferent, Aurelius the bishop reponed him to his former right, upon the unexpected birth of a son.

The rectifying of popish mortifications commendable, but not their misapplication, or extinction.

§ 19. By the 29th act, parl. 11. Jam. VI. popish benefices are annexed to the crown, or converted into civil uses. Consider that these mortifications were fraudulently elicited from persons, imposed upon by ways and means of priest-craft; and that they had been originally destinate to maintain an idolatrous and superstitious worship. Now, it being the public interest that none make a wrong, far less a sinful use of their property, it is incumbent on the orthodox magistrate, to convert what was mortified and fraudulently obtained for maintenance of idolatry, to the

maintenance

maintenance of the true worſhip of God: and in caſe there ſhall happen any excreſcence, over and above what may ſupport the ſame, and the miniſters thereof comfortably, then may not that be applied for ſome honeſt and neceſſary uſe in the republic, until the affairs of the church require the ſame again. This is confirmed by the Policy of the kirk, cap. 12. art. 14.

§ 20. The viſitors of hoſpitals are to be appointed by the ſovereigns, act 101. parl. 7. Jam. V. and accordingly by Will. parl. ſeſſ. 6. cap. 29, there is a recommendation to his majeſty to cauſe viſit hoſpitals, and inquire after mortifications. This is renewed ſeſſ 9. cap. 21. It would ſeem by the 27th act, parl. 2. Jam. I. that actions for bringing patrons and others to count for their intromiſſions with the rents of hoſpitals, may be intented at the Chancellor's inſtance, eſpecially in caſe no royal viſitation be appointed. *Viſitors of hoſpitals and mortifications to be named by the ſovereign.*

§ 21. In the 9th and 12th chapters of the heads of Policy of the kirk, they allow of a fourfold diſtribution of the churches partimony; one portion thereof to be aſſigned to the paſtor for his entertainment and hoſpitality: another to the deacons, elders, and other officers of the kirk and kirk-ſervants, ſuch as clerks of Aſſemblies, takers up of pſalms, beddals, and keepers of the kirk, joining with them alſo the doctors, and ſchools, to help their old rents where need requires; the third portion to be beſtowed on the poor members of the faithful, and on hoſpitals: the fourth for reparation of kirks, and other extraordinary charges as are profitable for the kirk, and alſo for the commonwealth if need require. *A fourfold diſtribution of the patrimony of the kirk.*

§ 22. In the 12th chapter of that book of diſcipline, the collection and diſtribution of all eccleſiaſtical goods or patrimony, properly belongs to the office of the deacons, (ſee the title of deacons) that the poor may be anſwered of their portion thereof, and they of the miniſtry live without care and ſolicitude, as alſo the reſt of the treaſure of the kirk may be reſerved and beſtowed to their right uſes. If theſe deacons be elected with ſuch qualifications as God's word requires, there is no fear that they will abuſe their office. Yet, becauſe the giving ſo great truſt to them, appeareth to many to be dangerous, let them be obliged to find caution for their fidelity, that the kirk rents be no way dilapidated. *Patrimony of the church collected by deacons, and why they are to find caution.*

BOOK III.

TITLE I.

Of Apostacy, and atheistical Opinions of Deists.

What an apostate is.

§ 1. Apostates are those who altogether desert the Christian Faith: Yet sometimes they are taken for such as desert that holy faith to which they are engaged at baptism, and become professors of a false religion. All heretics are not apostates.

The atheistical opinions of Deists.

§ 2. By the 21st act of Assembly 1696, all ministers are enjoined, where there is any apparent hazard of contagion from such persons as are of atheistical opinions, to detect the abominableness of their tenets; such as, the denying of all revealed religion, and the grand mysteries of the gospel, viz. The doctrine of the Trinity, the incarnation of the Son of God, his satisfaction to divine justice, justification by his imputed righteousness to them who believe in his name, the resurrection of the dead; and, in a word, the certainty and authority of all scripture revelation; as also, their asserting, that there must be a mathematical demonstration for each purpose, before we can be obliged to assent thereunto, and that natural light is sufficient to salvation.

The punishments of such Deists.

§ 3. By the 11th act of King William, parl. 1695, it is ordained, that whoever shall, in their writing or discourse, deny, impugn, or quarrel, argue, or reason, against the being of God, or any of the persons of the blessed Trinity, or the authority of the holy scriptures, or the providence of God in the government of the world, shall, for the first fault, be punished with imprisonment, ay and while they find bail to give public satisfaction in sackcloth to the congregation within which the scandal was committed; and, for the second fault, the delinquent shall be fined in one year's valued rent, and the twentieth part of his free personal estate, besides his being imprisoned, ay and while he give satisfaction again ut supra; and for the third fault, he shall

shall be punished with death as an obstinate blasphemer. See title of Blasphemy: Accordingly one Aikenhead was hanged for that crime betwixt Leith and Edinburgh, about the year 1697. All judges and ministers of the law are injoined to execute this act for the first fault, and all inferior magistrates of shires, regalities, stewartries, and their deputies, and magistrates of burghs, are to execute this act as to the second fault; and, as to the third fault, the execution thereof is remitted to the Lords of justiciary.

TITLE II.

Of Papists, Quakers, and Bourignianists.

§ 1. According to the canon law, "Hæretici sunt illi "qui vanæ gloriæ principatusque sui causa, fal- "sas opiniones gignunt vel sequuntur." Anciently the word Hæresis was taken for a firm opinion, whether the same was good or bad. It is committed by Christians when they pertinaciously propagate or follow opinions contrary to the received fundamental doctrine of the church. *Heretics who they are.*

§ 2. That no man should be compelled by temporal punishments to profess the true faith, is a doctrine universally received among the reformed churches. It is crimen mere ecclesiasticum, at least as to its cognition prima instantia. The reformed churches never deliver any they find heretics to the civil judge, or rather, according to the employment given the judges by Papists, the civil executioners. One continuing a heretic ought to be rejected and excommunicated, compare Titus iii. 10. with 1 Tim. i 20. Our sovereigns, by their coronation oath, are to root out all heretics that shall be convicted by the true kirk of God, from their empire of Scotland, which doth not oblige them to persecution, nor to pay blind obedience to the church, but only it binds them, at least chiefly, to execute the laws against Papists, who are declared common enemies to all Protestant states, Jam. VI. parl. 16. cap. 18. *Punishment of heresy.*

§ 3. The severity of our laws against Papists, will be further justified, if we consider, that by the law of God idolaters were to be put to death, Deut xvii. and agreeable thereto, popish idolaters are to be punished with death, by the 104th act, parl. 7. Jam. VI. By Jam. VI. parl. 6. cap. *Act of parliament against Papists.*

cap. 71. persons going out of the country for further knowledge of letters, are to have the King's licence, which shall contain this provision, that they shall adhere to the true religion, and do nothing against it, under the pain of barretry, (which with us is committed by those who go to Rome to buy benefices, and is punishable by infamy and banishment, Jam. VI. parl. 1. cap. 2.); and that within twenty days after their return, they make and give before their ordinary, the confession of their faith as now established, or otherways devoid the kingdom within forty days thereafter, or be pursued as adversaries to the religion. By James VI. parl. 7. cap. 104, none are to go on pilgrimage to kirks, chapels, crosses, or the like, keep saints days, sing carols within and about kirks, or observe other superstitious papistical rites, under the pecunial pains therein contained, for the first fault, and under the pain of death to the continuers therein. By King William's parliament, sess. 5. cap. 26, no Papist can make any gratuitous disposition or deed, in prejudice of their apparent heirs, declaring such disposition or deed to be null; and that it be judged gratuitous, unless the granter, writer, and witnesses, declare upon oath, before the judge of the bounds, that it was granted for an onerous adequate cause. By King William's parliament, sess. 9. cap. 3. these above mentioned acts are ratified, with all other laws made against Popery and Papists, especially these against Jesuites, priests, or trafficing Papists; and all sayers, and hearers of mass, and concealers of the same. Item, Whoever seizes any priest, Jesuit, or trafficing Papist, or their resetters, upon certificate of the conviction of the person seized by the judge, shall have 500 merks for his reward from the treasury, for which the receiver-general may be pursued before the Lords of session. Item, If it be proven that the said priest, Jesuit, or trafficing Papist, was held in repute such, or that he changed his name, and shall refuse the Formula of purgation subjoined to this act, it shall be sufficient ground for the council to banish him, never to return a Papist under pain of death, to be inflicted by the Lords of justiciary. Item, If any person be found in any meeting where there is any altar, mass-book, or other instruments of popish superstition, and shall refuse to purge, as above, it shall be sufficient ground to the council to banish, under

any

any certification they shall think fit, even to that of death; and whosoever discovers and seizes the said banished person, after his return, shall have the foresaid reward of 500 merks. Item, The 8th act, parl. 1. Char II. is ratified; and any Protestant relation, or his Majesty's advocate or sollicitor, may pursue for the exhibition and education of children in the keeping of Papists; and the Lords of session are impowered to modify an aliment out of the childrens or their parents means; and it is recommended to presbyteries to inform in this matter. Item, No Papist professed, or not purged, can receive any voluntary deed or disposition made to him of any lands, or real rights, or tacks of lands, or teinds. but the same are declared null, and to remain with the granter, and no action for warrandice or repetition of the price. Item, No Papist past the age of fifteen years, can succeed either as heir, or by other conveyance from the person to whom he may be heir, until he purge himself of Popery, as above; and if being educate in the Popish religion, he succeed as above, before the said age, then he shall be obliged to purge before he attain the same; and the person so succeeding, failing in either of these cases, devolves to the next Protestant heir, who is to be served as such to the defunct, and to have right to the estate and rents, from the said irritancy, ay and while the person excluded, or his heir, purge himself, as above; in which case he is to be reponed as before the exclusion. The intervening rents, with the burden of current annualrents of debts, remaining with the Protestant successor; but this exclusion to be without prejudice of creditors before the exclusion. Item, No Papist may grant any gratuitous deed in prejudice of his heir, but the same is declared null, save as to the affecting the granter's person and moveables. See the forecited 26th act, sess. 5. King William's parliament. Item, The Protestant on whom the succession devolves by the said exclusion, must prosecute his right within two years, else it falls to the next, and so on. Item, The Papist and his heir must renounce Popery within ten years after the said irritancy, (minority not reckoned), or is to be excluded for ever; and the estate thus devolving, devolves with all its lawful conditions and burdens. Item, No voluntary right by a Papist in favours of his apparent, heir also a Papist, shall be of force, though prior to this act,

act, unless cled with infeftment or poffeffion, or proceeded in judgement prior thereto. Item, All difpofitions or deeds in favours of cloyfters, or other Popifh focieties, are declared void, and to accrefce to the next Proteftant heir to the granter. Item, No adjudication is to expire in the perfon of a Papift, but coming in the perfon of a Proteftant, the legal being run, it expires within year and day thereafter, and no adjudication or real diligence is competent to a Papift, upon any gratuitous bond or deed. Item, That the Formula of purgation be taken before the council, or before the prefbytery, and reported within forty days to the council. Item, A Proteftant apoftatizing to Popery, forfeits his eftate immediately to his next heir, being Proteftant, as if he were dead; and this next heir, if in pupilarity, is to be reckoned Proteftant, if his education be fuch; or if it be Popifh, he is excluded until he purge, as above. Item, That no fufpected Papift be capable of any truft of the perfon or affairs of minors, and that none employ them in fuch trufts, until they purge as above, under the pain of a year's valued rent, or a thoufand merks, if the valued rent be lefs. Item, No fufpected Papift may teach any fcience, art, or exercife in families, or out with, nor may a Proteftant have a Popifh domeftic fervant, under the pain of five hundred merks, which may be purfued by any Proteftant; and, upon conviction, to have the fame for reward. By the 28th act, feff. 6. of King William's parliament, whoever perverts a Proteftant fubject to Popery, fhall be proceeded againft as a trafficking Papift; that a Proteftant fervant turning Papift in a Popifh family be punifhed as an apoftate; and the mafter, when required, is obliged to difmifs that fervant, never more to be received by him, or any other Popifh mafter, under pain of an hundred pounds; and that Popifh mafters allow their fervants due liberty to attend worfhip and catechifing, under the faid pain; and that thefe fervants ufe that liberty, under the pain of being banifhed the parifh. By the 5th act, parl. 1. Jam. VI. the fayers and hearers of mafs, or fuch as are prefent thereat, are punifhed by confifcation of all their goods, moveable and immoveable, and an arbitrary punifhment of their perfons for the firft fault, banifhment for the fecond, and death for the third fault. By the 122d act, parl. 12. Jam. VI. the fayers of mafs, refetters of Jefuites, feminary Priefts, and trafficking Papifts, againft the king's majefty, and religion

presently

presently professed within this realm, is, and shall be a just cause to infer the crime and pain of treason, provided how soon they satisfy the prince and the kirk the penalty foresaid shall not strike against the resetter. By the declaration of the estates, containing the claim of right, 11th April 1689, it is declared, that by the law of this kingdom, no Papist can be king or queen of this realm, nor bear any office whatsoever therein.

§ 4. The latest and most comprehensive acts of Assembly against Popery, are these: By act July 29. 1640, all idolatrous monuments are appointed to be taken down and destroyed; and presbyteries and synods are to see this work with all diligence performed. This is conform to the 64th and 90th canons, Concil. Carthag. " Ut reliquæ idolo-
" rum radicitus extirpentur, simpliciter placuit peti a glo-
" riosissimis imperatoribus, ut reliquæ idololatriæ non so-
" lum quæ sunt in statuis: sed quæ sunt in quibusuis locis
" vel lucis vel arboribus, omni modo deleantur." By Assembly 1642. sess. 7. and 1648. sess. 38. presbyteries are appointed to convene known Papists in their bounds, and oblige them, within a month, to put from their company Popish friends and servants, and give their children above seven years of age, to be educated at their charges, by such Protestant friends as the presbytery shall approve, and find caution, within three months, to bring home such of their children as are abroad, to be educated at the sight of the presbytery. The obstinate are to be processed *instanter*, and those who comply are to confer with professors in the next university, in order to their conversion. Item, The government is to be supplicate for an act, that in no regiment that goes out of the kingdom, any Papist bear office, and the colonel to find caution for this effect: but the substance of this desired act is already declared in the Claim of Right, and enacted by 9th act, parl. 1. Jam. VI. and the 5th act, parl. 2. Jam. VI. By the 8th act of Assembly 1699, they appoint all ministers to study Popish controversies more. Item, That all due endeavours be used to unite Protestants among themselves. Item, That ministers faithfully watch the flock committed to them, that so, by public preaching, private instruction and conference, apostacy may be prevented. Item, Ministers are to deal wisely and convincingly with those who have fal-

Act of Assembly against Popery.

len to Popery, and other corrupt practices, for their recovery. Item, When other means are ineffectual, presbyteries are appointed to proceed to church censure. Item, That according to the former acts of Assemblies, and acts of parliament, the names of Popish Priests and Jesuites, and trafficking Papists, and of those who have sent their children to Popish colleges and countries, be given in to each provincial synod, and by them transmitted to the respective magistrates, to the effect they be proceeded against according to law, Car. II. parl. 3. act 6. Item, The General Assembly resolves, that application be made to the civil magistrate, as often as need requires, for the vigourous execution of the laws against Papists, Popish schoolmasters, mistresses, governors and pedagogues, and Popish meetings; and for seeing to the training up of Popish youth in the Protestant religion. By the Assembly 1704, scandalous persons turning Popish, or pretending to do so, to evite censure, shall, after due pains to reclaim them, be excommunicated. By the 17th sess of Assemb. 1700, and 9th sess Assem. 1703, no private acknowledgement of a Papist's renouncing that religion verbally, is to be held sufficient to admit them into church privileges; but their reception thereunto must be the deed of a church judicature, not below a presbytery. By the 8th act of Assembly 1707, it is appointed that the synod in which these presbyteries are where Popery increaseth, do sometimes send ministers that are well acquainted with these controversies to assist the ministers of the bounds in conferring with the seduced, and for establishing others Item, Probationers, well seen in such controversies, are to be sent to assist the ministers in these parts, in preaching, that they may have the more time to instruct the people, and watch over them against Popery. All which acts and recommendations, as to ministers diligence against Popery, are revived by the 4th act of Assembly 1708. Calderwood, in his history, p. 594, tells us of an act against Papists made in that pretended Assembly holden at Linlithgow 1608, wherein they appoint, that at every service of any person as heir to his father, or any of his predecessors, he be not served by any judge without the testimonial of the bishop, and moderator of the presbytery, where he dwells, bearing the

confession

confession of his faith and integrity in the religion presently professed.

§ 5. By the 23d article cap. 14. of the French church discipline, all violence and unbecoming language against these of the Romish church, and even against priests and friars, shall not only be hindered, but also wholly suppressed, as much as possibly may be. *Papists not to be mocked.*

§ 6. By the 10th act of Assembly 1695, for preventing of the growth of these abominable heresies of the Quakers, it is recommended to all church judicatures to use all proper means for reclaiming of them, and in case of their obstinacy, to proceed against them with the censure of the church, but especially against the ringleaders, or these who have apostatised from our holy faith. *Apostate and ring-leading Quakers to be excommunicated.*

§ 7. The Assembly 1701, by their 11th act, finds, that the writings of M. Antonia Bourignion, are fraughted with impious and damnable doctrines, as they are represented in the apology for her, condemned by the immediately preceding act, which exhibites to the world an epitome of her errors in the fairest dress; such as, 1. The denying the permission of sin, and the inflicting of vengeance and damnation for it. 2. The attributing to Christ a twofold human nature, one of which was produced of Adam, before the woman was formed, the other born of the Virgin Mary. 3. The denying the decrees of election and reprobation, and the loading these acts of grace and sovereignty, with a multitude of odious and blasphemous aspersions, particularly, wickedness, cruelty, and respect of persons. 4. That there is a good spirit and an evil spirit in the souls of all men before they are born. 5. That the will of man is unlimited, and that there must be in man some infinite quality, whereby he may unite himself to God. 6. The denying of the doctrine of divine prescience. 7. The asserting of the sinful corruption of Christ's human nature, and rebellion in Christ's natural will to the will of God. And, 8. The asserting a state of perfection in this life, and a state of putrifaction in the life to come; that generation takes place in heaven, and that there are no true Christians in the world. *Errors of Antonia Bourignion condemned.*

TITLE III.

Of Schism and Prelacy, and of the Laws and Acts for preventing Innovations and Errors.

<small>Schism, what.</small> § 1. According to the canon law, "Schismaticus est qui ab unitate ecclesiæ se separat," schism is to the church what a cut is to the natural body, and it may be where no heresy in doctrine is: It is a breaking of that church union and communion which ought to be among her members.

<small>Schism about church-government.</small> § 2. Schism in church-government is either about the government itself, or about the persons in whom it is lodged; which difference may occasion the erecting of altare contra altare. Schism may be in worship, when both the same doctrine and government is acknowledged, but communion is not kept in the Lord's Supper, according to Christ's appointment. This seems in part to have been the schism among the Corinthians, occasioned perhaps through the corruption of some members with whom others have scrupled to communicate.

<small>When schism is to be proceeded against.</small> § 3. The understanding having such influence upon the will and affections, and union having so much interest in both, the same will be more easily attained by persuasive reasonings than authoritative injunctions. Though the authority of a church may be interposed to condemn heretical and scandalous members, yet it is rarely found to be the way of uniting a rent church, but rather the way to govern an united church; for it often happens, where such divisions arise, that parties do reciprocally decline each other's authority: indeed, where schism is only a spreading, or but among few, who cannot be otherwise gained. In that case, the censures of the church may be more successfully applied against them.

<small>Prelacy declared to have been abjured, to have been the cause of many evils, Prelatistsown that it is but of men. One</small> § 4. The General Assembly, by their act December 8. 1638, having considered the proceedings of this kirk, and acts of General Assemblies in former years, the vote was stated, Whether, according to the Confession of Faith, (i. e. the national covenant) as it was professed in the years 1580, 1581, and 1590, there be any other bishop, but a pastor of a particular flock, having no pre-eminence nor power

power over his brethren? And whether, by that confession, as it was then professed, all other Episcopacy is abjured, and ought to be removed out of this kirk? The haill Assembly most unanimously (one only hesitating) did voice, that all Episcopacy, different from that of a pastor over a particular flock, was abjured in this kirk; and therefore prohibites, under the pain of ecclesiastical censure, any to usurp, accept, defend, or obey the pretended authority of bishops in time coming. By the act of Assembly August 17. 1639, it is declared, that the changing of the government of the kirk from the Assemblies thereof, to the persons of some kirk-men, under the name of Episcopal government, was against the Confession of Faith 1580, against the order set down in the book of policy, and against the intention and constitution of this kirk, and which, from the beginning, hath been one of the chief causes of the bygone evils therein. The Assembly, in their answer, August 9. 1641, to the English ministers, declare, they are persuaded Presbyterial kirk-government to be of God, and Episcopal government to be only of men; and they resolve to hold the same constantly. Again, by their answer, August 3. 1642, to the declaration of the parliament of England, they say, the reformed kirks do hold, without doubting, their kirk officers and kirk government, by Assemblies higher and lower, in their strong and beautiful subordination, to be jure divino; yet Prelacy, as it differeth from the office of a pastor, is almost universally acknowledged by the Prelates themselves, to be but an human ordinance, settled by human law for supposed conveniency: wherefore, by human authority, without wronging any man's conscience, the same may be abolished upon so great a necessity as is a hearty conjunction with all the reformed kirks. Among the causes of that fast appointed by Assembly 1690, this is one, that the government of the church was altered, and Prelacy re-introduced without the church's consent, and contrary to the standing acts of our national Assemblies. From all which it appears, that the re-introducing of Prelacy, was always lay, and parliamentary only, and the government of the church by presbyters was orderly and synodically established by the guides and governors of the church, her preaching and ruling elders.

of the causes of national fasts; it never received the church's consent.

§ 5. The

Prelacy abolished by the Claim of Right; its toleration treasonable.

§ 5. The meeting of estates in their Claim of Right, April 11. 1689, declare, that Prelacy, and the superiority of any office in the church above presbyters, is, and hath been a great and insupportable grievance and trouble to this nation, and contrary to the inclinations of the generality of the people ever since the Reformation, (they having reformed from Popery by presbyters,) and therefore ought to be abolished. In pursuance whereof, it is abolished by the 2d act of parliament 1689; and by the 3d act of the 1st sess. of Queen Anne's parliament, it is statute and declared high treason to quarrel, impugn, or endeavour, by writing, malicious and advised speaking, or other open act or deed, to alter or innovate the Claim of Right, or any article thereof. Which act is as a hedge about the Revolution establishment; for after the same was voted and enacted, never durst any presume to offer any act or overture for a toleration to Prelacy; whereas, before that, some offered in parliament draughts of acts for a toleration to Prelacy, and moved that the commission of the late Assembly 1703 should be called to the bar for asserting in their address, that the parliament's granting a toleration to Prelacy would be to establish iniquity by law.

The licentiousness of the press, how restrained and censured.

§ 6. The Assembly 1638, December 20. inhibiteth all printers within this church to print any act of this or preceding Assemblies, any Confession of Faith, any debates about present divisions, or any treatise whatsoever, which may concern the church of Scotland, without warrant from the clerk of the Assembly, or to reprint the same by any other not appointed by him: and that under pain of ecclesiastical censure. By the 14th chap. art. 19. of the French discipline, all printers and stationers are warned, not to print or sell books that shall concern religion or ecclesiastical discipline, without the consistory's allowance, and no book is to be sold that tends to advance idolatry, and corrupt good manners. And by the 16th art. of the foresaid 14th chapter, ministers, nor any else in the church, cannot print books made by themselves or others, touching religion, nor any way publish them without allowance from the presbytery or synod, or from those authorised by the synod to licence books. By the 7th act of Assembly 1707, presbyteries are appointed to take special notice, of any book or pamphlet which has for its author or publisher any minister of this church, and examine if their be any thing therein contrary to her doctrine, worship, discipline or government, and that they censure such as shall transgress herein, according to the demerit of the cause. The sellers also and dispersers of erroneous and Popish books, are to be punished arbitrarily by the rubric of the 25th act, parl. 11. Jam. VI. But the statutory words run only against the home-bringers of such books, the books also are to be destroyed, and warrandice given to magistrates of burghs, with a minister, to intromit with them, without hazard of spuilzie: de praxi, sheriffs and other magistrates intromit with such books without a minister's presence or concurrence; see Mackenzie, tit Heresy.

§ 7 For preventing innovations, sudden alterations, by passing of acts which may threaten the peace of the church, it is enacted, that before any Assembly make acts which are to be new standing rules and constitutions to the church, the same be first past as overtures, to be transmitted to the several presbyteries, and their consent reported to the next Assembly, who may pass the same into acts, if the more general opinion of the church agree thereto. See Assembly 1634, August 30. Assembly 1641, sess 14. Assembly 1695, sess. 7. Assembly 1697, sess. 6. and by the act of Assembly 1700, sess. 17. any overtures of general concern proposed to the Assembly, after the first reading, are to lie on the table to be seen by all the members till the next day of the Assembly's sitting, and when transmitted, presbyteries are to consider of them, before the meeting of the synod, next after the Assembly, and their opinion is to be sent to the next Assembly in writing. When presbyteries observe this order, then the Assembly gathers the opinion of the church from the plurality of the written opinions returned; but in case a great number of presbyteries, should either be so well satisfyed, or so indifferent about the overture transmitted, or give such absolute trust and credit to their commissioners, that they give no opinion in the matter, in that case the opinion of the commissioners is to be looked upon as the opinion of their constituents. *How overtures are turned into acts of General Assembly.*

§ 8. The same authority and method that was necessary unto the framing of an ecclesiastic constitution, must be interposed *What acts of Assembly may be repealed.*

interposed and used at its repealing, " Nam nihil est tam naturale, quam eo genere quidque dissolvi, quo colligatum est." By the 8th act of Assembly 1706, commission books are only to be attested in a negative stile, even as those of synods; yet, by the 9th act of Assembly 1707, the actings and procedings of the preceding commission are ratified, and approven positively and solemnly, as former commissions had been, because of their extraordinary faithfulness, zeal, and diligence in addressing and petitioning the parliament against the dangers and evils feared from the then designed incorporating union with England.

Errors and separation, how censurable.

§ 9. By the 21st act of Assembly 1696, and by the 12th and 18th acts of Assembly 1704, all ministers and members of this church are discharged to publish or vent, either by speaking, writing, or printing, by teaching or preaching, any doctrine, tenet, or opinion, contrary unto any head, article, part, or proposition of the Confession of Faith of this church, and particularly the venting any Arminian or Socinian errors; and church judicatures are ordained to advert to any who shall teach or vent such errors, and proceed to censure them for the same. And also all presbyteries are enjoined to censure such persons within their bounds, who do carry on divisive courses, and withdraw from communion with this church, under a pretext of zeal to her doctrine, worship, discipline, and government, and that all means be used for reclaiming such misled people.

Ministers are to observe the public orders of this church.

§ 10. By the 6th act of Assembly 1690, it is recommended to presbyteries, to take notice of all ministers, whether the late conforming incumbents or others, who shall not observe fast and thanksgiving days, indicted by the church, or who shall be found guilty of administring the sacraments in private, or celebrating clandestine marriages without proclamation of banns, and to censure them accordingly.

The Confession of Faith to be subscribed with a Formula, and by whom.

§ 11. For retaining unity and soundness of doctrine, all probationers licensed to preach, all intrants into the ministry, and all other ministers and elders, all schoolmasters, chaplains, governors, and pedagogues of youth, are appointed to subscribe, at the sight of presbyteries, their approbation of the Confession of Faith, as the confession of their faith, Assem. 1690, act 7. Assem. 1700, 10th and 11th

11th acts. And by the 11th act of Assembly 1694, any of the late conform ministers may be received by the commission of the Assembly into ministerial communion, who shall acknowledge, engage, and subscribe, upon the end of the Confession of Faith, the following Formula. And by the 16th act of Assembly 1705, all students of theology licensed to preach, and all ministers and elders are in like manner to subscribe the same; the tenor whereof follows: "I A. B. do sincerely own and declare, the above
" Confession of Faith, approven by former General Assemblies, and ratified by law in the year 1690, to be
" the confession of my faith, and that I own the doctrine
" therein contained to be the true doctrine, which I will
" constantly adhere unto; as likeways, that I own and
" acknowledge the Presbyterian government of this church
" now settled by law, by kirk-sessions, presbyteries, provincial synods, and General Assemblies, to be the only
" government of this church, and that I will submit thereto, concur therewith, and never endeavour, directly
" nor indirectly, the prejudice or subversion thereof; and
" that I shall observe uniformity of worship, and of the
" administration of all public ordinances, as the same are
" at present performed and allowed." See book 1. tit. 4. sect. 7.

§ 12. The synods of this national church, in the year 1702, considering the great affair of the union of the two kingdoms, then under deliberation, did, for mutual edification, and strengthening one anothers hands in the Lord's work, appoint each minister and probationer, judicially, in their respective presbyteries, to profess and declare their resolutions and engagements to maintain, by God's grace, the true doctrine of this church, according to our Confession of Faith, and the purity of worship, discipline, and Presbyterian government of this church, founded on the word of God, and that they promise to disown all principles contrary thereto. *Synodical associations for securing the church government.*

§ 13. The fourth article of cap. 23. of the Confession of Faith, has these words; infidelity, or difference in religion, doth not make void the magistrates just and legal authority, nor free the people from their due obedience to him. Which are generally understood thus, viz. That the principles of our holy and peaceable religion, do not deny *How the 4th article of the 23d chapter of the Confession of Faith is generally understood.*

deny but infidels and Papists may be lawful magistrates in such countries or kingdoms where these false religions are established, and if any of our religion happen to sojourn in these territories, they ought notwithstanding to own their just and legal authority, and obey their lawful commands. But in other kingdoms or countries, such as this of Scotland is, where professing and defending of the Protestant religion is made a condition of government, betwixt the magistrate and people, in that case, if he shall either be of, or fall away to a false religion, and violate the said condition and agreement, then there is ground and reason for the peoples representatives, to claim their right, and declare him on that account to have forfeited his right to the crown, and declare the throne vacant, as did our meeting of estates, April 11. 1689.

Separatists not to be familiarly conversed with.

§ 14. The act of Assembly, Aug. 31. 1647, considering how the errors of independency and separation have spread in England so much, that exceeding great errors and blasphemies have issued therefrom, and are sheltered thereby: therefore, all persons are discharged from frequent and familiar converse with persons tainted with such errors, or to import, sell, or disperse, such erroneous books or papers; and it is recommended to the magistrate, to be assisting to ministers, in the execution of this act. There is a former act of Assembly, August 9. 1643, to the same purpose; and by the 10th act of Assembly 1701, the foresaid act 1647 is ratified. See § 6.

None are to withdraw from their own parish kirk.

§ 15. By the act of Assembly, Aug. 24. 1647, for preserving order, peace, and unity in the kirk, preventing of schism, and for maintaining that respect which is due to the ministers of Jesus Christ, every member of a congregation is ordained to keep his own parish kirk, to communicate there in word and sacraments; and if any person shall usually absent themselves from their own congregation, except in urgent cases, made known to, and approved by the presbytery, the ministers of those congregations whereto they resort, shall both in public, by preaching, and in private admonition, shew their dislike of their withdrawing from their own minister: likeas, the minister of that congregation from which they do withdraw, shall labour, first by private admonition to reclaim them, and if that fail, they are to be cited to the session, and censured as contemners of

§ 16. By the 6th act of Assembly 1708, all presbyteries and synods are strictly and peremptorily appointed to take particular notice of ministers, preachers, or others, who fall into irregularities or schismatical courses, that they duly censure them, according to the merit of their fault, even to deposition of ministers and elders. *Disorderly ministers and preachers to be particularly noticed.*

§ 17. The Assembly, Aug 4. 1641, doth charge all ministers and members of this kirk, to suppress all impiety and mocking of religious exercises, and that they eschew all meetings under the name and pretext of religious exercises, which are apt to breed error, scandal, schism, neglect of duties in particular callings, and such other evils. *Meetings merely on pretence of religion to be shuned.*

§ 18. For preventing of abuse to the kirk in general, and ministers in particular, the Assembly, by their act, Aug. 5. 1642, doth prohibite and discharge all and every one, to pretend or use the name of ministers to any petition, declaration, or such like, without their knowledge, consent, and assistance; and the transgressors hereof are to be proceeded against with the highest censures of the church. *The church's name is not to be used without her consent.*

§ 19. The General Assembly injoins all the members of this kirk to forbear the swearing, subscribing, or pressing of any new oaths or bonds, in the cause of reformation, without advice and concurrence of the kirk. See act and declaration July 28 1648. *No new oath in the cause of religion to be taken without advice of the the church.*

§ 20. In the General Assembly's answer, February 13. 1645, to the Assembly of divines in England, they seem to acknowledge, that they have some practices in this church which are in themselves indifferent; for they express themselves thus: nevertheless in other particulars, we are resolved, and do agree to do as ye have desired us in your letter; that is, not to be tenacious of old customs, though lawful in themselves, but to lay them aside for the nearer uniformity with the kirk of England; that rather than it fail on our part, we do most willingly part with such practices and customs of our own, and without the violation of any of Christ's ordinances. *Some customs of the church were acknowledged to be indifferent.*

§ 21. It is no small security to the Protestant religion, and tends much to the preventing of innovations and errors, that none are capable of civil trust, but true Protestants; *None but Protestants capable of any place of trust.*
for

for they who profess not the true religion, contained in the Confession of Faith, established by K. Jam. VI. his first parliament, may not be a judge, procurator, nor member of any court, cap. 9. parl. 1. Jam. VI. And by cap. 5. parl. 2. Jam. VI. this act is extended to all and whatsoever offices, without any exception, or restriction, in all time coming; and such churchmen as will not subscribe the above-mentioned Confession are deprived; and all such as refuse to subscribe the same, are to be repute rebels and enemies to the king and his government, cap. 46. 47. parl. 3. Jam. VI.

TITLE IV.

Of Witches and Charmers.

Acts of Assembly for preventing of witchcraft, grounds for apprehending of, and how to deal with them.

§ 1. OUR General Assembly, July 29th, 1640, ordains all ministers carefully to take notice of charmers, witches, and all such abusers of the people, and to urge the acts of parliament to be execute against them. By another act, August 19. 1643, ministers must be careful to instruct the people, press holiness of life upon them, and use the censure of the kirk against profane persons; moreover, let the people seek knowledge, study to believe, walk in holiness, and be instant in prayer; all which is proposed as means to prevent the growth of witchcraft; and further, presbyteries are ordained to take under consideration, by what other ways or means these sins may be tried, restrained, and condignly censured and punished, ecclesiastically and civilly. In pursuance whereof, the Assembly August 6. 1649, for advising anent the trial and punishment of witchcraft, charming, and consulting, there is a commission granted to one and twenty ministers, for a conference in the said matter, with nine lawyers, and three physicians: and in the Assembly 1700, among the unprinted acts, you will find a committee of ministers appointed to attend the Lords of council and justiciary concerning witchcraft, when called thereto by their Lordships. By the Assembly August 5, 1642, presbyteries are ordained to give up to the Lords of justiciary the names of witches, sorcerers, and charmers; and because such sins proceed often from ignorance, therefore all ministers are ordained

(especially

(especially in the North, where these sins are more frequent) to be diligent in preaching, catechising, and conferring to inform their people therein. By the forecited act of Assembly 1643, they declare the occasions of witchcraft to be these especially, *viz.* extremity of grief, malice, passion, and desire of revenge, pinching poverty, and solicitation of other witches. They say the reasons of Satan's prevailing are, gross ignorance, infidelity, want of love to the truth, and profaneness of life. The means they propose for bringing them to a just punishment, are, that a commission be granted to some gentlemen and magistrates, within the bounds of such presbyteries as shall crave it, giving them power to cause apprehend, try, and execute justice upon persons guilty of such crimes. They declare the grounds for apprehending witches to be these, A reigning report of witchcraft, backed with delations of confessing witches, being confronted with them; for it is found, that the delations of two or three confessing witches hath ordinarily proved true; as also, depositions of honest persons concerning evil deeds committed, or cures used by them, may be a ground for apprehending them. Mackenzie, on this title, says, that none should be apprehended for witches except it appear by the event of the inquisition, that they lie under many and pregnant presumptions, such as, that they are defamed by other witches; that they have been themselves of an ill fame, that they have been found charming, or that the ordinary instruments of charming be found in their houses; and it is to be remembred, that "Ad assumendas informationes, sufficiunt levia judicia, sed gravia requiruntur ad hoc ut citetur reus et ut judex specialiter inquirat." By the foresaid act of Assembly, after they are apprehended, honest and discreet persons should be appointed to watch them, to prevent their being suborned, and hardened by others, or destroying themselves; and ministers should be careful at all times, especially morning and evening, to deal with them, by prayer and conference, while they are in prison or restraint.

§ 2. Witchcraft was crimen utriusque fori by the canon law, and with us, the kirk session did use to inquire into it in order to the scandal, and take the confession of parties, or receive witnesses against them; but since so much weight

Who are judges competent thereto.

weight is laid upon the depofitions there emitted, they fhould be very cautious in their procedure. By the 73d act parl. 9. Queen Mary, although inferior judges may concur to the punifhment of this crime, by apprehending and imprifoning the parties fufpect, yet feeing the relevancy is oft-times fo intricate, and the procedure requires necefsarily fo much arbitrarinefs, and the punifhment is fo fevere, upon thefe confiderations, the cognition of that crime fhould be folely appropriate to the juftice court.

What is relevant to infer the crime of witchcraft. § 3. Paction to ferve the devil is certainly per fe relevant, without any addition, providing they acknowledge they knew him to be the devil. This paction is either exprefs, performed by a formal promife given to him, then prefent, to ferve him; or by prefenting a fupplication to him, or by giving the promife, to a proxy impowered by the devil for that effect, which he indulgeth to fome who dare not fee himfelf. There is likewife a tacite paction with the devil, when a perfon ufeth the words or figns which forcerers ufe, knowing them to be fuch; and this is condemned as forcery, and is relevant to infer the crime of witchcraft: but to ufe thefe words or figns, when the ufer knows them not to be fuch, if the ignorance be probable, and the ufer be content to abftain, it is no fuch crime. Renouncing of baptifm is moft relevant per fe to infer the crime of witchcraft. Witches ufe to confefs, that in fo doing they ufe this folemnity, by putting one of their hands on the crown of their head, and the other beneath the fole of their foot, at which time he gives them new names.

The devil's mark not per fe relevant. § 4. To libel the devil's mark is not per fe relevant, unlefs it be confefsed by them, that they got that mark by their own confent, quo cafu, it is equivalent to a paction. The prickers fay, if the place blood not, or if the perfon be not fenfible, then he or fhe hath the mark; which is given by a nip in any part of the body, and is blue, as is alledged; but it is hard to diftinguifh any fuch marks, a nævo, clavo, vel impertigine naturali. Where *Threatnings to do mifchief how relevant.* threatnings are fpecific, bearing a promife to do a particular ill, and when charms are ufed to obtain its execution, and when it is known that the threatner had a preceding enmity againft the perfon threatned, under thefe circumftances, "malum minatum & damnum fecutum" libelled,
would

would seem to be relevant: yet it is safer to punish these threatnings with some milder punishment than death, as crimen in suo genere, and not as witchcraft. Indeed if the person who used the charms, knew them to be such, as witches and sorcerers do make use of, for procuring such mischief, it is relevant to infer witchcraft, as hath been said. The using of magic arts or charms, though for good ends, as for the curing of diseases in men or cattle, has no place to make a relevant defence. Since the law cannot know exactly what efficacy there is in natural causes, it may very well discharge all such acts, wherein there is no necessary connection, inter causam & effectum, as it pleases, under the pain of witchcraft: nor can these who are accused complain of severity, since sibi imputent that use these forbidden things; and therefore, since the law and practice hath forbidden all charms, it is most just that these who use the same should be severely punished, whatever the pretext be upon which they are used, or after whatever way and manner, or to whatever end, whether good or bad. Consulting with witches, when done knowingly, intentionally, and in earnest, or a professing of necromancy, which was a prophesying by departed spirits, as also predictions and responses by the sieve, and the shear, and by the book, and all such cheats and species of sorcery. See the 73d act, parl. 9. of Queen Mary. When persons are delated by other witches, or per defamationem, which we call common report, and open fame, and thereupon libelled, that article is never sustained as relevant per se to infer witchcraft; yet sometimes articles that are of themselves irrelevant, are sustained relevant, being joined with that of fame and delation; but it is hard, and seems unjust to compose a relevant libel out of articles that are per se irrelevant.

Using of charms, tho' for good ends punishable.

Consulting with witches punishable.

What defamation by witches imports.

§ 5 The relevancy of this crime being discussed, the ordinary probation of it is by confession or witnesses. It should be evident, that the person confessing is not weary of life, or oppressed with melancholy. Albeit " hic non " semper requiritur ut constet de corpore delicti," this being a crime which consists in animo, yet the confession ought to be such, as contains nothing in it that is impossible. It is condescended by lawyers, that " succubi & in- " cubi sunt possibiles," that the devil may lie in the shape

When punishment follows on witches confession, or by probation of witches.

of a man with a woman, or in the shape of a woman with a man, having first formed to himself a body of condensed air; or that he may transport witches to their public conventions, and upon such confessions some have been punished as witches. The probation of this crime by witnesses is very difficult, and therefore *socii criminis*, or other confessing witches are adduced: but yet, these do not prove witchcraft solely, though dying and penitent: whereas it may be doubted if the consulting of witches may not be proved by two of them who were consulted; for if this be not a sufficient probation, it may sometimes be impossible to prove consulting any other way; but if such be sustained, why may not *socii criminis* be allowed as habile witnesses. The persons injured by witches, are admitted witnesses against them, but cum nota, women are received witnesses in this crime. Witches do rarely weep, because they are ordinarily hardened

Witches may be desired to take off diseases.

§ 6. It is thought lawful, by some, for all who are bewitched, to desire the bewitchers to take off the disease, providing the same can be removed by taking away the old charm, without any new application to the devil; which practice seems yet to be forbidden, Is. viii. 19. "And when "they shall say unto you, seek unto them that have fami- "liar spirits, and unto wizards that peep and that mutter: "should not a people seek unto their God? for the living "to the dead?" Yet it is not unlawful for any to remove the charm, or sign of it, if it be in their power to do it, without any application to the devil or his instruments.

How they torment by images, and of the punishment of witches.

§ 7. Witches do likewise torment mankind, by making images of clay or wax, and when they prick them, the persons do find extreme torment, which doth not proceed from any influence these images have upon the body tormented. but the devil doth by natural means raise these torments in the person, at the very same time that the witches do prick, or pounce, or hold to the fire those images. Witches confessing this manner of torment, may very judicially be found guilty, since " constat de corpore de- " licti, de modo delinquendi, & inimicitiis præviis." The punishment of this crime is with us death, and the doom ordinarily bears, to be worried at the stake and burnt.

Fortune-tellers, who, and how punished.

§ 8. Fortune-tellers are those who do profess to reveal and discover secrets, by means altogether inept or unlawful,

ful, and they are punished with us arbitrarily, not capitally; and by the law of England. cited by Mackenzie on this title, such persons are to be imprisoned for the space of a whole year, during which time they are to be pillored quarterly.

TITLE V.

Of Blasphemy, Cursing, profane Swearing, and Lottery.

§ 1. BLasphemy is a divine lese-majesty or treason, and is committed either by denying that of God which belongs to him, or by attributing to him that which is absurd. These who swear by the head or feet of God, are guilty of this crime by the canon law, "Videntur enim amplecti anthromorphitarum hæresin, que membra Deo tribuebat." They are also, according to them punishable, who delate not blasphemers. *Blasphemy, what.*

§ 2. By the 21st cap. parl. 1. Car II. it is appointed, that whoever, not being distracted in his wits, shall rail upon or curse God, or any of the persons of the blessed Trinity, be processed before the chief justice, and being found guilty, punished with death. From which act it is clear, that this crime can only be tried before the justices, and that distraction is only a relevant defence against the punishment. So that passion, rusticity, or raillery, excuse not. Yet if the denying of God's attributes, or any of the persons of the holy Trinity, proceed from ignorance, and the denial be not obstinately persisted in, they should be pitied rather than punished. It seems to me a good defence against the punishment of blasphemy, when one is compelled to blaspheme through torture, as the saints did through the torments and madness of Saul's persecution, Acts xxvi. 11. and Solomon, Eccl. vii 7. says, " Surely " oppression maketh a wise man mad ;" that is, it maketh him speak, or act, like a madman. *Its punishment, and defences against it.*

§ 3. By the 103d cap. Jam. VI. parl. 7. magistrates to burgh and landward, are ordained to appoint censors in public markets and fairs, with power to exact the pains of swearing, and that housholders delate offenders within their houses, under the pain of being esteemed as offenders them- *How cursing and profane swearing is punished, and the defences against its punishment.*

themselves. By cap. 16. parl. 5. Queen Mary, particular pains are ordained against profane swearers, with gradual augmentations, and ending in banishment: which acts are ratified by Charles II. parl. 1. sess. 1. cap. 19; and farther it is enacted, That who shall swear or curse, shall pay, the nobleman 20 pounds, the baron 20 merks, the gentleman, heritor, or burgess, 10 merks, the yeoman 40 shillings, the servant 20 shillings, *toties quoties*; and the minister the fifth part of his stipend, to be applied to pious uses, the one half in the parish where the offence was committed, and the other half to be betwixt the informer and prosecutor, and other uses, at the sight of the judges, as in the act about justices of the peace; and the insolvent to be punished in their persons. By the French church-discipline, cap 14. art. 24. profane swearers, who, through custom or anger, take the name of God in vain, after one or two admonitions, if they desist not, shall be suspended the Lord's table: so that custom and passion do not defend against punishment. But whether passion will excuse, at least in part, from being punished as a swearer and curser, when provocked thereto while employed about lawful honest business, I think needs be no difficult question; yet no lawyer will say, that anger doth lessen this vice, committed by him who is unlawfully employed, as in playing at cards, or in excessive and unseasonable drinking: see Mackenzie on the criminal law, p. 26.

Lottery sometimes lawful, and sometimes not. § 4. There is a lottery which is necessary, and useful in some cases, for ending of debates and controversies among men; as for example, where there is one adjudication in favours of divers creditors, they must have their preference by lot, in choice of the rooms of lands adjudged, See Stair's Instit. p. 75. 626, and 648. So the land of Canaan was divided among the Israelites by lot. But there is a lusory lottery, such as playing at cards, &c. which is condemned by the practice of most who have the commendation of good Christians in this church; and by the Assembly 1638, sess. 23. 24. art. 9. carding and diceing are noted as unlawful games: and by the 50th canon, Concil. sexti in Trullo, " Nullum omnium, sive clericum, sive laicum " ab hoc deinceps tempore alea ludere permittimus, siquis " autem hoc deinceps facere ab hoc tempore aggressus fu-
" erit, si sit quidem clericus deponatur, si laicus, segrege-
" tur."

" tur." To difcourage this kind of lottery, it is enacted, by James VI. parl. 23. cap. 14. that none play at cards or dice in any common houfe, town, hoftelry, or cook's houfe, under the pain of forty pounds to the keeper of the faid houfe for the firft, and lofs of liberty for the fecond fault; and that there be no playing in a private houfe, except where the mafter plays; and if more be won in twenty four hours than one hundred merks, it fhall be configned in the kirk treafurer's hands in Edinburgh, or in the collector for the poor his hands in the country. And magiftrates of burghs, and fheriffs, and juftices of peace in the country, are impowered to purfue for the fuperplus winning, or otherwife are declared liable to the informers for the double; whereof the half to himfelf, the other to the poor.

TITLE VI.

Of the Profanation of the Sabbath; of not obferving Faft and Thankfgiving Days; of Withdrawers from, and Difturbers of the Public Worfhip, and Obfervers of Superftitious Days.

§ 1. THE Affembly difchargeth the breach of the Sabbath by labouring either in feed-time or harveft, or by going of mills, falt-pans, fifhing falmon, or white fifh, under pain of incurring the cenfures of the kirk; and for preventing its profanation, they appoint both diets, fore and afternoon, to be kept even in landward for public divine fervice, 17th December 1638, and feff. 21 1639. The Affembly likewife declares, that thefe acts made againft breach of the Sabbath, fhall not only reach the fervants, who actually work, but alfo the fame fhall be extended againft their mafters and hirers, 14th Auguft 1643. By act of Affembly 18th June 1646, all fuch fkippers and failors who begin any voyage, or loofe any fhips, barks, or boats, out of road or harbour on the Lord's day, are to be cenfured. By feff. 38. 1648, elders are to take notice, how fuch as are within their bounds keep the kirk, and how the time is fpent before and after public worfhip. By the 25th act of Affembly 1690, all unneceffary failing and

How profanation of the Sabbath is cenfured and punifhed.

and travelling is prohibited on the Lord's day. Item, By act of Affembly 1705, feff. 1. minifters are to contribute their endeavours for fuppreffing grofs profaning of the Lord's day, efpecially idle ftrolling on the ftreets of Edinburgh, peer and fhore of Leith, King's-park, &c. and that by an impartial and prudent exercife of difcipline. By the 12th act of Affembly 1708, for the better obfervation of the Lord's day, they appoint fome to be fent from each presbytery within this church to attend the Lords of jufticiary, at their circuit within their bounds, and then to reprefent the profanation of the Lord's day by travelling thereupon, carrying goods, driving of cattle, and other abufes; and they ferioufly recommend it to the faid Lords, to reftrain and punifh the forefaid abufes, which the Affembly will acknowledge as a fingular fervice done to God and this church. And all minifters are injoined, to advertife their people, among whom fuch practices are, of the great hazard their immortal fouls are thereby in; and that if they continue therein, there will be a neceffity to reprefent them as fuch tranfgreffors to the forefaid Lords. So much refpect doth our law pay to the Sabbath or Lord's day, that it cannot be taken for redemption of lands, and a wood fetter cannot be obliged to attend and perform the requifites of confignation, by numeration of money, perufal of writs, and fubfcribing a renunciation on the Sabbath day. It is relevant to alledge, that an arreftment or horning is null, as being execute upon a Sabbath day; and poinding on the Lord's day, or on folemn days appointed by church or ftate for humiliation or thankfgiving, are void and punifhable, See Stair's Inftit. p. 3,6, 375, 411, and 728. And if the law did not thus order it, the confcientious obfervers of the Lord's day would certainly be molefted, and advantage taken of them by wordly wretches, and contemners of holy things. By cap. 70. parl. 6. Ja. VI. gaming, playing, paffing to taverns, or alehoufes, felling of meat and drink, and willful remaining from kirk in time of fermon or prayers, is difcharging under the pain of twenty fhillings, and if the offenders be unable to pay, they are to be put in the ftocks or joggs. Item, By cap. 18. feff. 1. parl. 1. Car. II. all falmon fifhing, going of falt-pans, mills or kills, hireing of fhearers, carrying of loads, keeping of markets, and ufing of merchandife on that

that day, and all other profanations thereof are difcharged, under the pain of twenty pounds for falt pan, mill, or kill, and ten pounds for each other profanation, to be applied as in title 5. § 3. and that the infolvent be punifhed in their perfons. By the 14th act of parl 1695, it is declared lawful to all burghs, not only of royalty, but of regality, barony, and villages, and kirk towns, whofe weekly markets are kept on Mondays and Saturdays, to change and alter the fame. And the faid burghs and villages are to make timeous intimation of the change to the next adjacent burghs, and providing they pitch not upon the market days of any burgh royal, or of any other market town within four miles.

§ 2. King Charles I. was prevailed on by Laud and his faction (little to his credit) to publifh his declaration concerning recreations on the Lord's day after evening prayer, dated 18th October, in the th year of his reign which he founds upon another of his father's to the fame purpofe in the year 1618. He declares his pleafure was, that his good people fhould not be hindered after the end of divine fervice on Sundays from their lawful recreations, fuch as dancing, either men or women, archery, leaping, vaulting nor from having of May-games, Whitfon-ales, Morris-dances, and fetting up of May-poles, or other fports therewith ufed, but he debars from the privilege of thefe fports all recufants that abftain from coming to church and divine fervice. How this agrees with the civil law; you may fee in the end of the title de feriis, in Juftinian's codex. "Dominicum diem ita femper honorabilem decernimus et venerandum, ut a cunctis executionibus excufetur, nulla quenquam urgeat admonitio, nulla fide juffionis flagitetur exactio, taceat apparitio, advocatio deliftecat. Sit ille dies a cognitionibus alienus, præconis horrida vox filefcat, refpirent a controverfis litigantes. Et poftea, nec hujus tamen religiofi diei otio relaxantes, obfcænis quenquam patimur voluptatibus ditineri, nihil eodem die fibi vendicet fcæna theatralis, aut circenfe certamen, aut ferarum lacrymofa fpectacula; et fi in noftrum natalem celebranda folemnitas inciderit differatur."

How fome proclamations allowing the profaning of the Lord's day, agree with the civil law.

§ 3. The non-obfervers of faft and thankfgiving days, may be punifhed as profaners of the Sabbath, I mean at leaft, with the like punifhment; for by the acts of parliament

Non-obfervers of faft and thankfgiving days punifhable.

ament 1693 and 1695 appointing fasts, the not-observers are punished more severely; and I know nothing to hinder the church from censuring such, as they do profaners of the Sabbath.

Disturbers of public worship, how punished.

§ 4. By cap. 27. parl. 11. Jam. VI. it is enacted, That troublers of the kirk, or who raise any fray therein, or in the kirk-yard, in time of divine service, be punished by loss of all their moveables. If the magistrate be present, no doubt, he may ordain the disturbers to be removed, and secured, till they find bail to answer therefor.

Observers of superstitious days censurable.

§ 5. By the act of Assembly 13th February 1645, it is unanimously ordained, That the observer of Yule-day, or other superstitious days, shall be proceeded against by kirk censures, and shall make their public repentance therefor in the face of the offended congregation. And if masters of schools or colleges grant vacancy on that day, they are to be cited to answer to the next Assembly by the ministers of the place; and no vacancy is to be granted at that or any time thereafter in compensation thereof. And schollars guilty herein, are to be corrected by their masters; but if they refuse to subject themselves to correction, or be fugitives from discipline, they are not to be received into any other school or college within the kingdom, By the 22d cap. sess. 2 parl. K. William and Q. Mary, the keeping of Yule vacancy, and all observation thereof, is discharged.

The church of Scotland hath no anniversary fast or feast days.

§ 6. This church hath no anniversary feast or festival days, but doth only set apart a day or days for thanksgiving or humiliation, as emergent providences do call for. By the 1st act, parl. 15. Jam. VI. the 5th day of August is appointed to be a day of thanksgiving to God, for King James his preservation from the treasonable attempt of the Earl of Gowrie and his brother; but the truth of this matter being much questioned by many, it never received universal obedience, and at length turned wholly into desuetude. By parl. 1. sess. 1. cap. 17. and parl. 2. sess 3. cap. 12. Car. II. the 29th day of May is appointed for the solemn commemoration of his birth and restoration; and, for that end, that it be set apart as a holy day unto the Lord But one of the reasons why the Presbyterians did not keep this day is, because, in the act of parliament appointing it, there is a long preface full of black aspersions

upon

upon the whole church and nation, and such reflections upon religion and the work of God, as cannot be read without horror. And they were followed with acts that destroyed the church-government, contrary to the national solemn engagements, and gave a deep wound to true religion; so that however the King's restoration might otherwise have been matter of joy, yet in this respect it could not be so to any in this land that had a true regard for the interest of religion. Our Prelatists did use to observe the 30th day of January, as an humiliation day, because upon it King Charles I. was beheaded in England, by the authority and power of the usurpers and sectaries there; but though that horrid fact was still detested and abhorred, both by this church and kingdom, yet we never would observe it, because of our notour innocence in that matter. It is true, it is our duty to mourn for the sins of others, but not as our own sins, except we have had some sinful active accession thereto.

§ 7. It is not to be reputed an observing of superstitious days, when people, in obedience to civil authority, do refrain from work thereupon, according to the 21st act, cap. 14. of the French church discipline. *What is not a superstitious observing of days.*

TITLE VII.

Of slandering, and assaulting of Ministers, beating and cursing of Parents, and Injuries personal and real.

§ 1. RAising of scandals and prejudices against ministers, being so obstructive to the success of the gospel, the Assembly, by their act August 6. 1642, doth ordain presbyteries and synods to proceed diligently against all persons that shall reproach ministers, with the censure of the kirk, even to the highest, according to the degree and quality of the scandal. *Slandering of ministers to be censured.*

§ 2. By the 27th act, parl. 11. James VI. and act 7. parl. 1. Car. I. and act 5. sess. 1. parl. 2. Car. II. it is appointed, that who invades or puts violent hands, or offers violence to ministers, by themselves, their men, tenants, or servants, or any others of their hounding out or allowance, for whatever cause, shall be punished by tinsel of moveables, *Violence offered to ministers how punished.*

ables, the one half to the King, and the other half to the party offended, for the violence allenarly; but prejudice of greater punishment, if any higher crime concur, such as mutilation or slaughter; and that landlords, heritors, and chiefs of clans, where the invaders dwell or haunt, be holden, upon complaint of the party, to exhibite them; and if, after legal intimation made to the said landlords, &c. the said delinquents be found within their bounds, haunting openly for ten days, that they be holden as connivers, and be obliged to exhibite them under the like punishment: But by the 27th act of parliament 1685, it is ordained, that whosoever shall be found guilty of assaulting the lives of ministers, or of invading or robbing their houses, or actually attempting the same, shall be punished with death.

Beating and cursing of parents how punishable. § 3. By the 20th act, sess. 1. parl. 1. Car. II. beating or cursing of parents is declared to be punishable by the law of God with death, and therefore ordains, that whatsoever son or daughter, above the age of sixteen years, and not distracted, shall beat or curse his father or mother, he shall die without mercy; but if they be within the age of sixteen, and past pupillarity, they are to be punished arbitrarily.

Verbal injuries what. § 4. Verbal injuries are committed by unwarrantable expressions, as to call a man a cheat. Calvin, in his lexicon juridicum, says, That " Diffamare est per diversas " partes famam divulgare, facta vitiorum commemorati- " one." In libelling of such injuries, there is requisite, 1st, that the particular expressions be distinctly condescended on, that the injury may be accordingly estimate. Next, that the calumniandi, or injuriandi animus, the design of injuring, as well as the injuring words, must be libelled and proven, except the words infer so clearly the injury, that there is no necessity to libel the design. In the last place, that the pursuer did presently resent the injury, and thereupon did signify, either expressly, or by some other acts, his dissatisfaction therewith; for, if he was of such a temper as not to signify any resentment thereof at first, the law will not allow him to repent of that good humour. Bockelman, in his compend. of the institutions of the civil law, says, that " injuria est delictum, quo quid ad contume- " liam vel dolorem alterius admittitur." And by the canon law, it is " dictum vel factum alterius famam vel dignita- " tem

" tem minuens." Sometimes injuries are inferred, not only from exprefs words, but even from the prefumptive meaning of the fpeakers, as to look in a man's face and fay, I am not fuch a lyer as others are; or, to fay flantingly to a clergyman, you are a fine church-man indeed.

§ 5. Since injuries are eftimate, according to the defign of the offender, it follows that men who are fools, idiots, very young, or very drunk, are not punifhable for verbal injuries, except the offender did become drunk upon defign to offend: and great paffion, which breaks off all defigning, *jufta et non affectata ira*, excufeth alfo in this cafe. The relating alfo of what we have heard from good authors, who defign no prejudice, is fufficient alfo to defend againft the punifhment due to injurers. *What defends againft the punifhment due to injurers.*

§ 6. Real injuries, according to that forecited Civilian, are " cum quis pugno pulfatur, fuftibus cæditur, verbera-
" tur, cumque bona ejus qui nihil debet ut debitoris pof-
" fidentur cum quis vexandi caufa, in jus vocatur, aliudve
" quid ad invidiam alterius fit vel geritur." Mackenzie, on this title, tells us, real injuries are committed by hindering a man to ufe what is his own, by removing his feat out of its place in the church, by giving a man medicaments which may affront him, by arrefting his goods unjuftly, by wearing, in contempt, what belongs to another man as a mark of honour, by razing fhamefully a man's hair, or beard, or by offering to ftrike him in public. *Real injuries what.*

§ 7. *Libelli famofi*; that is, infamous libels are the moft permanent of all injuries; for the offender in them fhews more defign, and therefore are more feverely punifhed; which, with us, is arbitrary, except where the prince is malicioufly and defignedly abufed. He who writes, dictates, or affixes infamous libels, or caufes write, dictate, or affix them, is punifhable. If the offender was a minor, or was provoked; or if he did tear it before it was fully written, or after it was affixed, confeffed his fault, and faid he only did it out of paffion; or, if what was faid was true, thefe things will leffen the punifhment. *Infamous libels called by Civilians libelli famofi, how punifhed, and its defences.*

§ 8. According to our law, verbal injuries are punifhed by the commiffars, except they were committed againft a magiftrate: in which cafe, the council or criminal court ufes to amerciate them, efpecially when he is fpoken againft in the exercife of his office: but real injuries may be purfued *Who are judges competent.*

sued before the council or criminal court. By the civil law verbal injuries are extinguished, if they be not pursued within a year, or by posterior express friendship.

How church judicatures are to behave in processes for calumny.

§ 9. When the complaint consists of some injury done to the complainer, it is fit that the church should endeavour to compose and remove such differences privately; but if the bringing of it before them cannot be got avoided, let it rather be tabled by order of the eldership, than pursued at the instance of the complainer, because thus the thing as scandalous may be more abstractly considered, the person more easily convinced, and the heat of parties prevented. But if parties will enter their own complaint, let them be acquainted, that they are not to expect that the church can civilly punish the injury, but they are to be exhorted to pardon it as to any vindictive humour, and told, that it is only their business to remove the scandal, and gain and please parties, to their edification. And I suppose the calumniator complained of should prove what he alledged against the pursuer, yet even that cannot vindicate him altogether, except the end of his devulging it appeareth really to be his brother's edification: See Durham on Scandal. Upon the whole, where there is no probable ground to expect edification in giving way to such processes, according to that author, it were expedient for the church altogether to wave them.

TITLE VIII.

Of Bribery, Partiality, and Negligence of Judges.

Bribing what.

§ 1. IT is to no purpose to make good canons and constitutions, if the execution of them be not committed to just and diligent persons; as it is to no purpose to have an exact balance, if that balance be not put in a good hand. Bribing is the taking of money or other good deeds, either for doing of justice, or committing of injustice. And if they be taken upon that account, whether by the judges, their wives, children, or servants, the judge is thereby guilty as if done by himself, providing the same be done by his command or ratihabition.

Partial judges who.

§ 2. Judges are partial, when they are moved to act, or forbear, either for fear of angering and disobliging parties,

or

or from a design and love to gain their favour. By the act of Assembly 10th August 1648, impartial church procedure is proposed as a general remedy against the growing of sins in the land. And the Assembly 11th June 1697, appoints ministers and members of kirk-sessions impartially to exercise church discipline; and excites them thereunto, by putting them in mind, that in these matters, they have to do with the great and terrible God, whose honour and favour is to be preferred, and whose wrath and anger is to be feared before all other considerations whatsoever. By the 104 act, parl. 7. Jam. V. consulting, or giving partial judgement, or taking of bribes, is declared infamous in any judge. By the 93d act, parl. 6 Jam. VI. the taking of bribes is discharged to the lords of session, their wives and servants, under the pain of infamy and deprivation.

§ 3. By the laws of this and other well governed nations, judges negligent in putting laws to execution, are punishable for their remissness and negligence. And by act of Assembly January 30. 16 , it is enacted, that whatever minister or member of session, be found faulty in neglecting to pursue the scandals therein mentioned, in their stations, the said minister or member of session be complained of, and censured by the presbytery for the first fault, and that the censure be recorded, and that the second negligence be delated to, and censured by the synod; and for the third neglect, they be censured by the synod with suspension from their office, which is to be recorded in the synod register, See book 4. tit. 5.

<small>Negligence of ecclesiastical judges censurable.</small>

TITLE IX.

Of Deforcement of Officers.

§ 1. HOW citations are sometimes appointed to be execute, for preventing of deforcement, see lib. 1. tit. 2. sect. 6. deforcement is that force or violence which opposeth church officers while they are in the execution of the orders and appointments of church judicatures. But if any officer want his orders in writing along with him, the violence offered to him in that case cannot be espoused by church-courts, as an indignity offered to them, otherwise strangers might be emboldened to affront others

<small>Deforcement what.</small>

others, by assuming and pretending their authority Therefore, when any injury is offered or committed against so unexact and negligent church officer, it is only to be resented as if it had been done him when going about his own affairs.

Who are habile witnesses of deforcement.

§ 2 Whoever may be admitted witnesses for proving of other offences may be sustained as witnesses to prove the deforcement, otherwise it may never be proven, but then the witnesses must not be pursuers or complainers, even though they were abused; and if they do depone of any wrong done to themselves, they may be rejected as prejudicate witnesses.

TITLE X.

Of Murder, Paricide, Duels, and Self-Murder.

That these crimes come under church cognizance.

§ 1. AMong the ecclesiastical remedies enacted against profaneness, August 10. 1648, art 5. it is proposed to the consideration of presbyteries, how murder should be censured, in case the magistrate do not his duty in punishing it capitally. And in that form of process, hereto subjoined, enacted by Assembly 1707, cap 6. art. 1 murder, among divers horrible crimes, is there enumerated as the object of the church's cognizance. It is not improper that church-men understand somewhat of the laws and customs relating to criminal matters, the relevancy and punishment of many crimes being either founded upon or expressed in the word of God, whereof they are the authorised ministerial interpreters. It is true, it may be feared, that church discipline shall have but small success upon obdured or monstrous criminals; yet, it being a mean appointed by Jesus Christ for reclaiming of sinners, it should on that account be tried, and no more neglected than his word and sacraments, which very often have no better effects. This church hath very clearly expressed her opinion about the extent of the object of church discipline, Assem. 1638, sess. 22. 24. art. 13. where they ordain, that discipline in kirk-sessions (for there all processes against church members do first begin) strike, not only upon gross sins, as blood-shed, &c. but against all sins repugnant to the word of God.

§ 2. Civilian

§ 2. Civilians define murder to be the killing man by man, unlawfully; and they divide it into that which is committed cafually, in defence, culpably, or wilfully. Cafual homicide is, when a man is killed without either the fault or defign of the killer, as if an ax head fhould fall off and kill a by-ftander, or a rider fhould kill with his horfe's hinder feet: cafual flaughter or homicide then, is that which is occafioned by miftake and juft ignorance; for if it proceed from affected ignorance, as for inftance, if a man will not know what he may know, his ignorance in that cafe will not make the murder following upon it to be conftructed cafual homicide; but if it proceed from grofs and *fupina ignorantia*, it may be punifhed by an extraordinary or arbitrary punifhment, but not by death. It is then neceffary, that the committer ufed all exact diligence to evite the crime, elfe he is not in the cafe of cafual homicide. Further inftances whereof are, if a mafon, before he through down ftones, advertife all below, tho' in the throwing he kill, he is to be cleared from murder. Or if a hunter fhoot at a beaft, but a man come in the way and be killed; and yet if either the mafon cry not, or if the hunter did fhoot in a place where people ufe to be, he is judged by fome lawyers to be guilty of faulty murder. If the committer do what is againft the law of nature, or what is criminal; or if what he doth may produce ill confequences and murder, though he defigned not the fame: in all which cafes he ought to be liable, and it feems reafonable, that he who killed, when he was doing what was unlawful, may be arbitrarily punifhed, though he did exact diligence to fhun killing.

Murder what, and of cafual homicide.

§ 3. *Homicidium neceffarium*, or homicide committed in felf defence is, when a man being purfued, or reduced to inevitable neceffity, has no way left him to evite his own death, but by killing the aggreffor: this is in law called *inculpata tutela*, or, *moderamen inculpatæ tutelæ*; within which moderation, if the defender contain himfelf, he is no way punifhable; and fo favourable is felf-defence, that the exceeder is not liable to the ordinary punifhment, but is punifhable according to the excefs, at the difcretion of the judge. This moderation is faid to be exceeded in thefe three, 1ft, In arms, as if the aggreffor have only a ftaff, and the defender wound him with a fword or piftol, the defender

Homicide committed in felf-defence, and how lawful bounds are exceeded.

defender is in that case punishable. And yet this conclusion is not infalliable; for if the defender was much weaker than the aggressor, he might be excused to use such unequal weapons, according to Mackenzie on this title. 2dly, the defender is said to exceed in time, if he strike the aggressor, "antequam sit in actu proximo occidendi," for else it should be lawful to every man, upon the first apprehension of fear, to kill the aggressor. If he threaten to kill, and be one who is known to have any design to murder, or be a person who useth to execute what he threatens; and if he have a sword, though not drawn, or a pistol, though not cock'd; if he hath either of these, according to the forecited author, he may be lawfully killed, because he is "in actu proximo offendendi;" and yet he thinks the defender may be arbitrarily punished. 3dly, the defender is said to exceed in the measure, as if he killed him for wounding, whom he might have shunned, or if he followed the aggressor. Although much be left to the arbitration of the judge, as to all the three; yet the general rule is, that if the defender exceed only in either of the three, as *v. g.* in the arms or time, the excess is said to be "culpa levissima:" if in two of these, as in time and arms, then it is accounted "culpa alevis," and is punishable: but if the defender exceed all the three, as in time, arms, and way of prosecution, then it is "culpa lata;" but yet he is not punishable as if he had *dolose* murdered, for though it be a rule *in civilibus*, That "culpa lata æ-"quiparatur dolo," yet it is a rule "in criminalibus, that "culpa lata nunquam æquiparatur dolo, ubi agitur de "pœna corporis afflictiva." This exception of self-defence must be proponed against the relevancy, and must be condescended upon, thus, the defender or pannel nowise acknowledging the killing, yet if he kill'd, it was done in his own defence, in so far as the defunct drew a sword, and thrust, or offered a pistol. And though he prove not his exception of self-defence, he will not therefore be condemned, except the pursuer prove the libel. The way of proving this exception of self-defence is so favourable, that it may be proved by presumptions, and by witnesses, otherwise declinable, as cousins, servants, and witnesses who depone only upon credulity.

How self-defence is proponed and proven.

§ 4.

§ 4. *Homicidium culposum,* or faulty flaughter, is, where the murder was not defigned, and yet it was committed merely by accident, as if one fhould hound a dog at another, who fhould bite him at whom he was hounded, fo that he fhould die thereby, in that and the like cafe, the offender is not to be punifhed with death, but arbitrarily, becaufe " aberat animus occidendi." The difference between this and cafual homicide, is in this, the committer " verfatur in illicito," but not fo in the other, yet they both agree in this, that they wanted all defign of killing.

What is homicidium culposum, or faulty homicide.

§ 5. Wilful murder is committed by fore-thought fellony. and if he who intended to kill one, did not by a miftake kill him, but killed another, yet he is to die, becaufe he killed a man defignedly. Since the defign of killing depends much upon the nature of the wound given, then where the wound was not deadly, the inflictor thereof cannot be punifhed as a murderer, though the perfon wounded thereafter die: and though fome be of opinion, that if the party live three days after receiving of the wound, the fame is thereby prefumed not to be mortal: yet generally this is referred to the arbitriment of the judge, who is in this to follow the opinion of phyficians, or of one phyfician. if more were not prefent: but if they vary, then the judge fhall not incline to punifh by death, but by an extraordinary punifhment. For murder is not to be inferred but from a concluding probation: and if the wound be but fmall, and a fever follow, then it is prefumed that the party died rather of a fever, efpecially if the perfon wounded walked a foot for forty days: and feeing ordinarily, wounds that are mortal do kill the receiver in that time, it were therefore not hard to conclude, that he who dies thereafter, dies not of his wounds, if he has walked a foot all that time.

Wilful murder what, and what wound is to be judged mortal.

§ 6. Night thieves, robbers, and murderers, may be killed without any punifhment, when private perfons are warranted to purfue them by fheriffs, juftices of the peace, or privy confellors, and the robber or murderer refifts to be apprehended. And by the civil law, it was lawful for a father to kill his own daughter, if he found her committing adultery, and to kill alfo her adulterer; and if the hufband kill the adulterer of his wife, he was only to be punifhed by fome arbitrary punifhment,

Killing of robbers, murderers, and adulterers, how warrantable.

nishment, but not by death. See the tittle of the Pandects, *de adulter*. But there is no such decision yet happened in this country. In the memoirs of the Marquis of Langallery, printed at London this year 1708, p. 85. the following passage is related, viz. a citizen of Madrid, finding a Frenchman and his wife on the bed, stabbed them both. After the execution, he goes out with his dagger in his hand, stained with the blood of these two persons, and presents himself before the judges, who were then upon the bench. The court of justice, without any other formality, upon the recital of the action, declared him innocent; this he says happened in the year 1700, and the Frenchman was a gentleman of the retinue of the French ambassador.

Fighters of duels how punished and censured.

§ 7. *Monomachus*, or, the fighter of a single combat, is, " singulus qui pugnat cum singulo." By the 12th act of the 16th parl. Jam. VI. all such fighters are punishable with death, although none of them be killed, and the provoker is to be punished with a more ignominious death than the defender. The giving or accepting challenges to fight, and those who carry them, and the seconds of such, may be punished by the council arbitrarily, although combat follow not, because they tend to disturb the peace. The General Assembly by their act 1648, discharges duels, and ordains all who shall fight them, or make, write, or receive, or with their knowledge carry challenges, or go to the fields, either as principals or seconds to fight, the contraveners are to be brought into public twice, once in order to their being rebuked, and again, in order to the professing their repentance; (but the method of censuring such now, is to be regulate according to the Form of Process enacted by Assembly 1707, of which more hereafter, Book 4.) if the person guilty be elder or deacon, he is to be deposed, and whosoever shall refuse to submit to the censure appointed by the church, shall be processed to excommunication. And by cap. 14. art. 32. of the French church-discipline, the same, upon the matter is enacted.

Self-murder how punished, and what defends against its punishment.

§ 8. Self murder is punished with confiscation of moveables, and Christian burial is denied them. Furiosity and madness ought to defend against this punishment, even though he hath lucid intervals, seeing it is more humane to presume

presume he killed himself in his madness, except it can be proved, that he used even in his lucid intervals to wish he were dead, or to commend self-murder. An endeavour to kill one's self, is punishable by confiscation, as self-murder. But it may be reasonably feared, that the inflicting that punishment upon it will tempt the poor creature to renew its endeavour with better success. Self-murder may likewise be committed by omission, as if a man should designedly starve himself.

§ 9. Parricide is a crime which is committed by killing our parents, or, by the civil law, ascendents or descendents in any degree. By the 220th act, parl. 14. Jam. VI. parricide is punished only in him who kills his father, or mother, good-fire, or good-dame, and they are ordained to be disinherited in linea recta. *Parricide what, and how punished.*

§ 10. By the 21st act of King William and Queen Mary for preventing the murder of children, it is enacted, that if any woman shall conceal her being with child during the whole space, and shall not call for, and make use of assistance in the birth, the child being found dead or a-missing, the mother shall be holden and repute the murderer of her own child, though there be no appearance of bruise or wound upon the body of the child. *Murder of children how proven.*

§ 11. The taking of potions to cause abortion, after the child was quick, should be capitally punished, though the using such means before the " fœtus fuit animatus," or to hinder conception, is to be punished arbitrarily. By the 91st canon Concilii sexti in Trullo, it is thus determined, " eas quæ dant abortionem facientia medicamenta, et que " fætus necantia accipiunt, homicidæ pœnis subjicimus." *Abortive potions how punishable.*

§ 12. If the exposed infants do thereby die, the exposers are as guilty as the takers of abortive potions, especially if the place was solitary and remote from society, and where beasts might devour them: But if they were exposed where people resort, and might easily be seen, these who laid them down are only to be punished arbitrarily. Since in this land most rarely are children lawfully begotten, ever exposed, therefore we are not obliged to repute them otherwise than unlawfully begotten, see Matthæus de crim. expos. infant. The parish where such children are found, is certainly at first, to bear the burden of their maintenance and education. *The exposers of infants how punished, and if they be bastards.*

TITLE

TITLE XI.

Of Incest, Adultery, Bigamy, Rapes, Fornication, et de Venere Monstrosa.

Incest what, its kind, and how punished.

§ 1. Incest is defined by Civilians, to be, "fæda et nefaria maris et fæminiæ commixtio, contra reverentiam sanguini debitam;" and they divide it into two kinds, *viz.* That which is against the law of nature; of this sort is all copulation between ascendants and descendants; the other branch, is that which is against the municipal law of the country; but our laws does not observe this distinction: for it is enacted by parl. 1. Jam. VI. act 14. That whosoever polutes his body with such persons in degree as God's word doth contain, Levit. xviii. shall be punished with death. By the act of Assembly 1648. sess. 38. incestuous persons, in case the magistrate doth not punish them capitally, are to make public profession of repentance for the space of fifty-two Sabbaths; but this act is innovate and amended by the 4th act of assembly 1705, and the 11th act of Assembly 1707.

Adultery what.

§ 2. Adultery is the violation of anothers bed: Hence some give its derivation " ad alterius thorum ;" and is committed by married person's lying with an unmarried, or an unmarried person's lying with one who is married. If the woman with whom the adultery is committed was at that time living as a common whore, and the committer was a single man, and knew nothing of her being married, his punishment should be moderated on that account; but if the man was married, the crime is the same, whether the woman was a whore or not, it being still a violation on his part. And that the lying with a man's betrothed or affidat spouse, may be construed adultery; because he who lies with one who is to be shortly married, renders the succession as doubtful as he who lies with a married wife.

The difference betwixt single and notour adultery.

§ 3. Notour adultery is by the 74th act of parl. 9. Q. Mary declared to be punishable by death, after premonition is made to abstain from the same manifest and notour crime. Yet by the explanation of this act given by the 105th act parl. 7 Jam VI that is only declared to be notour adultery, where, 1st, There are bairns ane or mae
pro-

procreated betwixt adulterers. 2dly, When they keep company or bed together notoriously known. 3dly, When they are suspected of adultery, and thereby give slander to the kirk, whereupon being admonished to satisfy the kirk, they contemptuously refuse, and for their refusal are excommunicate. If either of which three degrees be proved before the justices, the committers are punishable by death.

§ 4. Although there be no express law for inflicting death upon ordinary adulterers, yet Mackenzie, on this title, thinks, that judges are not hindered to inflict the punishment of death upon ordinary adulterers, by any thing expressed in that forecited act Jam. VI. otherwise, it should be an act in prejudice of the law of God, which expressly ordains adulterers to be put to death, Deut. xxii. By Justinian's 134th N. cap 1. the civil law is altered, appointing death to be inflicted upon adulterers. And by the law of most nations, adultery is only punished by pecuniary mulcts. With us notour adultery has been punished with death, and single adultery arbitrarily. *Adultery how punishable.*

§ 5. By the act of Assembly Aug. 5. 1642. all presbyteries are ordained to give up to the Lords of justiciary the names of the adulterers and incestuous persons, witches and sorcerers, within their bounds, that they may be processed and punished according to law. By Assembly 1648, sess. 38. a person being once guilty of adultery, is to make public profession of repentance twenty-six Sabbaths in sackcloth; and a relapse in adultery three quarters of a year: but this act is innovate and amended by the forecited act 4 of Assembly 1705. And by that same act 1648, persons guilty of relapse in adultery are to be more summarily excommunicated. *How the church censures adulterers.*

§ 6. Since adultery is only committed by married persons, it is therefore requisite that the libel in adultery bear, That such persons were married; and except it be proven or be notour to the assize, they should not file the pannel, though copulation be proved. Adultery may be proven by strong and violent presumptions, as the being in bed together alone, and being naked, and the being frequently alone together; likewise gifts, love-letters, close doors, the wife's being abroad all night, the entertaining persons that are known to be pimps, and cohabitation, are all presumptions, upon which it is ordinary for assizes to file pannels, with the assistance of any other probation. *The marriage ought to be proved, and what probation is requisite in adultery.*

§ 7. By the 11th act of Assembly 1707, cap. 4. if the woman who hath brought forth the child, doth declare she knoweth not the father, and that she was not forced, whether married or unmarried, the same censure is to be inflicted upon her as in the case of adultery. But if she alledge she was forced in the fields by a person unknown, in that case the former behaviour of the woman should be inquired into, and she seriously dealt with to be ingenuous; and if she hath been of entire fame, she may be put to it to declare the truth, as if she were upon oath, but not without the advice of the presbytery, and no formal oath should be taken.

<small>How she is to be censured who lies with an unknown man.</small>

§ 8. In our law a man marrying two wives, or a woman marrying two husbands, commits bigamy: and this is accounted by the 19 act parl. 5. Q. Mary, a breach of the oath made at marriage, and therefore is punishable as perjury, by confiscation of all their moveables, warding of their persons for year and day, and longer during the Queen's will, and as infamous persons never to bruik office, honour, dignity, or benefice, in time coming. It may be doubted if Quakers can be punished as perjurers, seeing they give no oath at marriage, and certainly they should, seeing marriage implies a vow, though no explicite oath be given. It may be doubted also if the two persons marrying be guilty of bigamy *eo ipso* that they marry, though because of some intervening accident they bed not, but seeing by the second marriage they give contrary oaths, certainly they are guilty of perjury: for perjury being the medium peccati in this crime, and not copulatio or coitus, as in adultery. "Reatus contrahitur per contrariæ vota."

<small>Bigamy what, and its punishment.</small>

§ 9. Rape, or ravishment, is that crime which is committed in the violent carrying away a woman from one place to another, for satisfying the ravisher's lust, and is in the civil law punishable by death, L Un C. de Rap Virg. &c. The canon law describes it thus: "Est rapina " et violentia quædam, qua mulier de cujus nuptiis nihil " actum est antea, abducitur, invitis parentibus." By the 4th act, parl. 21. James VI. it is declared, 'That although the consent and declaration of the woman ravished, declaring that she went away of her own free will, may free the committer from capital punishment, yet shall it not free him

<small>A rape what, and its punishment.</small>

him from arbitrary punishment; which act insinuates that the crime with us is otherwise capital.

§ 10. Since minors are punishable for adultery, much more ought they for a rape; for men in these years are more prone and liable to perpetrate such extravagancies than when at a greater age. Though it may seem that whores are " infra legum observantiam," and ought not to have protection from law who offend against it; yet if the whore be now become a penitent, and reconciled to the church, and for a long tract of time hath had a chaste and laudable conversation, it may be doubted if the ravisher of such a person may not be punished " pæna ordinaria." *Minors, and such as force common whores, how punishable.*

§ 11. Fornication is committed by the carnal knowledge of unmarried persons. The canon law distinguisheth thus: " stuprum (say they) est virginis destoratia, et illicitus cum " vidua concubitus." That law commands such abusers of virgins to marry them, the parents consenting thereto; and if they refuse to do so, his body is to be chastised, and himself excommunicated. But if the father of the corrupted virgin will not bestow her upon him in marriage, then the man is obliged to give her such a dowry as virgins of her degree and quality use to get. That same law says, simple fornication is " concubitus soluti cum soluta et im- " pudica," the punishment whereof is left unto the judge's discretion. That there should be a distinction of punishment inflicted upon the deflowerers of virgins, and abusers of honest widows, from these who abuse themselves with such women who have sinned so already, is very reasonable. By the act of Assembly August 10. 1648, fornicators are to make profession of their repentence three several Sabbaths; who is guilty of a relapse therein, six Sabbaths; who is guilty of a trilapse, twenty-six Sabbaths; and of a quadrilapse, three quarters of a year, all in sackcloth, and are first to appear before the presbytery, confessing their sin there, before they be admitted to public profession of repentence for it; but this act is reformed and amended by the Form of Process. By cap. 38. sess. 1. Car. II. fornication is finable in 400 l. to noblemen, 200 l. the baron, 100 l. the gentleman and burgess, and 10 l. every inferior person; and that the pain be doubled *toties quoties*, and to be levied off the man as well as the woman, to be applied to pious uses: but if fornicators be insolvent *Fornication, what, and how punished and censured.*

vent, they are to be punished corporally, according to the 13th act, parl. 1. James VI.

What defends against the punishment.

§ 12. Although the subsequent marriage of fornicators may defend them from civil punishment, and likewise legitimates the children begotten before marriage, according to the present practice, yet the church doth not judge the scandal given to be thereby removed; and therefore, by their act 11th June 1646, they appoint all married persons, under public scandal of fornication before marriage, although the scandal thereof hath not appeared before marriage to satisfy publicly therefor, their being in the state of marriage notwithstanding, and in the same manner they should have done if they were not married.

Venus montrosa, how punished.

§ 13. According to Mattheus de Criminibus, "Montstrosa Venus est quæcunque vel virum vel fæminam mencitur." With us the confession of sodomy itself without any other adminicles, is sufficient to infer the punishment of death, except the confessor be known, or at least suspected to be distempered. Bestiality is likewise punishable with death; and the endeavour is as highly punishable, if the delinquent was only hindered by others. In both these crimes witnesses who are liable to exceptions will be received, because of the attrocity of the crime, as some authors think; see Mackenzie on this title. We have reason to bless God that these crimes are rarely committed, and some of them not so much as known in this land; and therefore never any particular statute against them hath yet been made: but our libels against them bear, that altho' by the law of the Omnipotent God, as it is declared Levit. xx. as well the man who lieth with mankind, as the man who lieth with a beast, be punishable with death, &c. The ordinary punishment in both these is burning, and the beast is also burnt or drowned with which the bestiality was committed; partly for the preventing of monstrous births, and partly to blot out the memory of so loathsome a crime.

TITLE XII.

Of Penny-Bridals, Promiscuous Dancing, Stage-Plays, Immodesty of Apparel, Drunkenness, Tippling, and Acts in general against Profaneness.

§ 1. PEnny-weddings are neither by our civil nor ecclesiastical constitutions absolutely discharged, for that were to deprive the poorer sort of the satisfaction of meeting with their friends on that occasion. But our Assembly, considering that many persons do invite to these penny-weddings excessive numbers, among whom there frequently falls out drunkenness and uncleanness, for preventing whereof, by their act February 12th 1645, they ordain presbyteries to take special care for restraining the abuses ordinarily committed at these occasions, as they shall think fit, and to take a strict account of the obedience of every session to their orders thereanent, and that at their visitation of parishes within their bounds; which act is ratified March 8. 1701. And by the 12th sess. Assembly 1706, presbyteries are to apply to magistrates for executing the laws relating to penny-bridals, and the commission, upon application from them, are to apply to the government for obliging the judges, who refuse, to execute their office in that matter. By the 14th act, parl. 3. Car. II. it is ordained, that at marriages, besides the married persons, their parents, brothers, and sisters, and the family wherein they live, there shall not be present above four friends on either side. And if there shall be any greater number of persons at penny-weddings, within a town, or two miles thereof, that the master of the house shall be fined in the sum of 500 merks.

Penny-weddings, how restrained.

§ 2. The General Assembly, by their act July 19th 1649, finding that scandal and abuse rises from promiscuous dancing, do therefore discharge the same; the censure thereof is referred to the several presbyteries, which is ratified March 8. 1701. By the church discipline of France, cap. 14. art. 27. these who make account to dance, or are present at dancing, after having been several times admonished, shall be excommunicated upon their growing obstinate

Promiscuous dancing censurable.

and rebellious, and all church judicatures are to see this act put to execution. By the 5 d canon concilii Laodiceni, "Non oportet Christianos ad nuptias venientes ballare vel saltare. sed modeste cænare vel prandere, ut decet Christianos."

Stage-plays, &c. condemned.

§ 3. By the 28th art. of the forecited cap. of the French church discipline, Christian magistrates are exhorted not to tolerate hocus pocus, and slight-of-hand plays, nor puppet and stage players, neither shall it be lawful for believers to assist at comedies or tragedies, and such other plays, acted in public or private, seeing that in all ages they have been prohibited among Christians, as tending to the corrupting of good manners. Nevertheless, when in colleges it shall be thought fit that youth may represent some history, it may be tolerated, providing it be not contained in the holy scriptures, and done very seldom, and even then by advice of the colloquy, which shall first be satisfied with the composition. In the third book of the Digests, tit. 2. de his qui notantur infamia, book. 2. § 5. sub fin. "Eos enim qui quæstus causa in certamina descendunt, et omnes propter præmium in scænam prodeuntes, famosos esse."

Immodesty of apparel condemned.

§ 4. By the 29th art. of the above-cited cap. of the French church discipline, the churches shall advertise believers to use great modesty in apparel, and shall give order to abate the superfluity therein committed. Nevertheless the churches shall make no law thereabout, the making of such appertaining to the magistrate. And by art 6. all persons who wear habits to have open marks of dissoluteness, shame, and two much newness, as painting. naked breasts, and the like, the consistory shall use all possible means to suppress such badges of immodesty by censures. All obscene pictures, which are apt to dispose and incite to unclean thoughts and desires, are most improper furniture for the houses of Christians, and therefore the users of them may fall under church censure, if they be not removed.

Means and considerations for preventing drunkenness.

§ 5. Temperance is the golden mids between abstinence and intemperance; for attaining whereof, when we are sufficiently strengthened and refreshed with our ordinary diets, we should abstain betwixt them, and if we will not suffer ourselves to be thus rationally bounded, I cannot see how we can otherwise eschew the evil of being tempted to excess

excess in drinking, bot from the specious pretences and solicitations of our own voluptuous tempers, and the enticement and example of others; and if we transgress the bound above proposed, we cannot but fall into temptation: for Card. Bona, de vitæ Christi næ principiis, saith, " sæpe " nescimus utrum subsidium petat inevitabilis corporis cu- " ra, an fallacia concupiscentiæ nos decipiat, et in hac in- " certitudine hilarescit infelix anima, ut salutis obtentu in- " temperantiam excuset." Our law seems to approve and appoint this manner of bounding, for the 20th act, parl. 2. Jam. VI. dischargeth all haunting of taverns and ale-houses after ten hours at night, or any time of the day, excepting time of travel, or for ordinary refreshments, under the pain of being punished as drunkards. And therefore, if one accused for drunkenness deny the same, or impute the signs and effects thereof proven against him to other causes, as sickness of the stomach, giddiness of the head, or the like, these defences, though they may be true, yet are not relevant to defend the accused against the punishment of drunkenness, providing his tippling be proven by the unseasonable haunting of taverns; and it needs not be thought hard that no distinction is made betwixt drunkenness and tippling, seeing it is a common observation, that tipplers are harder to be reclaimed than drunkards themselves.

Tippling punishable, as drunkenness.

§ 6. Among the remedies proposed against the corruption of the ministry, by Assembly 13th June 1646, act 11. ministers are not only to forbear drinking of healths, called Satan's snare, leading to excess, but likewise to reprove it in others, and the following act of parliament, punishing the sin of drunkenness, doth appoint excessive drinking, especially under the name of healths, to be punished. The act I mean is 19th, sess 1. parl. 1 Car II which enacts, that who drinks to excess, or haunts taverns, as above, shall pay, the nobleman 20 l. the baron 20 merks, the gentleman, heretor, or burgess, 10 merks, the yeoman 40 shill. and the servant 20 shill. *toties quoties.*, and the minister the fifth part of his stipend: which fines are to be applied as the fines for other immoralities, and the insolvent are to be punished in their persons.

Drinking of healths a snare, drunkenness how punished.

§ 7. Such as commit crimes in their drink, are sometimes, for want of design and malice, more meekly punished than others, especially if they were cheated, upon design, into

If such as are drunk be punishable for crimes, and can contract.

that condition by others And in this case, the law distinguisheth inter ebrios, who are rarely drunk, and ebriosos, who are habitually such; for these last should be most severely punished, both for their drunkenness, and the crimes occasioned by it. And such as make themselves drunk, upon design to excuse or lessen thereby the sin they are to commit, merit no favour; and such as know they are subject to extravagancies in their drink, merit as little. Persons that are incapable and stupid through drink, the law not only forbids people to contract with them, but makes all contracts then made reducible on that head. The law is so far from countenancing fraud, that it repairs the injured against it See Stair's Instit. p. 98. and 60.

Presbyteries may appoint informers against vice, and how judges refusing to punish the same are liable.

§ 8. By the 10th act, sess. 4. parl. King William and Queen Mary, presbyteries are ordained to appoint informers against and prosecutors of profane persons, within their bounds, before the civil magistrate. And by the 13th act of the following session of that parliament, all magistrates are strictly required to execute the laws against profaneness at all times, and against all persons, whether officers, soldiers, or others, without exception. And if any of these judges shall refuse or delay to put the said laws to execution upon application from minister, kirk-session, or any in their name, giving information, and offering sufficient probation against the offender, that every one of the judges so refusing or neglecting, shall, *toties quoties*, be subject and liable to a fine of an hundred pounds, to be applied for the use of the poor of the parish where the scandal was committed: declaring hereby, that any for the kirk-session or minister, having their warrant, may pursue any of these negligent judges before the Lords of session, who are ordained to proceed summarily; and that it shall be a sufficient probation of the judges refusal, if the pursuer instruct, by an instrument under a notary's hand, and witnesses thereto subscribing, and deponing thereupon, that he made application to the said judge, unless the judge so pursued, condescend and instruct, that within the space of ten days after the said application, he gave orders to cite the party complained on, within the space of ten days, and at the day of compearance, he was ready to have taken cognition of the scandal complained on, and instruct and condescend on a relevant reason why the laws were

were not put in execution. By the 31st act, sess. 6. of K. William's parl. it is ordained, that in every parish, where any of the ordinary inferior judges happen to reside, they shall execute the laws against profaneness, and mocking religion and the exercise thereof, at the instance of any person whatsoever who shall pursue the same; certifying them, if they fail therein, either by themselves, or their deputes, the Lords of session will appoint judges in that part. And in other parishes where no such magistrates do reside, it is ordained, that the foresaid persons shall appoint deputes for the said parishes, with the power and for the end foresaid, such as shall be named to them by the heritors and kirk-session thereof. But, really, it is foreign to members of a kirk-session, considered as such, to chuse or present a civil magistrate, even as it is to a civil court, as such, to chuse or present the members of a kirk-session. And farther, they discharge advocation, simpliciter, of processes, against immorality from these parish judges; and likewise, all suspensions of their sentences, without consignation or liquidate discharges. It is also ordained, that in case of calumnious suspending, the Lords of session decern a third part more than is decerned, for expences; and likewise, they appoint the fines to be instantly paid in to the parish collector for the poor, or the party imprisoned till sufficient caution be found for payment of the same, or otherwise to be exemplarly punished in his person in case of inability. It is also enacted, that no pretence of different persuasion in matters of religion, shall exeem the delinquent from being censured and punished for such immoralities, as by the laws of this kingdom are declared to be punishable by fining. And it is recommended to the privy council, to take further effectual course against profaneness, and for encouraging of such as shall execute the laws against it.

Parish magistrates for punishing vice, their sentences not to be advocate or suspended.

Difference in religion exeems not from church censure.

§ 9. By the acts of Assembly for suppressing profaneness, they appoint as follows: That church judicatures execute discipline faithfully against all scandalous conversation, and in particular, against drunkenness and swearing, but with that gravity, prudence, and meekness of wisdom, as may prove most effectual for reclaiming them. And ministers are to be free with persons of quality for amending of their faults; and if it be found needful, presbyteries

Discipline to be faithfully exercised, and how the quality is to be admonished.

byteries are to appoint some of their number to concur with the minister in admonishing such. Masters of families are to receive no servants, but such as have testimonials of their honest behaviour; and none ought to get testimonials, but such as are free of scolding, swearing, and such like more common sins, as well as fornication, adultery, drunkenness, and other heinous gross evils And the ordinary time of giving testimonials is to be in face of session; but if an extraordinary exigent happen, let it be given by the minister, with consent of the elder of the quarter. If they have fallen, or relapsed into scandalous sins, let their testimonials bear both their fall and repentance; but it were more charitable, that the scandal were suppressed, and remembered no more. And persons of quality removing to Edinburgh, or elsewhere, with their families and followers, if they carry not testimonials along with them, the minister from whom they remove, shall advertise the minister to whom they come, if to his knowledge they be lying under any scandal It is recommended to ministers, presbyteries, and sessions to meet together for private fasting and prayer, and conference about the state of the church, with respect to the growth and decay of godliness, and success of the gospel; and in these days the presbyteries ought to pass their privy censures, and both synods and they are exhorted to perform them with more accuracy, diligence, and zeal. It is appointed, that ministers be frequent in private personal conference with those of their charge, about the state of their souls And presbyteries are to take special notice of ministers, who do converse frequently and ordinarily with malignants, and with scandalous and profane persons, especially such as belong to other parishes. Whereas men of business for their too late sitting in taverns, especially on Saturdays night, do pretend relaxation of their minds; therefore it is recommended to ministers, where such sinful customs are, to represent the evil thereof both publicly and privately, and call such to redeem that time, which they have from business, and employ the same in conversing with God. It is appointed likewise, that carriers and travellers bring testimonials from the places where they rested on these Lord's days wherein they were from home, to their own ministers. An abstract of all acts of Assemblies against profaneness is to be got and printed; and also

Who grant and use testimonials, their contents.

Sessions and presbyteries are to keep days for prayer, and pass privy censure duly, and ministers to be frequent in converse.

Men of business not to be excused for tarrying late in taverns, and carriers must have testimonials.

Abstracts of acts of parliament and as-

so it is overtured, that an abstract of all acts of parlia- *sembly a-*
ment against the same be gotten. And each presbytery is *gainst vice to*
to hear the same read twice a year, at two diets to be ap- *be got.*
pointed for that effect. And it is likewise recommended
to presbyteries, to prepare overtures to General Assemblies,
that they being found proper means for curbing of vice,
may by them be enacted. It is appointed, that persons *Gross igno-*
grosly ignorant be debared from the communion; for the *rance how to*
first and second time suppressing their names; for the *be censured.*
third time expressing their names; and for the fourth time
let them be brought to public repentance: this is to be
understood of those that profit nothing, nor labour for
knowledge; for if they be labouring to profit, they ought,
by the act of Assembly, to be treated with more forbearance. All which means for suppressing of profanity are
enacted by Assemblies August 10. 1648. April 14. 1694,
January 24. 1698, January 30. 1699.

TITLE XIII.

Of Theft, Sacrilege, Usury, Falsehood, Beggars and Vagabonds.

§ 1. THeft is described by lawyers to be "fraudulo- *Theft what,*
"sa contrectatio, lucri faciendi gratia, vel *how punish-*
"ipsius rei, vel etiam usus ejus possessionisve, quod lege *ed, and when*
"naturali prohibitum est." By the word *contrectatio,* *exculable.*
they understand, not only the away-taking of a thing; for
theft is committed not only by concealing what was taken
from another, but likewise the using a thing deposited or
impignorate to other ends and uses than was agreed upon.
When one is urged by necessity, not from a desire to gain,
to take food or raiment from the owners thereof, without
their consent, he is not to be despised, but rather pitied
and pardoned, Prov vi. 30. By the 83d act, parl. 11.
Jam. VI. it is statute, that whosoever destroys plough, or
plough-graith, in time of tilling, or wilfully destroys the
corns, shall be punished therefor by the justices to the
death as thieves; but our practice in this is a little arbitrary and uncertain. By the 26th act, sess. 1. parl. 1. *How stollen*
Car. II. it is appointed, that the persons from whom goods *goods are to*
are stollen, pursuing the thief, usque ad sententiam, shall *be recovered.*
have

have his own goods again, where-ever they can be had, or the value; and he is to have his expences of prosecuting the thief, out of the readiest of the thief's goods.

Sacrilege what, and how punished

§ 2. *Sacrilegus dicitur qui sacra legit.* By the canon law, sacrilege is committed, either properly, when a thing sacred is taken out of a sacred place; or less properly, when a sacred thing is taken out of a profane place, or when a profane thing is taken out of a sacred place: This crime is likewise committed when sacred things are imbezzled. Though with us, there be no formal consecrations of churches, vestments, cups, &c. yet to steal any thing destinate to God's service, or even to steal any thing out of a church, ought to be looked on as an aggravation of the crime of theft.

Usury what, its several branches, how it is proven and punished.

§ 3. The taking of more annualrent than the quota stated by law, is the first branch of usury; the second is, to take annualrents before the term of payment; the third is, to take wadsets in defraud of the law; by doing this, they do not take more annualrent directly than what is prescribed by the law, but they take wadsets of land from the debtor for more than their annualrents can extend to, and then they set back-tacks to him for payment of what is agreed upon. The fourth branch of usury with us, is, to take bud or bribe for the loan of money, or for continuing it. But it were against reason, that by lending money to my friend, I should become incapable of a donation from him. By the act 7. parl. 16. Jam. VI. it is appointed, that usury shall be proved by the oath of the party receiver, of the unlawful annualrent, and witnesses insert, without receiving the oath of the giver of the usury, for eviting perjury. The pain of usury with us, is, that the debtor shall be free from his obligation, or have back his pledge; or if the debtor conceal, then the revealer shall have right to the sums, act 222. parl. 14. Jam. VI. and by the 248 act, parl. 15. Jam. VI. it is appointed, that the usury bond or contract shall be reduced; and being reduced, the sum shall belong to his Majesty or his donators, and the party to have repetition of the unlawful annualrent paid by him, in case only he concur with the donator in the reduction. Usury is called *crimen utriusque fori*, and how ministers are to be censured for it, See book. 4. tit. 5.

Falsehood what.

§ 4. Falsehood is a fraudulent suppression, or imitation of truth, in prejudice of another. This description of *crimen falsi*

falsi, or falsitas, doth agree with that given by the Canonists, *viz* " Est fraudelenta sive dolosa veritatis imitatio, vel " occultatio " This crime is committed in writ, either by producing a false writ, if they knew it to be false, and abide by it, or by fabricating a false writ. Again, it is committed by omission, in a notary's not setting down what he was required to insert in his instrument, or the omitting to express the day and place, when the omitting thereof might have been disadvantageous. By the 22d act, parl. 23. Jam. VI. the makers or users of false writs, or accessory to the making thereof, are to be punished with the pains of falsehood; and the counterfeiter, falsifier. or accessory, cannot, by passing from the writ quarrelled, free himself from the punishment. The punishment of forgery is declared, by act 22. parl. 5. Q. Mary, to be proscription, dismembring of the hand or tongue, and other pains of the canon or civil law. The second species of falsehood is, that which is committed by witnesses in their depositions, by taking money to depone or not depone; by concealing the truth, or expressing more than the truth, though they received no money. And, thirdly, by deponing things expresly contradictory; but in this case, the contradiction must be palpable. and not consequential, " Nam omnis in- " terpretatio præferenda est ut dicta testium reconcilien- " tur." By cap. 46. parl. 6. Queen Mary, false witnesses, and their inducers. are to be punished by piercing their tongues, escheat of moveables, and infamy, and farther at the judge's discretion. Perjury differs not much herefrom, for it is defined by lawyers to be a lie affirmed judicially upon oath, and it is punishable by confiscation of all their moveable goods, warding of their persons for year and day, and longer during the Queen's will, and that, as infamous persons, they shall never be able to bruik office, honour, dignity, nor benefice in time coming. For this see the 19th act, parl. 5. QueenMary. There is a third species of falsehood committed by forging true money, without authority, by coining false money, or by mixing and allaying worser with nobler metals in current coins, or by venting and passing the adulterate money coined by others, or entertaining the forgers, or being art and part with these coiners. This crime is commonly punished by death. The fourth species of falsehood is committed by using of false weights and measures.

Falsehood in writ.

Falsehood committed by witnesses.

Perjury what, and how punished.

Forging of money, how punished.

measures. By the 19th parl. act 2. Jam. VI. the users of false weights and measures, are to tine their haill goods and gear. Having of false weights in the shop presumes using, except this presumption be taken off, by alledging that the weights are presently bought or borrowed, or laid aside as light. Falsehood is also committed by assuming a false name, and by presenting one person for another at the subscribing of papers: for such impostors the punishment of death hath been inflicted. Decemb. 12. 1611, mentioned by Mackenzie on this title.

§ 5. By the 22d act, parl. 4. Jam. V. no beggar born in one parish is to be allowed to beg in another, and badges are to be made by the headsmen of each parish for that effect; which law agrees with those of other nations, see Matth. de crim. de improba mendicitate. And by book 11. title 25. of the Codex de validis mendicantibus, they are distinguished from the poor, and punished as we do sturdy beggars and vagabonds. Car. II. parl. 1. sess. 3. cap 10. it is ordained, that all masters of manufactories, may, with advice of the magistrates of the place, seize vagabonds, and idle poor persons, and employ them in their work, and exact off the parishes where they were born, or if not known, the parishes where they have haunted for three years before, two shillings per diem, in manner prescribed in the act, and thereafter may retain them in their service for seven years for meat and cloaths. Sturdy beggars and vagabonds should be proceeded against by the sheriffs, and other judges, and they may exact caution of them: but if they find none, they should be denounced fugitives, and they may be sent to public work-houses, or correction-houses, or put in the stocks; and if they be reset after they are denounced fugitives, their resetters are liable for the perjudice sustained, and the parties damnified will have action against the magistrates within whose bounds these vagabonds are willingly reset. See Jam. VI. parl. 1. cap. 97. and parl. 11. cap. 97. parl. 12 cap. 124. 144. 147. and parl. 15. cap. 268. and Car. II. parl. 2. sess 3. cap. 18. By the act of the General Assembly September 1. 1647, it is recommended to presbyteries, to consider of the best remedies, for preventing abuses committed by beggars living in great vileness, and many of their children wanting baptism.

- - - - -

TITLE XIV.

Of Art and Part.

§ 1. THESE who are assisters by counsel or other- *Art and part* wise, are in our law said to be art and part of *explained.* the crime. By art is meant, that the crime was contrived by their art and skill, *eorum arte*; by part is meant, that they were sharers in the crime committed, when it was committed, *et quorum pars magna.* The Civilians used, in place of art and part, *ope et consilio*; by our law such assisters are called complices.

§ 2. By the 151st act, parl. 11. James VI. it is ordain- *How far ad-* ed, that nothing can be objected against the relevancy of *vice imports accession.* that part of the summons, which bears, that the persons complained upon are art and part of the crimes libelled: but the judge here is to consider, whether the adviser gave the counsel upon the account of former malice conceived by himself; or if it was only given in resentment of any wrong done to the committer, and is to be more severely punished in the first case than in the last. 2dly, In the case of advice, the adviser's age is much to be considered; for though minors, and those who are drunk, may be punished for murder, yet it were hard to punish them for advice. 3dly, The words in which the advice was conceived should still be interpreted most favourably for the adviser; for words are capable of several and distinct senses, as they are understood by the respective speakers, and they vary by the very accent or punctation. 4thly, If the adviser retracted his opinion, he ought not to be punished with the ordinary punishment, if he thereafter and instantly intimated to the person against whom the advice was given, what danger he was in, and also dissuaded the committer from following the advice given.

§ 3. He who allowed his house to the adulterers, for *Who are pu-* perpetrating that crime, or for consulting about the com- *nishable as accessories in* mitting thereof, is certainly punishable, though it was not *adultery.* committed. He who retains his wife, after he found her committing adultery, and lets go the adulterer, is punishable as a leno, pimp, or baud, providing he take money to conceal the adultery, " Nam lenocinium est, ubi mari- *What is le-* " tus *nocinium.*

"tus quæstum facit de corpore uxoris." He who gives warrant and order, or hires others to commit adultery, deserves the same punishment with the adulterer, and in effect he is most guilty, seeing he wants the natural temptation of the adulterer, and commits the crime in contempt of the law

Panders, &c. and innkeepers how punishable for whoredom and drunkenness.

§ ... Panders, pimps and bauds, making gain of the whoredom of others by their help and advice, deserve severe punishment as accessories to their wickedness. As likewise, the keepers of taverns and alehouses, who furnish their guests with liquors unto drunkenness, or sell those liquors at unlawful times, or to drunkards, are to be punished themselves, as drunkards, according to the instructions given to the justices of the peace in the 1.th act parl. 1. sef. 1. Car. II. And there seems to be good reason for it, seeing the best of druggs given to excess, either as to quantity or quality, and whatever overpowers our nature, is poisonable.

BOOK

BOOK IV.

TITLE I.

Of Scandals and Church-discipline in general. Of the Method of proceeding with the Scandalous, and how Scandals are to be tabled before Church-judicatures.

§ 1. WE are not here to understand by scandal, a thing actually displeasing the party offended; nor is it always to be judged by the matter, seeing offence in lawful matter may be taken, where it is not given, as in that eating and drinking mentioned Rom. xiv. Or in taking wages for preaching the gospel, 1. Cor. ix Neither is it the pleasing of men that doth always edify them, nor the displeasing of them that doth stumble or scandalize them; but scandal is something accompanying word or dead, with such circumstances as maketh that word or deed inductive to sin, or impeditive of the spiritual life, or comfort of others. *Scandal what.*

§ 2. Church discipline serves chiefly to curb and restrain the more peccant humours of professors, and therefore sins of infirmity, strictly so called, which are not in themselves so scandalous to others, should not be any part of the object thereof, otherwise its exercise might prove more molesting and offensive than edifying and sanative. Again, offences from disputable practices, or things indifferent, are not properly the object of church censure, because there is not a solid ground therefrom for thorough conviction of the party. Further, offences which the church may find cannot be proven, ought not to be prosecute, for thus her authority is much weakened, and neither is the offender edified. In the last place, though some gross scandals (which are not public or flagrant) may be proven by two or three witnesses, (especially if it be against a person otherwise orderly) yet he is not therefore to be cited to appear in public, except upon supposition of his obstinacy to acknow- *When offences are to be brought to public, and when not.*

ledge

ledge the offence to thofe who knew and were offended therewith; which method is agreeable to that of Chrift's prefcribing, Matth. xviii. for the removal of private offence. But, on the other hand, fcandal fhould be taken public notice of, when they are of their own nature grofs and infectious; next, when the offence becometh public, though at firft it was not fo, and when it is accompanied with contempt of private admonition, or with frequent relapfes therein.

The ends and ufe of church difcipline.

§ 3. Church difcipline and cenfures are for vindicating the honour of Chrift, that fuffers in the mifcarriage of any member: again, they are inflicted on the church's account for preferving of her authority, difcipline being as the ecclefiaftical whip for that end, and for preferving her from corruption by the fpreading of the leaven of profanity. Another end of church difcipline is for the offender's good, that they may be afhamed to the deftruction of the flefh, and faving of the fpirit in the day of the Lord Jefus, 1 Cor. v. 5. act 11. Affem. 1707. cap. 1. fect. 3.

Offences of the fame kind, not to be always managed after the fame manner.

§ 4. The fame offences upon the matter are not to be profecute at all times, nor againft all perfons, and in all places, in the fame manner: thus we fee the Apoftle Paul in fome cafes cenfuring corrupt men, as Hymeneus and Philetus, 1 Tim. i. 20. fometimes he threateneth, and yet fpareth, although the fcandal did merit cenfure, Gal. v. 12. he faith, I wifh they were cut off that trouble you; yet he cuts them not then off, becaufe he found not the prefent circumftances of the church to require it. See alfo 2 Cor. x. 6. where he faith, having in a readinefs to revenge all difobedience, when your obedience is fulfilled; therefore it ought not always to be accounted partiality, when fuch differences in church procedure are obferved; providing nothing be done with refpect of perfons, on civil or natural accounts: and alfo, providing the difference be rather in the manner and circumftances of proceeding againft fome offences, (efpecially if they be fuch where no rule how to proceed againft them is fixed,) than in difpenfing with what feemeth to be material.

The order prefcribed, Matth. xviii. to be obferved, and what it implies.

§ 5. The order prefcribed by our Lord Jefus Chrift, Matth. xviii. for repairing and profecuting of private offences, implies, 1ft, That whether they be in leffer particulars, or in greater, yet if known to but a few, they are

are not inſtantly to be brought to public, (except ſome circumſtance neceſſitate the ſame for greater edification) which order ought to be obſerved by miniſters, elders, and private perſons, act 11. Aſſem. 1707, cap 2. ſect. 1. It implies further, that when the perſon offending doth accept of a private admonition, there is then no more mention to be made thereof. Again, if that private admonition prevail not, then the perſon offended is purpoſely and ſeriouſly to take two or three with him, for the further reclaiming and admonition of the offender, before it come to the church, which may be fitly done at miniſterial viſitation of families. Moreover, it implies, if this hath not the deſired effect, then is the offence to be delated unto the church-ſeſſion; and when it is brought there, it were fit, that ſome who had been witneſſes to the private admonition, were brought with the parties, to inform the judicatory, and inſtruct that the offender hath been ſeriouſly admoniſhed in private, but without ſucceſs: therefore it is convenient that the witneſſes to the private admonition be members of the ſeſſion. In the laſt place, we may draw from this order, that if the ſeſſional admonition have weight with the offender, ſo as to reclaim him, and ſatify thoſe he had ſcandalized, there is no need for rebuking him before the congregation, except the forbearing a congregational rebuke may hazard the infection of others, and encourage them to follow the offender's practice.

§ 6. One is obſtinate when he doth refuſe either to hear private admonition, or doth decline to appear and anſwer before church judicatures, after a third citation, either perſonally apprehended, or a copy thereof left at his dwelling houſe: but one citation given, apud acta, is peremptory, and diſobedience thereunto may infer contumacy likewiſe, act 11. Aſſem. 1707, cap. 2. ſect. 4. 5. In the next place, it is contempt in one, when appearing, to juſtify his offence, or deny it when evidently proven. It is alſo contempt, when one acknowledges his offence, but with a proud and inſolent behaviour; or, who uſeth haughty, reflecting, or irreverent expreſſions. Such an offender doth thereby vilify the ordinance of Chriſt more than if he had made no compearance at all. Laſtly, it may be conſtructed a not hearing of the church, when one

When a perſon is to be accounted obſtinate.

continues

continues to commit the same sins, notwithstanding of his serious-like penitence for the same.

What satisfying, and what not, for removing of scandal.

§ 7. Every verbal acknowledgement and promise of amendment, ought not always to be so satisfying as to sist procefs; for notwithstanding of all that, the offender's gesture when compearing, his expressions elsewhere, and his common walk and conversation, may convince the judicatory that he is but a mocker; on the other hand, church officers ought not to delay the removing of an offence, till they be satisfyed that the offender is sincerely and graciously penitent, for that would engage church judicatures to decide as to the state of some souls, which is bold for them judicially to dive into, and when all is done impossible to arrive at any certainty about it. It is to be noticed, that in church-discipline a difference is to be made between what is satisfactory unto a church judicature, so as to admit the offender unto all church privileges, as if the offence had never been; and what may be satisfying, so as to sist procedure for the time. Upon Simon Magus his confession, Acts viii. 24. it is probable, that as he then did thereby prevent excommunication; so upon it, it is not probable that he was thereupon immediately admitted into church communion. There is requisite then in the offender, who intendeth to have access to church privileges, a sober, serious acknowledgement of the offence, with the expression of an unfeigned-like purpose to walk inoffensively, and especially to watch against relapses; and if there appear no ground for hindering the judicature to esteem the offender one, who purposeth as he expresseth, they should accept of his expressions as satisfactory.

Who are to be admitted to public repentance, and when to be absolved.

§ 8. By the act of Assembly 1596, ratified 1638, it is appointed, that none falling into public slanders be received into the fellowship of the kirk, except the minister have some appearance and warrant in conscience, that he hath both a feeling of sin and apprehension of mercy, and for this effect that the minister travel with him in doctrine, and in private instruction, to bring him hereto, and especially in the doctrine of repentance; which being neglected, the public place of repentance is turned into a mock. By the 4th act of Assembly 1705, they do appoint and ordain, (with respect to scandals, the grossness whereof makes it necessary to bring the persons guilty oftner than once before

fore the congregation,) that after such persons are convict before the session, it be judicially declared unto them, that they have rendered themselves incapable of communion with the people of God in sealing ordinances, and that they be appointed to appear in public to be rebuked for their sin, whether they appear penitent or not, conform to the divine institution, 1 Tim. v. 20. And it is referred to the respective church judicatures concerned, to determine how often such delinquents shall appear in public; and they ordain, that after a public rebuke, the minister and elders be at further pains in instructing the minds of the scandalous, and that the session, upon satisfaction with their knowledge, and sense of their sin, do admit them to public profession of their repentance, in order to absolution: But if, after taking pains on them for some competent time, they still remain grossly ignorant, insensible, and unreformed, the session is to advise with the presbytery; and if the presbytery shall see cause, that then the sentence of the lesser excommunication be pronounced against them in face of the congregation, from which they are not to be relaxed, nor admitted to make public profession of their repentance, in order thereto, till the session be satisfied with their knowledge, seriousness, and reformation.

§ 9. By the 11th act, Assembly 1707, cap 3. in offences, such as swearing, cursing, profaning of the Lord's day, drunkenness, and other scandals of that nature, ordinarily the guilt for the first fault would be spoken to in private by the minister or an elder, and on promise (from a sense of guilt) to amend after admonition, they may sit there; but if the person relapse, he should be called before the session, and if found guilty, may be there judicially rebuked, where the session, on promise, from a due sense to amend, may again sit; but if the person amend not after that, the session should orderly proceed, unless repentance appear, and due satisfaction be offered, till they inflict the censure of the lesser excommunication. *Drunkenness, swearing, &c. how to be proceeded against.*

§ 10. Perhaps an offender may make such satisfying acknowledgements for his scandal, that the judicature cannot but judge them sufficient to remove the same, but only he refuses to appear in the accustomed place, where scandalous persons do publicly profess their repentance; in which case, I am sure, that formality and circumstance of a fixed place *Public place of repentance how a civil punishment.*

place is not of such moment, as to bear the stress and weight of one satisfying the church. For the apostolical order, 1 Tim. v. 20. joining all who have offended publicly to be rebuked before all, is sufficiently answered by their receiving a public rebuke for their scandal, in the usual place and seat where they hear the word preached. and that without putting of their person under arrest in some certain place, for some time.

Keys of doctrine and discipline how they differ.

§ 1. The key of doctrine differs from the key of discipline, thus; the first doth only absolve a sinner upon the condition of saving grace, but the other doth absolve upon an outward serious profession of repentance; by the one mens faults are only reproved, but by the other particular persons are by name reprehended. Though a person be guilty of some alledged scandalous sin, yet a minister cannot, in public, give him an ecclesiastic rebuke for it, without the previous trial, and thereafter the sentence of a church judicature, otherwise he usurpeth their authority, and sheweth more of himself than of respect to church order and edification. Indeed I confess a minister may sometimes very consequentially from his text reprove such sins, and their aggravations, as may make impression upon all the hearers, that the application does agree with such circumstantiate sins, whereof they know such persons to be guilty. In which case, the reproof is to be regarded as coming from the word of God: but if there must be a plain deviation from the text, before the preacher can get that sin then reproved, in that case it looks somewhat like a design, and cannot but be feared it may want its due authority. Now a minister may easily prevent this, if he shall but chuse those texts which point, without any violence, against such sins.

When necessary that offenders should speak in public, and how a public rebuke is to be given.

§ 2. At the offender's first appearance, he is to acknowledge himself guilty of the sin for which he is to be rebuked. Again, he should edifyingly declare his sorrow for it before absolution, that the congregation may the more cordially readmit him into their communion. But much or oft speaking is to be demanded or allowed, as it may be found most edifying: yet all recantations of errors are always to be made explicitly. A public rebuke ought to be so managed, that there be no ground given for constructing it a penance, punishment, or mark of reproach, but the minister

minister is to carry therein, as one much affected and afflicted with the sin: he is to behave authoritatively, having words fitted for edifying the congregation, and humbling of the offender. And that the authority and solemnity of the rebuke may have the deeper impression on all, it were fit that God were addressed in reference thereto, either before or after the rebuke.

§ 13. Matters may fall under the cognition of church judicatures several ways; as, first, by accusation, when a party formally appeareth as an accuser, and is content " inscribere in crimen"; that is, to bind himself to underly the same censure, (he not proving the accusation) which the defender would have merited, had the libel been proven. If, upon trial, there be found any presumptions of guilt, or, if it appear that there was a " fama clamosa" for what is libelled, the pursuer in that case ought not to be repute a columnious accuser, even though he succumb in his probation. No infamous person can be admitted an accuser. Infamy, by Matthæus de criminibus, is defined, " Ignominia seu existimationis læsio, quæ quis virorum ho-" nestorum numero eximitur." Neither are such as are contemners of church authority, or who have been in former pursuits rash and calumnious, to be admitted accusers. A formal accuser is not necessary when the offence is public. If a party cited either upon accusation, or order of the judicature, be found innocent and acquitted, these who inform them thereof, whether the party require it or not, ought to be noticed, either for their calumny or impudence, as they shall find cause, act 11. Assembly 1707, cap. 2. sect. 8.

Inscribere in crimen, what, who is a calumnious accuser; and who cannot accuse, how informers are to be censured.

§ 14. An accusation, though unduly given, should have this effect, as to prompt the judicatory to inquire and search into the truth of the things represented. This gives no allowance to search and prey into faults " ex levibus " conjecturis;" but the warrant for it should be founded upon " fama publica, clamosa, et frequens." A delation is a verbal information or intimation made against some persons, for faults and offences, unto the members of a church judicature. By the canon law, an informer or delator doth differ from an accuser in this, that he is not obliged, " in- " scribere in crimen;" neither incurs he any penalty, although the information be not proven; and by the 11th act,

Scandals tabled by inquisition, delation, and exception.

An informer may be a witness. act, Assembly 1707, cap. 7. sect. 10. the informer may be a witness, except in the case of pregnant presumptions of malice against the person accused, or where he formerly complained for his own interest. Many times offences and scandals are discovered to church-judicatures, by the exceptions or objections proponed by parties against each other; I confess there useth to be too much liberty taken for recriminations in processes, which at any other time were more inexcusable

Where scandalous persons are to satisfy, and what warrants a kirk-session to admit process for uncleanness. § 15. When persons guilty of uncleanness live in different parishes, the process and censures against them are to be before that session where the woman liveth, or where the scandal is most notour. If the uncleanness be committed where neither party resides, as perhaps in the fields, or in time of fairs or markets, in these cases, they are to be processed and censured where their ordinary abode is, except the place of their abode be at a considerable distance from the place where the sin was committed, and the scandal be most flagrant where it was committed. The session, where the sin is to be tried and censured, is to acquaint the other session where any of the parties reside, who are, ex debito, to cause summon them to compear before that session where the scandal is to be tried. Church sessions are not to enter upon processes for uncleanness where there is not a child in the case, unless the scandal be very flagrant; for, upon the one hand, many of these actions, which gave occasion to the raising the scandal of uncleanness, are such as are not themselves alone publicly censurable, but are to be past by with a private rebuke; yet, on the other hand, some of these actions, which come under the name of scandalous behaviour, may be so lascivious and obscene, and cloathed with such circumstances, as may be as offensive and censurable as the act of uncleanness itself, act 11. cap. 4. Assembly 1707,

TITLE II.

Of the Transaction, and Prescription of Scandals.

Transactions betwixt parties doth not sist process. § 1. THough a party who commenced a process of scandal, doth disclaim or renounce the same, yet the church may proceed; for transactions between parties

ties cannot take away the church's interest in removing offences; yea, even though a party hath been dismissed for a time, through want of probation, if it shall afterwards emerge, the process may thereupon be wakened.

§ 2. By the 11th act, Assembly 1707, cap. 1. sect. 4. the several judicatures of this church ought to take timeous notice of all scandals; but it is judged, that if a scandal shall happen not to be noticed in order to censure, for the space of five years, it should not be again revived, so as to enter in a process thereanent; (unless it be of a very heinous nature, or become again flagrant;) but the consciences of such persons ought to be seriously dealt with in private, to bring them to a sense of their sin and duty. And for the same reason, persons who have resided in parishes, for the space foresaid, should not ordinarily be challenged for want of testimonials. When nothing hath been objected by the members of presbyteries or sessions, against any of the ministers or elders, at the privy censures of these respective judicatures, the members thereafter ought not to be heard, in their accusations against one another, for any thing that was committed before the last privy censure; and neither should the people be heard in their accusations against any of their ministers or elders, or any of the ministers or elders against one another, for any thing that was committed prior to the last presbyterial visitation of the parish, because then it was the season, and hour of cause, to have propalled it, if private methods had not succeeded for removing the same; and the insisting, after such an omission, is rendered most suspicious, unless satisfying reasons be given for it. See cap. 7. sect. 9. of the forecited act of Assembly.

The time for prescription of scandals, and requiring of testimonials.

TITLE III.

Of Libels, Probation, and Citation.

§ 1. A Libel is a law syllogism, consisting of the proposition or relevancy, which is founded upon the laws of God, or some ecclesiastical constitution agreeable thereto, as, whosoever is absent from public divine service on the Lord's day, ought to be censured. The second part consists of the subsumption or probation, which condescends on matter of fact, viz. But such a person did, upon

A libel what.

upon such or such a Lord's day, absent unnecessarily from the public worship of God. The third part consists of the conclusion or sentence, which contains a desire, that the profaner of the Lord's day, according to the laws and customs mentioned in the first part, may be censured.

<small>A copy of the libel, with a list of witnesses, to be delivered; it must condescend on time and place.</small>

§ 2. By cap. 2. sect 7 act 1 assembly 1707, the moderator is to inform the offender appearing, of the occasion of his being called, and to give him, if desired, a short note thereof in writing, with the names of the witnesses that are to be made use of against him, that so he may be prepared to defend himself, which is agreable to the common principles of justice and equity. The libel must condescend on time and place, when and where the facts and offences libelled were committed, that so the offender may not be precluded from proving himself to have been absent, and so impossible for him to have done such a deed, or so offended, at the time and place libelled.

<small>What is a relevant libel. It is unlawful to be witnesses or on the assize of irrelevant libels.</small>

§ 3 The relevancy of the libel is the justness of the proposition, whether the matter of fact subsumed be proven or not; and therefore, if the thing offered to probation be obviously irrelevant and frivolous, it ought to be rejected, and not admitted to proof: for nothing is to be admitted by any church judicature, as the ground of a process for censure, but what hath been declared censurable by the word of God, or some act or universal custom of this church agreeable thereto, as said in cap. 1 sect. 4. forecited act. Although one article of the libel *per se* be not relevant, yet if three or four articles *conjunctim* be relevant, the same may be admitted to probation. The relevancy of a libel is so much to be regarded, that, I think, it is unlawful for any to be either witnesses or members of inquest upon irrelevant libels. What? Is not this to be a witness against thy neighbour without cause, Prov xxiv. 28. It was a truth that Abimelich the priest gave hallowed bread, and the sword of Goliah, to David; yet it was a bloody sin for Doeg the Edomite, to inform the wicked King against the Lord's priest, 1 Sam. xxi. and xxii. It was a presbyterian minister's duty to preach the gospel under the late persecution, secretly and cautiously, to honest hearers at their desire; yet it would have been a Doeg like sin, to have witnessed the truth in that matter before our then judges, seeing, by the 8th act of parl. 1685, it was death for such even to preach in houses. What is here said against such witness bearing, strikes with as much force against the members of inquests finding such irrelevant libels proven; for though it was both true, what the one witnessed, and the other found, yet I would be affraid, if I were in their case, that before God I should be condemned as accessory to the shedding of innocent blood. Before the witnesses be judicially examined the accused party is to be called, and the relevancy of the libel discussed, sect 10. cap. 2. act foresaid. But in causes intricate and difficult, the discussing of the relevancy may be delayed till probation be taken; and then, greater light being thereby given, both relevancy and probation may be advised jointly, as the Lords of session and privy council have often times done.

When the relevancy is to be discussed.

§ 4. When the libel is read, the defender sometimes proposeth a defence, which, if admitted and proven, exculpates and clears him from the fault libelled, either in whole or in part: as, if the libel be murder, and the defence *inculpata tutela*; or if the libel be adultery, at such a time and place, and the defence be *alibi*. But the party accused must, before probation, offer the grounds of exculpation to be proven by witnesses; in which case the moderator and clerk, if required, are to give warrant to cite witnesses upon the parties charges, the relevancy of the offered exculpation being first sustained by the judicature: and if the exculpation be fully proven, all further proof of the libel must there sist. But if the substance of the scandal be once proven, there can be no place for exculpation, unless it be as to some extenuating circumstances, not contrary to, but consisting with the depositions already taken.

Exculpation described, and when to be granted.

§ 5. Probation is that whereby the judge is convinced, that what is asserted is true; and he must be convinced either by confession or oath of party, or writ, witnesses, or presumptions, as follows: probation by confession, if judicial, is the strongest of all probation; but if men confess a crime, rather from weariness of or aversion to life, than from conscience of guilt; or, if there appear any signs of distraction or madness, then such confessions ought not to be rested upon, except they be adminiculate with other probation. Confessions before a church judicature are not rested upon before civil courts, except they be renewed before

Probation, what, and by confession.

before themselves; and so it is *e contra,* for men may incline to confess things before church judicatures, knowing that church discipline is " medicina, non pœna," or " ob levamen conscientiæ," which ought not to be discouraged: whereas they may deny the same fault, and resile before the civil judge, for fear of corporal punishment.

Oath of calumny, verity, and credulity, what.

§ 6. An oath of calumny may be exacted of either party, whereby they swear that they believe or judge, that the points they insist on, are both just and true, and they will be holden as confessed, if they refuse to depone when required. By an oath of verity, or for confirmation, the swearer positively affirmeth by his oath, that what he asserteth is true; and it is the only oath sworn by a party which can terminate the plea and strife. But by an oath of credulity, the swearer doth not assert the verity of the matter, but the verity of his belief of the matter, which only terminates the plea in so far as to exclude him who sweareth, from insisting on these points contrary to his own belief or persuasion; See Stair's Instit. p. 698. 701.

Probation by oath of party instanced; it is not to be pressed.

§ 7. If the delated father of a child, after private conferences, do still deny, then the session is to cause cite him to appear before them: if he persist in his denial, when compearing, he is to be confronted with the woman, and the presumptions held forth as particularly as possible: and if after all this he deny, though the woman's testimony can be no sufficient evidence against him, yet pregnant presumptions, such as, suspicious frequenting her company, or being " solus cum sola, in loco suspecto," or in suspected postures, and such like, which he cannot disprove, may so lay the guilt upon him, as to shew him, that there appears no other way of removing the scandal, but his appearance to be publicly rebuked therefor: if he will not submit himself to be rebuked, it is safer that a true narrative of the case be laid before the congregation, and intimation given, that there can be no further procedure in the matter, till God in his providence give further light, than that an oath be pressed, and upon refusal, proceed to the higher excommunication. But if the person accused do offer his oath of purgation, and crave the privilege thereof, the presbytery may allow the same, the form whereof may be as follows.

§ 8. I

§ 8. I A B now under process before the presbytery *Style of the* of   for the sin of   alledged to be committed by *oath of pur-* me with C D. and lying under that heavy slander, being *gation.* repute as one guilty of that sin: I, for ending the said process, and giving satisfaction to all good people, do declare before God, and this   that I am innocent and free of the said sin of   or having carnal knowledge of the said C D and hereby I call the great God the Judge and Avenger of all falsehood, to be witness and judge against me in this matter, if I be guilty, and this I do by taking his blessed name in my mouth, and in swearing by him who is the great Judge, Punisher, and Avenger, as said is, and that in the sincerity of my heart, according to the truth of the matter, and my own innocence, as I shall answer to God in the last and great day, when I shall stand before him, to answer for all that I have done in the flesh, and as I would partake of his glory in heaven, after this life is at an end.

§ 9. But this oath is not allowed to be taken in any *When and* case but this, when the presumptions are so great, that *where this* they create such jealousy in that congregation and session, *allowed and* that nothing will remove the suspicion but the man's oath *taken; and* of purgation; and when his oath will indeed remove the *its effects.* scandal and suspicion. In all other cases this oath is in vain, and so should not be admitted, and never but by advice of the presbytery. It is to be taken, either before the session, presbytery, or congregation, as the presbytery shall determine. And if it be taken before the session or presbytery, it is to be intimate to the congregation, that such a person hath taken such an oath, and the party may be obliged to be present in the congregation, and may be put publicly to own his purging himself by oath, and thereupon be declared free from the alledged scandal. All what concerns this oath, is recommended by cap. 4. sect. 6. &c of the forecited act of Assembly.

§ 10. After an end is made, as above, with the per- *How the wo-* son delated as father, the woman is to be dealt with to *man is to be* give the true father; and if after all serious dealing and *when the fact* due diligence, she give no other, she is to be censured *is not proven* according to the quality of the offence confessed by her, *against the* without naming the person delated; the judicature reser- *man.* ving place for further censure, upon further discovery.

E e   § 11. If

§ 11. If a person do voluntarily confess uncleanness where there is no child, and the case be brought to the kirk-session, they are to inquire whether it floweth from disquietness of mind, or from sinistrous design; as when a man suing to a woman for marriage, is denied, but spreads the report that he hath been guilty with her. If it be found that there is no ground for the confession, the person confessing is to be censured as defaming himself, and likewise as a slanderer of the other party; and withal, application is to be made by the session to the civil magistrate, that he may be punished according to law: see that fore-cited fourth chapter of the act of Assembly.

How a voluntary and malicious confessor of uncleanness is to be censured.

§ 12. It is rare to prove a scandal by writ, but yet it may happen so to be proven, and the want of the writer's name and witnesses, ought to be no objection in church courts against writs, more than in bills of exchange. If one denieth that to be his subscription, it is hard to sustain its being proven to be his " per comparationem literarum." which is but a presumption; and men's hands may be sometimes so artificially imitated, that it shall be hard to discern which is which; besides, one man's writ may differ from its self at several occasions.

Probation by writ.

§ 13. Probable presumptions, and many concurring, may do much to prove, especially in such things which rarely can be proven with ordinary clearness. The presumption of cohabitation, after the parties are discharged, is sufficient, as may be seen on that title, to infer adultery: also, cohabitation, and behaving as man and wife, for some considerable time, presumeth marriage: and the depositions of witnesses, are sometimes founded upon presumptions, as when they depone upon things which depend upon acts of the mind, as, ebriety, and dolus malus. But when a libel is only proven by presumptions, it is not so safe to pass the ordinary censure thereupon, as if it had been proven by unexceptionable witnesses and full probation.

Probation by presumptions.

§ 14. Witnesses may be cited on fewer days than parties. The diligence against them may run in this form, viz. Mr A. B. moderator, &c forasmuchas pursuer &c. having applied to us for a diligence to cite witnesses in the said matter, in manner and to the effect underwritten: Therefore we require you, that upon sight hereof,

Form of a diligence against witnesses, their non compearance to be censured.

ye

ye pass and lawfully summon   personally, or at
their dwelling places, to compear before us within the
kirk of   upon the   day of   in the
hour of cause, with continuation of days, to bear leal
and soothfast witnessing, upon the points and articles of
the said process, in so far as they know, or shall be inquired at them; with certification as effeirs. And this our
precept you are to return duely execute and indorsed.
Given, &c. by warrant, &c. If witnesses refuse after
three citations to compear, then they may be proceeded
against as contumacious: or, if judged needful, after the
first or second citation is disobeyed, application should be
made to the civil magistrate, that he may oblige them to
appear; see that 9th sect. cap. 2. of that frequently above
cited act of Assembly.

§ 15. In church judicatures, women and minors past *Objections a-*
fourteen years of age, are received witnesses. If the defen- *gainst wit-*
der appear, he may object against any of them, and if the *nesses.*
objection be relevant, and made evident to the judicature,
the witnesses are to be cast: for which see that same act.
The objections of infamy, or enmity, are relevant to cast
any witness: but the design of church courts being "ad
" tollendum scandalum, & ad eruendam veritatem," they
will sometimes receive witnesses cum nota, against whom
some common and general objections have been made, reserving to themselves to consider how far they will make
use of their testimony at advising the sufficiency of the
probation.

§ 16. Witnesses are to be sworn thus, lifting and hold- *How witness-*
ing up the right hand, they swear by God, and as they *es are to be*
shall answer to him, they shall tell the truth, and nothing *sworn, exa-*
but the truth, concerning the articles and points of the pre- *mined, and*
subscribe the
sent process, in so far as they know, or shall be asked. *initialia testi-*
Which oath the moderator is judicially to administer, and *monii.*
though there be no relevant objection against the witnesses,
yet they are to be solemnly purged of malice, bribe, or
good deed, done or to be done, and of partial council, by
which some understand prompting or consulting for making of the process. The witnesses are to be sworn and
examined in presence of the accused party, if compearing,
and he may desire the moderator to propose such questions, or cross questions, to the witnesses, as may tend to his

exculpation, which f the judicature think pertinent, are to be propofed The initialia teftimoniorum, fuch as, their age. married, or unmarried, or foluti, that is, widows. and the like, are propofed, that the deponent's veracity may by thefe be traced If witneffes cannot fubfcribe their names to their depofition, the clerk is to mark that they declare they cannot write, and the moderator is always to fubfcribe the fame, whether they can write or not. If they can but fubfcribe the initial letters of their names, they fhould do it, and the clerk is to write about their mark thus (Adam A. B. Bruce his mark).

Singularity of witneffes, what.

§ 17. A fingular witnefs is one that hath no concurring witnefs. This fingularity is either, " obftativa," which is, in a crime not reiterable; as if one fhould depone, that a man was murdered at one place, and another depone he was murdered at another place. Again, there is a " fin-"gularitas adminiculativa," which is, where the witneffes do not concur in their depofitions; yet they are not contrary but the one affifts the other, as in the proving that an horfe was ftolen, one fhould depone that he faw the thief go in without a horfe, and another faw him take the horfe. In the third place, there is a " fingularitas diverfificativa," when witneffes depone different acts in a crime, which is reiterable; as if one witnefs depone upon an adultery, committed at one time, and another of an adultery committed at another time. Is that perfon's being guilty of adultery fufficiently proven?

Probation by notoriety, and if judges may be witneffes.

§ 18. Of things notour, there are fome which cannot be proven, and yet are true, as fuch a man is another's fon: other things can be proven which are " facti permanentis," fuch as, that there is a palace or fountain in fuch a town, " fed notorium non indiget probatione." Again, there are things notour, which need no probation, which are " fac-" ti tranfeuntis," as that fuch a perfon did publicly commit murder. Although judges cannot be both judges and witneffes, yet, he is a witnefs and a judge too of what he fees and hears in judgment, for thefe are counted as notour; See Stair's Inftit, p 704.

How parties are duly fifted before a churchjudicature, and the requifita citationis.

§ 19. It is repugnant to the laws of God and man, to condemn any that is abfent or unheard, unlefs his abfence proceed from his own fraud or ftubbornnefs: therefore in order to a due hearing, citations muft be given to parties con-

concerned, in writing, especially if they be called before presbyteries, and other superior judicatures of the church; see the 2d cap. of the forecited act of Assembly. The citation must bear, 1. The judicature before which the person cited is to appear. 2. The name of the pursuer, (if the party be not cited by order of the judicature) 3. The name of the defender. 4. The cause for which the person is cited. 5. The place where compearance must be made. And lastly The time when they must compear. And this is to be observed, that all parties and witnesses cited before church courts, are to be designed in these citations as they are or may be commonly in all other writs. If they be residing within the parish, they may be cited upon forty eight hours advertisement.

§ 20. It hath sometimes been practised, to cite parties even when out of the country, a particular instance whereof is, the commission of Assembly 1644, caused cite some Scots, then about Oxford in England, (for emitting a malignant declaration) at the mark-t-cross of Edinburgh, pier and shoar of Leith, to appear before the then next ensuing General Assembly, upon sixty days warning, counting from the day of the citation. *Parties out of the country how cited.*

§ 21. If the persons be charged with scandal, who live within the bounds of another parish, the kirk session of that parish where that person resides, should be desired to cause cite them to answer before the session in whose bounds the scandal happened, and the same course is to be followed in such cases by the other judicatures of the church. *Parties in another parish how cited.*

§ 22. Citations are called dilatory for the first and second, that the party may appear; and the third, or one given *ad actu*, is called peremptory, wherein the judicature certifies the person cited, that they will proceed to the cognition of the cause, though he appear not, or that they will proceed against him as contumacious. If the person do not compear upon this peremptory citation, and no relevant excuse therefor be proposed and sustained, the judicature is to proceed to take cognition, either by examining of witnesses, or by other documents, for the verity of the scandal, and that before they censure him for contumacy; see cap. .. sect 6 of the forecited act. If any under process for scandal, abscond, they should be cited first from the pulpit of the parish where the process depends, and where they *Citations dilatory and peremptory, how to proceed with those who disobey or abscond.*

they reside; and if they do not thereupon appear, they are next, by order of the presbytery, to be cited from the pulpits of all the kirks within their bounds, to compear before them; and if they do not then appear, they are to be declared fugitives from church discipline in all the kirks within that bounds, desiring that if any know of the said fugitives, they may give notice thereof, and the presbytery is to sist there, until they get some further account of these persons; see § 18. of the forecited cap. and act. This citation is commonly called *edictal*, and likewise takes place when the person to be cited takes methods to hinder a copy to be given in the usual way, or, when it is dangerous for the officer to travel to that place.

<small>Style of a summons, and of the copy and execution thereof, and of caution to appear.</small>

§ 23. Sometimes the warrant for citing bears the libel, and then a full copy thereof is given, but sometimes it bears not the libel, and then the defender is cited to hear and see the informations against him, and must, when appearing, be treated as in § 2. of this title; the form of which summons may run thus: Mr A. B. minister and remanent members of the church session of   to   our officer, we require you, that upon sight hereof, ye pass and lawfully summon   personally, or at his dwelling-house, to compear before the said session, within the session-house at   the   day of   next to come, in the hour of cause, to answer to the information or libel against him, for the sin and scandal of   laid to his charge: with certification, &c. given at   the   day of   by warrant of the said session, A. B. sess. cls. Besides the general certification of the church censures, which is the method ecclesiastic courts do take, to procure obedience to their orders, there are some proper certifications, as in transportation of ministers, and their edicts of ordination and admission, of which already in book 1. Now the copy of a summons may run thus: I   church officer of   by virtue of an order directed from them, lawfully summons you   to compear &c. with certification, &c. conform to the principal warrant, dated at   the   day of   this by warrant of the said session I give, before these witnesses,   &c. A. B. officer. He is to return the summons execute in these terms, viz. upon the   day of   I   church officer

officer of   paſt at the command of the within written order directed from the church ſeſſion of   and by virtue thereof, lawfully ſummoned the within mentioned   perſonally apprehended, and delivered to him a true copy of the ſaid warrant, to compear before the ſaid ſeſſion, day and place within ſpecified, to anſwer for the ſin and ſcandal of   laid to his charge; and made certification as is within expreſſed. This I did conform to the within written warrant in all points; before theſe witneſſes, A. B, &c. And for the more verification hereof, we have ſubſcribed thir preſents at   the day of, &c. The execution muſt bear, that either citation was given to the party perſonally, as above, or left at his dwelling-houſe, with his wife, bairns, or ſervants, if the officer get entry; or by affixing a copy on the door, after knocking ſeveral times, if he get not entry. If any man bind as cautioner for another, that he ſhall undergo the diſcipline of the church, under a pecunial pain for the uſe of the poor, he ſhould bind to the magiſtrate, and not to the church.

§ 24. When minors are convened before church judicatures, their curators are not to be cited as before civil courts, though they may be acquainted therewith, that their pupils may receive ſuitable advice and inſtruction from them. A minor, that is, a male paſt fourteen, and a female paſt twelve years of age, may be called before church judicatures, when guilty; as for pupils under that age, it will be rare if ever they be concerned as delinquents, except " ubi " malitia ſuppletætatem ;" that is, where ſtrength of nature is as far advanced in them as it uſeth to be in others of riper years. The concluſion of all church proceſs, being againſt the defenders themſelves, none can appear for them; nay, advocates are not ſo much as allowed to plead for compearing parties, otherwiſe pleas would probably be more frequent, and tedious too: and the truth hath been many times expiſcate by the countenance, behaviour, or expreſſions of parties themſelves, which would have been concealed by advocates. In the M. S. acts of Aſſembly at Edinburgh 1575, they refuſe to allow advocates to plead before them in a proceſs of dilapidation againſt the biſhop of Dunkeld, but ordains him to anſwer himſelf; and if he think fit, may chuſe any miniſter to reaſon for him. When

All defenders muſt appear perſonally, even though minors, and how ſocieties appear.

incor-

incorporations are cited, it is necessary they be allowed to answer by some commissioned from their body, who must be members of that society, or reside therein. If a burgh royal were cited, they would not be allowed to appear by him who resides not among them, but only is one of their honorary burgesses; and no party sustains great loss thereby, seeing they may advise with whom they please in drawing of answers, and the like.

TITLE IV.

Of the vocational and personal Faults of Ministers and Probationers, how they are censured, and of the Method of proceeding to censure, and of reponing them against these Censures.

Non-residence what, and how censured, who are deserters, and how censured, and defences against the same.

§ 1. BY the 132d cap. parl. 8. James VI. non-residence is declared to be, when a minister resides not within the parish, but is absent therefrom, and from his kirk, and using of his office, for the space of four Sabbaths in the year, without a lawful cause, allowed by the presbytery; which non-residence is deprivation. By parity of reason, the same pain may be applied against principals, and masters of universities, who attend not upon their charges. The ministry is said to be *militia spiritualis*, they are watchmen fixed by their superiors as centinals at such posts, which, if they desert without warrant, all the order of the spiritual discipline is overturned. Agreeable hereunto is the act of Assembly 1596, ratified by Assembly 1638, whereby it is appointed, that ministers not resident with their flocks be deposed, according to the acts of the General Assembly, and laws of this realm, otherwise the burden is to lie on the presbytery, and they to be censured for the same; and by the th article of the same act, it is appointed, conform to the old acts of Assemblies therein mentioned, that ministers reside in their own parishes, or at their ordinary manses By the 4th cap. of the policy of the kirk, they who are once called of God, and duely elected by man, and have once accepted the charge of the ministry, may not leave their functions, otherwise the deserters are to be admonished, and in case of obstinacy, excommunicated.

ted. And by the M. S. acts of Assembly at Edinburgh, 1570. It is appointed that ministers at their public instalment, shall promise solemnly never to leave their ministry at any time thereafter, under the pain of infamy and perjury. Conform hereunto, in the cap. 1. art. 14. of the French church discipline, ministers, with their families, must actually reside in their parishes, under pain of deposition: and by art. 23. deserters of the ministry shall be excommunicated, if they do not repent, and reassume the office God hath committed unto them. By the Assembly 1691, sess. 15. although ministers have received their ordination from foreign churches, yet, if they have a standing relation to any charge in this church, they are not to remove out of the kingdom, without consent of the respective judicatures of this church, otherwise they may be treated as deserters. See the ordination engagements, book 1. If persecution be particular against one minister, in that case, it is generally thought, he may warrantably flee, without being esteemed a deserter; but it will scarcely defend against desertion, when the persecution becomes general. A minister seems to be particularly tied to wait upon his charge in the time of a public calamity; and therefore the commission, 16th May 1645, found that Mr Mungo Law, minister at Edinburgh, could not be spared from his charge, to attend the General's regiment, in respect of the fear of the infection in the city.

§ 2. Supine negligence is, an habitual or customary neglect of some one or other of the pastoral duties; but every escape cannot infer it, the pastoral office being in some sense a burden too heavy for the shoulders of angels. By our law, supine negligence is relevant to infer deposition, even as error, scandal, ignorance, and contumacy are; see the act of parl. 1690, settling the church government. And by the forecited act of Assem. 1596, it is appointed, that such ministers as be slothful in the ministration of the sacrament of the Lord's Supper, be sharply rebuked; and if they continue therein, that they be deposed. And by the act of Assembly June 13. 1646, among the enormities and corruptions of the ministerial calling, the following is mentioned, viz. idleness, that is, seldom preaching, as once on the Lord's day, or in preparation for public duties, not being given to reading and meditation,

Supine negligence what, and how censured.

meditation, but only now and then, not like other tradesmen, continually at their work.

Dilapidation what, and how censurable.

§ 3. Dilapidation of benefices is, the deed of any churchman, whereby his rents are wasted, diminished, or altered to the worse from what they were. And the punishment is, disannulling of the deed, and deprivation to the granter, Jam. VI. parl. 7. cap. 101. by that forecited act of Assembly 1596, it is declared, that delapidation of benefices, demitting of them for favour or money, without advice of the kirk; interchanging of benefices by transaction, or transporting of themselves by that occasion, without advice of the kirk, are precisely to be punished, Suchlike, setting of tacks without consent of the Assembly, is to be punished as dilapidation.

Simony what, and how proven and punished.

§ 4. Simony is the buying or selling of any spiritual thing, or of what is annexed thereto. The canonists describe it to be, "Studiosa voluntas, seu cupiditas emendi "vel vendendi spiritualia, vel spiritualibus annexa." Thus Simony may be committed by making advantage of administrating the sacraments. By Jam. VI. parl. 21. act 1. any condition made by the intrant with the patron, reserving to himself a sufficient maintenance answerable to the state of the benefice, is declared not to be Simony. In this crime, witnesses who are not very habile, or " omni exceptione majores," such as whores and infamous persons, may be admitted, and it may be proven by presumption or oath of party, according to the opinion of some lawyers, and all because it is ordinarily carried on with much privacy and clandestine dealing. "Ambitus" is " crimen mere ecclesiasticum," and not usually punished by laicks. By the forecited act of Assembly 1596, it is provided, that none seek presentations to benefices, without advice of the presbytery; and if any do in the contrary, they are to be repelled as *rei ambitus*. They further appoint that it be inquired, if any by solicitation or moyen, directly or indirectly, press to enter into the ministry; and if it be found, the person so soliciting, is to be repelled; these three crimes, Dilapidation, Simony, and Ambitus, do often meet in one and the same person, and the crime is denominate from that which most predominates in it.

Ambitus, what, and how censured.

§ 5. By the 23d act of Assembly 1696, it is recommended to all synods and presbyteries, that they advert to the

the many irregularities committed by vagrant unfixed mi- *Intruders* niſters: and preſbyteries, where any difficulties occur, *and vagrant* are to conſult their ſynods, before they proceed to cen- *miniſters,* ſure. By the 27th act of that Aſſembly, they ſuſpend *cenſured.* one from the exerciſe of his miniſtry, becauſe he exerci- ſed it in a vagrant diſorderly way. And by the 18th act of Aſſembly 1701, preſbyteries are appointed to ſend in to the commiſſion an account of ſuch miniſters, or preach- ers, as intrude into pariſhes, that application may be made to the government for removing them, that the kirks intruded into may be orderly planted. Aſſem. 1694. ſeſſ. 14. the Queen by her proclamation, dated at Windſor, September 20. 1708. in purſuance of ſeveral acts of par- liament made in favours of the preſent church eſtabliſh- ment, particularly the act 1695, againſt intruders, doth require and command, all ſuch as have intruded upon churches or manſes, to remove therefrom, and all magi- ſtrates and judges within their reſpective juriſdictions, are to ſee the ſame executed, by decerning accordingly, and procuring letters of horning and caption thereupon to be directed *in communi forma*. By the diſcipline of the French church, cap. 1. art. 26. the miniſter that ſhall intrude him- ſelf, although he were approved by the people, is not to be approved by the neighbouring miniſters or others, but notice muſt be given to the colloquy thereof, or provin- cial ſynod. And by the 55th article of that chapter, the names of vagrant miniſters are to be proclaimed through all the churches.

§ 6. By the foreſaid act of Aſſembly 1596, ratified *Vocational* 1638, it is enacted, That ſuch miniſters as ſhall be found *faults of mi-* not given to their books and ſtudy of the ſcripture, not gi- *cenſured.* ven to ſanctification and prayer, that ſtudies not to be powerful and ſpiritual, not applying the doctrines againſt corruptions, which is the paſtoral work, obſcure and too ſcholaſtic before the people, cold and wanting in ſpiritual zeal, negligent in viſiting the ſick, or caring for the poor, or indiſcreet in chuſing parts of the word not meeteſt for the flock, flatterers, and diſſembling of public ſins, and e- ſpecially of great perſonages in their congregations: all ſuch miniſters are to be cenſured according to the degree of their fault, and continuing therein are to be deprived. Item, Such as be ſlothfull in the miniſtration of the ſacraments,

F f 2   and

and irreverent, or profaners thereof, by admitting the ignorant or profane thereto, and omitting the due trial of such as are to be admitted, or using but light trial, or having respect in their trial to persons; all such ministers are to be sharply rebuked; and if they continue therein, are to be deposed. Item, But if any minister be found a seller of the sacraments, he is to be deposed *simpliciter*: and such as collude with scandalous persons, by overlooking them for money, do incur the like punishment. Item, All ministers, who neglect the due exercise of discipline, and continue therein after admonition, are to be deposed.

Personal faults of ministers how censured.

§ 7. By the forecited act 1596, it is appointed, that such ministers as are light and wanton in their behaviour, as in gorgeous and light apparrel, or in speech, or in using light and profane company, or that are guilty of dancing, carding, diceing, and the like, if they continue therein after due admonition, shall be deposed as scandalous to the gospel; and agreeable hereto is the 54th canon concilii Laodiceni, " Quod non oportet sacratos, vel clericos in nupti-
" is vel conviviis aliqua spectacula contemplari, sed priuf-
" quam ingrediantur Thymelici, surgere et secedere de-
" beant." Item, Ministers found to be swearers or banners, profaners of the Sabbath, drunkards or fighters, are to be deposed *simpliciter*. By the 27th and 42d of these canons, called *apostolical*, " Episcopum, vel presbyterum,
" vel diaconum verberantem fideles peccantes, aut infide-
" les injuriam facientes, ac per hoc timeri volentem, ab
" officio deponi mandamus." And by the other canon,
" Episcopus, presbyter, aut diaconus, aleæ vacans, aut
" ebrietatibus, vel desistat, vel gradu suo dejiciatur." Item, Ministers that are detractors, flatterers, breakers of promise, liars, brawlers, and quarellers, after admonition, if they continue therein, they are to be deposed. By the 53d canon, called *apostolical*, " Si quis clericus in cau-
" pona comedens deprehensus fuerit, a communionis so-
" dalitate secernatur, præter eum qui vitæ necessitate di-
" verit in hospitium." And by the 55th conon concilii Laodiceni, " Quod non oportet sacratos vel clericos, ex
" collatione, convivia peragere, sed neque laicos." And by the 43d canon, concil. Carthaginen " Ne in caupo-
" na iversentur clerici, nisi hospitio accepti. Ut clerici
" comedendi, vel bibendi gratia, non ingrediantur, nisi
hospitii

" hospitii necessitate compulsi " By our law, (vid. tit. 13. book. 3. the haunting of taverns at unseasonable hours therein condescended upon, is equally punishable with drunkenness. So that a minister's drinking temperately in change-houses, though with good company (but at forbidden hours) will not defend him against the punishment of drunkenness. Item, Ministers are not to take usury, and if they continue therein, they are to be deprived. By the 44th of these canons called *apostolical*, " Episcopus aut " presbyter, aut diaconus, usuras exigens a debitoribus, " vel desistat, vel ordine mulctator." Item, Ministers given to unlawful trades and occupations, for filthy gain, such as, keeping of inns, bearing of wordly offices in noblemen and gentlemen's houses, merchandise, and such like, buying of victual, and keeping it to the dearth, and all such wordly occupations, as may distract them from their charge: All such are to be admonished, and if they continue therein, are to be deposed. By the 6th of these apostolical canons, " Episcopus, aut presbyter, aut diaco- " nus seculares curas non adsumat, alioqui deponatur." And by the 20th canon, " Clericus se fidejussionibus im- " plicans gradu suo dejiciatur." Calderwood, in his history, p. 458. acquaints us, that by acts of Assembly ministers are prohibited to join with their ministry, the office of a notary, husbandry, or hostilary, &c under the pain of deposition. In the M. S acts of Assembly 72, the regent desiring some learned ministers to be planted senators of the college of justice, the Assembly finds that none were able to bear both the said charges. The Assembly 1643, (in the index of their unprinted acts you may find some of it), considering that Mr William Bennet minister at Ancrum, did vote in the election of a commissioner to the convention of estates from the shire of Roxburgh, as one of the barons and freeholders there, they do recommend it to him to abstain from civil courts and meetings. As also, they understanding, that Mr Andrew Murray minister at Ebde, had come to succeed to the Lord Balvaird, they appoint him to exercise his calling of the ministry, and to reject such temporal honours during his own life, as being incompatible with that calling, and very good reason that the lesser and least useful should cede to the greater and better work. Item, by the forecited Assembly, act 1596, ratified by the
Assembly

Assembly 1638, all their members are discharged from attending the court, and affairs thereof, without the advice, and allowance of their presbytery: And that they intent no civil action without the said advice, except in small matters. Calderwood, in his history of Assembly 1600, saith to this purpose, " Qui ambulat in sole coloratur, qui tan-
" git picem inquinatur, qui frequentat aulam et curiam
" profanatur; forum pontificis Petrum ad abnegationem
" Christi adegit quæ est corporum constitutio, ea est et mo-
" rum, circumposito aere calido calescimus, et rursus fri-
" gido frigescimus; cum sanctis sanctus eris, cum perver-
" sis perverteris." Item, Ministers are to use godly exercises in their families, such as, teaching of their wives, children and servants, in ordering prayers, reading of the scriptures, and such like other points of godly conversation; whoever be found negligent therein, after due admonition, are to be deposed. Item, Ministers that are not spiritual, and profitable in their ordinary converse, are, upon due trial, to be sharply rebuked. Item, No minister is to countenance or assist a public offender challenged by his own minister for his public offence, or to bear with him, as if his own minister were too severe upon him, under pain of admonition and rebuke.

Remedies against vocational and personal faults of ministers.

§ 8. The General Assembly, by their act 13th June 1646, provide the following remedies against the evils both in the calling and lives of ministers, and appoints them to be observed: *Imprimis*, None are to be taken in to be a helper, or second minister, but such as are able for the same charge. Item, That presbyteries be faithful in the trial of intrants, and in loving admonitions one of another secretly, and that absents from synods and presbyteries be censured. Item, The moderators of presbyteries are to see that godly conference be entertained at presbyterial meetings, even in the time of their refreshments. Item, Ministers are to have more frequent converse among themselves, for strengthening one another's hands, and begetting and cherishing of friendship, and removing of misconstructions. Item, Ministers are to cherish weak beginnings in the ways of God, and couragiously oppose all revilers and mockers of the godly. Item, Silence, or ambiguous speaking in the public cause, and not speaking against the corruptions of the time, are to be seasonably censured;

censured; and such as mock, upbraid, or threaten, stop, or disturb ministers for freedom in preaching, and the faithful discharge of their conscience, are to be processed; see Assembly 1648, sess. 26.

§ 9. A presbytery is not to proceed to the citation of a minister, or any way begin the process, until there be first some person, who, under his hand, gives in the complaint, with some account of its probability, and undertakes to make out the libel, at least under pain of being censured as a slanderer. This informer or accuser ought to be of good report; for it were of dangerous consequence to admit every body to accuse. By the 21st canon, concilii Chalced. "Clericos vellaicos, Episcopos, aut laicos ac-"cusantes, non indiscriminatim, nec citra inquisitionem, "admittere ad accusationem, nisi eorum existimatio primo "examinata fuerit." Yet presbyteries may proceed against ministers, when a "fama clamosa" of the scandal is so great, that for their own vindication, they find themselves obliged to begin the process without any particular accuser, after they have inquired into the rise, occasion, broachers, and grounds of the said common fame. *What warrants a presbytery to enter in process against a minister: and how accusers are to be admitted.*

§ 10. After the presbytery has considered the libel raised against the minister, then they order him to be cited, to get a full copy, with a list of the witnesses names to be led for proving thereof, and a formal citation is to be made in writ, either personally or at his dwelling-house, bearing a competent time allowed to give in answers unto the libel, and his just defences and objections against witnesses, at least ten free days before the day of compearance; and the citation should bear the date when given, and the names of the witnesses to the giving thereof, and the execution bearing its date, with the names and designations of the witnesses, should be made in writ, and signed by the officer and witnesses: which being accordingly returned, he is to be called. As to the form and manner of citations, it is not to be understood as a privilege restricted to ministers only, but it is to be extended to all who are convened before church judicatures, with little difference, as has been observed on title Citations. *The manner of citing ministers*

§ 11. If the minister compear, the libel is to be read unto him, and his answers thereunto are to be read, in order to the discussing of the relevancy. If the libel be found *How to behave towards a minister compearing and confessing* found relevant, then the presbytery is to endeavour to bring him to a confession: If the matter confessed be of a scandalous nature, such as uncleanness, or the like, the presbytery, whatever be the nature of his penitence, are *instanter* to depose him *ab officio*, and to appoint him in due time to appear before the congregation where the scandal was given, and in his own parish, for removing the offence, by the public profession of his repentance.

How towards one absenting or contumacious.

§ 12. If a minister absent himself by leaving the place, and be contumacious, without making any relevant excuse, after a new public citation, and intimation made at his own church, when the congregation is met, he is to be holden as confessed and to be deposed and censured *instanter* with the lesser excommunication; but if after some time he do not subject himself to the censures of the church, he may be proceeded against till he be censured with the greater excommunication.

How towards him who compears, and denies, but against whom the libel is proven.

§ 13. If a minister accused do appear, and deny the fact, after the relevancy is found, the accused is to be heard object against the witnesses, and allowed to be present at the examination, and modestly to cross-interrogate. If after consideration of the reputation, hability, and depositions of the witnesses, the judicature shall find the scandal sufficiently proven, they are to proceed to censure, as in the case of confession.

How to carry towards a minister charged with errors.

§ 14. If the errors be not gross, and striking at the vitals of religion, or if they be not pertinaciously stuck unto, or industriously spread, with a visible design to corrupt, or that the errors are not spreading among the people, then lenitives, admonitions, instructions, and frequent conferences are to be tried in order to reclaim. And unless the thing be doing much hurt, so as it admits of no delay, the synod or General Assembly are to be advised with, and the reference intimated to the minister concerned, which is agreeable to the 12th act of Assembly 1694. And by that act all the judicatures of the church are forbidden to censure any minister whatsoever for not qualifying themselves in the terms of the act of parliament, by taking the oaths to the civil government. It is true, that appointment continues only till the next Assembly; but the same reason for making that temporary, may make it a perpetual act.

§ 15. If

§ 15 If the libel against a minister be for a multitude of *How to carry* smaller things laid together, the presbytery in proceeding *towards a* therein are to make a presbyterial visitation of that minister's *minister charged with a* parish. And if they find these things, laid to his charge, *multitude of* to have been committed since the last visitation, or find a *smaller things* satisfying reason wherefore they were not then tabled, they *laid together.* are to inquire how far the minister hath been guilty of giving offence, after he was acquainted that offence had been taken at these things he is charged with: it should be likewise inquired, if any of the complainers did first in a private way inform any of the neighbouring ministers of these things now publicly complained of? and the presbytery is to judge accordingly. If they find upon trial, the complaint to resolve on the minister's having committed such acts of infirmity or passion; as, considering all the circumstances, may be either amended, and the people satisfied, and that the offence was taken by the minister's own people, only or mainly, then the presbytery is to take all prudent ways to satisfy and reclaim both minister and people.

§ 16. By the 4th act, sess. 2. par. 1. Car. II. ministers are to be suspended that absent from the diocesan synod for *Absence from* the first fault, and that such a censure may be inflicted *synods censured by suspen-* where no excuse is offered, is not to be doubted. Yet our *sion, and why* church judicatures are rather inclinable to threaten, and be *so called.* in readiness to revenge every disobedience, than actually to inflict the censures they may upon every just provocation. Ministers are said to be suspended, because their restoring or deposing is yet doubtful, and doth much depend upon their future behaviour, or upon further discoveries and clearer probation

§ 17. By the General Assembly April 1682, as related *Grounds of* in Calderwood's history, the causes of deposition were judg-*deposition,* ed to be these, viz Heresy, Popery, blasphemy, per-*what.* jury, adultery, incest, fornication, slaughter, theft, common oppression, common drunkenness, usury against the laws of the realm, non-residence, absence from his kirk, and neglect of his office for forty days together in a year, without a lawful impediment allowed by the next General Assembly; plurality of benefices, (but the act of parliament says, plurality of benefices having cure), dilapidation thereof, and simony. Which crimes are likewise declared causes of deprivation, by cap. 132. of parl. 1584. It is to be observed, that the church doth not, except in some most horrid crimes, depose and excommunicate both at once. By the 25th of the canons, called Apostolical, "Episcopus, aut presbyter aut diaconus in scortatione, vel perjurio, vel furto deprehensus, ordine suo summoveatur; ab ecclesia tamen non excludatur," ministers are not to employ deposed ministers in any exercise of the pastoral calling, or entertain ministerial communion with them, under pain of deposition. By the 11th of these forecited canons, "Si quis clericus cum deposito, ut cum clerico, simul oraverit deponatur et ipse," if any deposed minister shall apply to the civil magistrate for redress against that sentence in so doing he acknowledgeth in the civil magistrate a privative power, to hinder the church from exercising that jurisdiction she hath received from Christ, and therefore he puts himself out of all hopes of almost ever being restored. By the 12th canon concil. Antiocheni, "Si quis a proprio episcopo depositus, presbyter vel diaconus, vel episcopus a synodo, ausus fuit, imperatoris auribus molestiam exhiberi, cum oporteat ad majorem synodum converti, et jus quod se habere putat ad plures episcopos referre, eorumque examinationem et judicium suscipere: qui itaque his contemptis imperatori molestus fuerit is nulla venia dignus, neque sui defendendi locum habeat, nec restitutionis futuræ spem expectet."

§ 18. By deprivation, a minister is removed only from his particular charge, and loseth the benefice, as was done against the ministers of Linlithgow and Bathgate, by the synod of Lothian in May 1660; but instances of this kind are rare. By deposition, a minister is deposed *simpliciter* from both office and benefice. This church doth not make that distinction, which the canonists do, betwixt deposition and degradation: for they say, that deposition is pronounced verbally, by his superiors removing him from his office, but in degradation, the ensigns and vestments of the several degrees of orders he had been invested with, are pulled off him, and thereafter his person is delivered to the civil magistrate, to be punished for his crimes.

§ 19. The custom of this church is, that when they enter upon a process of deposition, the name of God is solemnly called upon for light and direction. Solemn prayer er is likewife made before they enter upon the grounds for reponing of depofed minifters. The act of depofition runs in this or the like form: At   the which day, anent the fummons and complaint purfued before the prefbytery of   at the inftance of   againft minifter at   mentioning, &c. and anent the citation, &c. to have compeared, &c to have anfwered to the faid complaint given in againft him, and the famen being proven, to have heard a fentence of depofition, or fuch other cenfure given and pronounced againft him, by authority of the faid presbytery, as he fhould be found to deferve, conform to the acts and practice of this church, obferved in the like cafes, or elfe to have alledged a reafonable caufe in the contrary; with certification, if he failed, the faid prefbytery would proceed, and do therein as they fhould find juft. Which fummons being oft and divers times called, &c. puefuers prefent and compearing, the faid   defender abfent; the faid prefbytery having confidered the articles of the faid fummons and complaint; and being well and ripely advifed therewith, they found the fame relevant by the acts and practice of this church to infer depofition; as alfo, they found the articles of the faid complaint fufficiently proven, by the depofitions of feveral famous witneffes, lawfully fummoned, folemnly fworn, purged and interrogate thereupon. That, &c. (here narrate the particular things found proven) as the depofitions of the faid witneffes extant in procefs, bear; and, therefore the faid presbytery did by their vote, depofe the faid   likeas they hereby do, in the name of the Lord Jefus Chrift, the alone King and Head of his church, and by virtue of the power and authority committed by him to them, actually depofe the faid   from the office of the holy miniftry, prohibiting and difcharging him to exercife the fame, or any part thereof, in all time coming, under the pain of the higheft cenfures of the church. Extracted, &c. The fentence of fufpenfion runs in this form: They do fufpend the faid   from the exercife of his miniftry till a definite time, prohibiting him to exercife the fame during the faid fpace, till he be orderly reponed thereto, under the pain of depofition. The Affembly Auguft 5th, 1648, confidering, that according to the antient order and practice of this kirk, the cenfures of fufpenfion and depofition are both

And the form of acts of depofition and fufpenfion.

No depofed or fufpended minifter is to intromit with the benefice.

"ab

"ab officio et beneficio," therefore they discharge deposed or suspended ministers to exercise any part of the ministerial calling, or intromit with the stipend, under pain of excommunication to the deposed minister; and of deposition to the suspended. See also act of Assembly Dec. 18. 1638, sess. 14.

For what probationers are to be censured.

§ 20. By the 2d article of the 10th act of Assembly 1694, if probationers malverse in doctrine or conversation, they shall be accountable to and censurable by presbyteries; and if they refuse subjection, or prove contumacious to such censures, whether of suspending or recalling their licence, intimation thereof shall be made to the church judicatures where they reside or haunt, that so none may employ them to preach.

When the Assembly only can repone and what judicature can repone.

§ 21 By the act of Assembly 2d August 1641, ministers deposed for the public cause of reformation, and transgressing the order of this kirk, shall not be suddenly received again to the ministry, till they first evidence their repentance both before their presbytery and synod, and thereafter the same be reported to the General Assembly. The Assembly 12th August 1642, considering that sentences of superior judicatures should stand effectual, till they be taken away by themselves, therefore synods are discharged to repone ministers deposed by Assemblies, and presbyteries from reponing any minister deposed by either.

He cannot be restored to his former parish, nor yet to that of another deposed for the same fault.

By act of Assembly 13th February 1645, it is ordained, that no minister deposed shall be restored again unto that place where formerly he served, as being a thing prejudicial to the congregation, and derogatory to the weight of that sentence of deposition, and it being almost impossible that ever he can prove useful in that parish again. See the form of process on this head. By act of Assembly August 1.. 1648, it is enacted, that no minister deposed for being an enemy to the government of this church, when it shall fall out, that he be put in a capacity of readmission to the ministry, shall enter into the congregation of any other minister, who also hath been deposed for that same fault.

Ministers deposed for horrid crimes not to be reponed.

By the 53d article of the French church discipline, ministers who have been deposed for crimes which deserve signal punishment, or that bear marks of infamy, cannot be restored to their office, what acknowledgement soever they make. And as for other less faults,

after

after due acknowledgement made, they may be restored by the national synod, to serve in another church, and not otherwise, which agrees with these acts of our Assemblies just now cited.

§ 22. By the 13th act of Assembly 1690, all sentences past against any minister, hinc inde, by any church judicature, upon the account of the late differences among Presbyterians from the year 1650, till the reintroduction of Prelacy, are declared to be of themselves void and null, to all effects and intents. *How a great many ministers were reponed against sentences past during the late divisions.*

TITLE V.

Of Sentences and their Reviews, of Declinatures, References and appeals.

§ 1. JUdicial sentences are either interlocutors, that is, a sentence intermediate between the dependence and termination of processes; or they are definitive, that is, they terminate processes. And these are either absolvitures, whereby the defender is freed and assoilzied from the conclusion of the libel or process, or they are condemnatory, whereby the conclusion of the process is found just and true against the defender; or they are mixed, whereby the defender is absolved from some part of the conclusion of the process, and is condemned in other parts thereof. *Several kinds of sentences.*

§ 2. The moderator of no judicature ought to give forth their sentence, till the same be first put in writing, and then he is to order the clerk to read it in presence of all parties. Thus no judicature can be in the least wronged by any clerk's unfaithfulness or omission. *Sentences must be written before they be pronounced.*

§ 3. When it is doubtful what sentence should be past, it is the safest side, and the least error, either to drop the process for the time, or else to absolve the defender, conform to that maxim in law, " Satius est impunitum relin- " qui facinus nocentis, quam innocentem damnare, l. 5. " d de pæn," for in absolving the guilty there is but an omission, whereas in condemning the innocent there is committing of iniquity and injustice. *In doubtful cases it is safest to absolve.*

§ 4. Before a judicature can think to pass a sentence, parties being first fully heard, must close what they have to say, and after they have concluded their defences and answers, then the judicature begins to advise what sentence *Conclusion of the causes.*

to pronounce; and seeing the pursuer speaks first by his libel, the defender is allowed to be the last speaker.

Some sins not to be tried publicly.

§ 5. When faults are singular and monstrous, it is the laudable practice of judges, to order the punishment and trial of such crimes in private; I am sure, to acquaint the people of some unnatural sins, whereof they had never heard, were but a scandalous and pernicious instruction. See the 51st art. 1. cap and 10th and 11th art. of the 5th cap. of the French church discipline.

Nullity of sentences.

§ 6. Sentences are in themselves null, when pronounced against the general acts of the church, or by an incompetent judge, such as the sentences of kirk sessions against ministers, or even by presbyteries and synods, when the process is carried and admitted before their superior judicatures.

The nature, use, and end of reviews, and who can review.

§ 7. When the party neglects to use the ordinary remedy of appeal, he is allowed (where the sentence is palpably gravaminous) to pursue a review thereof before a superior judicature. They are like reductions, and ought to be so libelled, calling the parties and judge to produce what is craved to be reviewed. They are not much in use with us, and if they were, some self-will'd and litigious persons would take too much encouragement from it. Assemblies, from which their lies no appeal, may review or recal their own sentences, on some new or extraordinary discovery. But inferior-judicatures, from which parties may appeal, are not to determine but to refer the desired review or reduction to their superior judicature. If a party shall omit to propone a competent and proper defence, with a fraudulent and vexatious intention to protract and resume debates; in that case he ought not to be heard in his making thereof out of due time and order. But to hear emergent and new-discovered defences since the conclusion of the cause, is but just.

The magistrate is to interpose his authority for getting obedience to church censures.

§ 8. In the latter part of the 23d act parl. 1693, it is statute, that the Lords of their Majesty's privy council, and all other magistrates, judges, and officers of justice, give all due assistance, for making the sentences and censures of the church, and judicatures thereof to be obeyed, or otherwise effectual as accords.

§ 9. Declinatures are " ante latam sententiam definitivam;" but appeals are made from, and after that sentence

These·

These declinatures are of two sorts, the first unwarrantable, when a judicature is declined as having no authority, as if a minister should decline his own presbytery, or the other superior judicatures of the church to be his lawful judges, which is a higher degree of contumacy than that which follows upon non-compearance, and may be warrantably censured with deposition by the 5th act of parliament 1690. There is a warrantable declinature, when a judicature is declined as having committed injustice in some interlocutory sentence. There is likewise a warrantable declinature, which may be made against particular members, who are related to the party by consanguinity or affinity, nearer than a cousin german, or who have behaved themselves as parties in the cause. It is just now said, that appeals are properly made from definitive sentences, but they are likewise made from interlocutory sentences, when they contain such damage to the party, whereof no reparation can be expected, from the definitive sentence that is to ensue. Thus, Paul's appeal was just, Acts xxv. 9. for although his accusers could not prove their libel against him, yet his judge did not absolve him, but partially and unjustly remitted him to the judgement of his false and malicious accusers.

Difference between references and appeals; when warrantably made, and when not.

§ 10. *Appellatio* is by lawyers said to be "Iniquitatis " sententiæ querela, a minore judice ad superiorem pro- " vocans;" the design of appeals is to redress wrongs done by the iniquity, unskilfulness, or precipitancy of judges.

What an appeal is; its end.

§ 11. As to the effect of appeals, "non sortiuntur ef- " fectum suspensivum sed devolutivum tantum," and consequently resolve only in the nature of protests for remeid of law against a sentence pronounced by the Lords of session, and not in the nature of suspensions. By the last article, cap 5. act. 11. assem. 1707, an appeal being made by parties, should sist the execution of the sentence appealed from, only while the appeal is duely and diligently prosecute, and may thereby be determined, otherwise not; unless the judicature appealed to, receive the appeal and take the affair before them: and in that case the judicature appealed from is to sist till the appeal be discussed.

The effect of an appeal, and how it sists execution.

§ 12. By the act of Assembly August 30. 1639, appellations are discharged to be made by leaping over either presbytery or synod, except it be after the synod is past,

The manner of making appeals, and to whom made.

and immediately before or in the time of the sitting of the General Assembly. The Assembly 1648, sess. 30. orders thus, that where the appeal after sentence is not ready to be given in, the party shall protest for liberty to appeal, and accordingly, within ten days, give in his written appeal to the judicature or moderator thereof, otherwise it falls; which order and method is further cleared by the 8th act of Assembly 1694, whereby it is appointed, that verbal appellants give in their subscribed appeals, within ten days to the clerk of the judicature appealed from, (notwithstanding the judicature may be up before the time) and also intimate the same to the moderator, by leaving with him an authentic copy thereof, with the reasons of the same, to be registered by the clerk, and summons direct thereupon against parties defenders, and extracts thereof, with the citation foresaid, are to be produced by the appellants at the discussing thereof, declaring that any appeals or insistings thereupon, otherwise made, shall be rejected.

When an appeal is to judged deserted.

§ 12. When the judicature *ad quem* meets, the party appealed, and oftentimes the judge *a quo*, craves that the appellant may be called, and if he appear not, the appeal is holden as deserted; in which case *firmatur sententia*. If appellant fail, then to insist, it *ipso facto* falls, becomes void, and the sentence of the judicature appealed from is to be put in execution. See the Form of Process on this head enacted 1707. Unless the appellants send full instructions and documents for the necessity of their absence. See cap. 9 art. 9. French church discipline.

How parties are sisted by bills and references.

§ 13. By the act of Assembly August 3. 1643, it is appointed that all bills whatsoever of particular concernment, whereunto all parties having interest are not cited, should be rejected. As also, that they be first presented to the inferiour judicatures of the kirk, who may competently consider of them, and from them, be orderly *et gradatim* brought to the Assembly, and references are to be made by the inferior to the immediate superior judicatures in the same manner. Likewise upon a reference made and intimate, all parties present are thereby cited, *apud acta*, to the judicature referred unto: But if absent, the clerk must be ordered to direct summons against them, which if omitted, the reference cannot be received.

§ 15. When an appeal is brought from the kirk-seffion to the presbytery, they are to consider, whether the cause is of that nature, as it behoved at length to come to the presbytery, by the course of discipline, before the final determination thereof: as, if it be in a process of alledged adultery or such like; in which case, they may, to save themselves time, fall upon consideration of the affair without insisting upon the *bene* or *male appellatum*, even tho' it seem to be preposterously appealed. But if the cause be such, as the kirk-seffion are the competent and proper judges of, to its ultimate decision, and if there hath no cause been given by the seffion, through transgreffing the rules of an orderly process, or by the incompetency of the censure, the presbytery is not to sustain the appeal; and if they do not sustain it, but find the appellants to have been malicious, litigious, or precipitant, then they are to inflict some censure, such as reproof before the presbytery, or appoint them to acknowledge their precipitancy before their own seffion, and that besides remitting the process to them. If the appeal to be sustained, and yet upon proceeding in the cause, the presbytery find the appellant censurable, they are to order him to be censured accordingly: but if they find, that the kirk seffion hath unwarrantably proceeded, either to the contributing to the raising of a scandal, or inflicting a censure without a sufficient cause, they are then not only to absolve the appellant, but to take proper ways for vindicating his innocence: yet so as not to weaken the kirk-seffion's authority; for which end they may give that seffion suitable instructions and rules to walk by, or private admonition, or to call for a visitation of their seffion register. See that forecited Form of Process, Assembly 1707.

When the bene or male appellatum is to be discussed

When the appeal is not to be sustained.

When the appeal is to be sustained.

TITLE VI.

Of the Order of Proceeding to Excommunication.

§ 1. IF a guilty person continue in that condition mentioned tit. 1. of this book, or lie under the censure of the lesser excommunication for a considerable time, after intimation thereof hath been made, both in the congregation where it was inflicted, and also in that to which he belongeth, and yet be found frequently relapsing in these vices

When to proceed from the lesser to the higher excommunication, and grounds for both.

ces he was censured for, it may be construed such a degree of contumacy, and so aggravate the crime as to found a process for the censure of the higher excommunication, which is to be inflicted or not, as may most tend to the reclaiming of the guilty person, and edification of the church. Where there is no obdurate contumacy, the lesser excommunication needs only have place. Again, where no scandalous practice hath been proven, only there is a simple contumacy following by not appearing, in that case, the lesser excommunication is length enough. But if the scandal be of an heinous nature, and that it is spreading and infectious, as in heresies or schism in the church, in which cases, contumacy is to be proceeded against.

Every error or difference in judgment not sufficient ground for excommunication.

§ 2. Yet every error or difference in judgement about points wherein learned and godly men may differ, and which subverts not the faith, nor is destructive to godliness, or when persons, out of conscience, do not come up to the observation of all these rules, which are or shall be established by authority for regulating the outward worship of God, and government of his church, the censure of excommunication should not be inflicted for such causes. See Durham on scandal. The letter from the Assembly of divines at Westminster, with the answer of our General Assembly 1645.

How the presbytery proceeds with persons present or absent in order to this censure.

§ 3. The kirk-session having brought the process to the lesser excommunication, before they proceed further, they are by a reference to lay their whole proceeding in writ before the presbytery, who finding them to have orderly proceeded, and that the lesser excommunication is not sufficient, they are to cause cite the scandalous person. If he appear, and deny the scandal alledged and libelled, then they are to lead probation as in other cases. If he appear not, then the citation is to be renewed till he hath got three.

After three ordinary citations, three public admonitions.

§ 4. If he contemn these three citations, then he is to be admonished out of the pulpit, to appear and submit three several Sabbaths; and a presbytery-diet should intervene betwixt every one of these admonitions. By these admonitions intimation is to be made, that the presbytery will proceed to inquire into the guilt, although the delinquent be absent, and threatning him with the highest censure of the church, if he continue impenitent; and therefore the

minister

minister is gravely to admonish the party present or absent to repent and submit himself to the discipline of the church.

§ 5 If after all, the person continue impenitent or contumacious, the presbytery appoints the minister to pray for him publicly in the congregation, and he is to exhort them to join with him in prayer, that God would deal with the soul of the impenitent, and convince him of the evil of his ways. Which prayers of the church, are to be put up three several Sabbath days, a presbytery interveneing betwixt each prayer. *After three admonitions, follow three public prayers.*

§ 6. The scandalous person still continuing impenitent, and making no application or submission, the presbytery is then to appoint the minister to intimate their resolution to proceed upon such a Sabbath as they shall name for pronouncing that dreadful sentence, unless either the party, or some for him, signify some relevant ground to stop the procedure, that so, upon the congregation's tacite consent and acquiescence, the sentence may have its due weight and intended effect. *Edict for excommunication.*

§ 7 All these slow and several steps of the church's proceedings to this high censure, do shew their tenderness towards their lapsed brother, their earnestness to have him reclaimed, and also to create a greater regard and terror of that dreadful censure, both in the party and all the people. Let not those who deserve it, or upon whom it hath been orderly and justly inflicted, mock and say, *parturiunt montes*, &c. for whatsoever the church shall so bind on earth, our Lord hath said it shall be bound in heaven, Matth. xviii 18. and this censure is like a seal to all the threatnings of God in his word, which shall verily be execute against impenitent sinners. *The reason of this slow procedure.*

§ 8. The day being come, the minister is to preach a sermon suited to that solemn occasion, concerning the nature, use, and ends of church censures; Then, after the ordinary prayers and praises of the congregation are performed, the minister is to narrate all the steps of the process, shew the obstinate impenitency of the scandalous person, and that now there remained only that mean of cutting him off from the society of the faithful. Then he is to desire the congregation to join with him in prayer, that God would grant repentance to the obstinate person, would *The ministers behaviour before he pronounce the sentence.*

graciously

graciously bless his own ordinance, to be a mean for reclaiming him, and that others may fear.

The form of the sentence of excommunication.

§ 9. Then immediately after prayer that terrible sentence is to be pronounced, in these or the like words, speaking to him, in the second person, if present, and of him, in the third person, if absent. Whereas thou N. hast been by sufficient proof convicted of (here mention the sin) and after due admonition and prayer, remainest obstinate, without any evidence or sign of true repentance: Therefore, in the name of the Lord Jesus Christ, and before this congregation, I pronounce and declare thee N. excommunicated, shut out from the communion of the faithful, debars thee from their privileges, and delivers thee unto Satan for the destruction of thy flesh, that thy spirit may be saved in the day of the Lord Jesus.

What is meant by delivering to Satan.

§ 10. Why the apostle, 1 Cor. v. 5. expresses excommunication by delivering to Satan may be for this, among among other reasons, that Satan is called the god of this world, as world is taken in opposition to the church of God, so that delivering to him implies no more than that Matth. xviii. 17. if he neglect to hear the church, let him be to thee as an heathen man and publican, thereby letting us know how dreadful a thing it is to be shut out from the ordinary means of grace and salvation, and exposed to the temptations of our grand adversary the devil.

When pronouncing the sentence may be stopped.

§ 11. If after prayer, or before pronouncing of that sentence, the scandalous person make any public signification of his penitency, and of his desire to have the censure stop, the minister may, upon any apparent seriousness in him, delay pronouncing him excommunicated, upon his public engagement and promise to appear before the presbytery at their next meeting, of which the minister is to make report, and the presbytery is thereupon to deal with the scandalous person as they shall see cause.

The effects of this sentence.

§ 12. After the pronouncing of this sentence, the minister is to warn the people of the effects thereof; such as, that they hold that person to be cast out of the communion of the church, and therefore they are to shun all unnecessary converse with him; nevertheless excommunication dissolveth not the bonds of civil or natural relations. By the act of Assembly 1596, revived Assembly 1638, art. 16. sess. 23. such are appointed to be excommunicated as
will

will not forbear the company of excommunicated perſons. By the 10th of theſe canons called *apoſtolical*, " Si quis " etiam domi cum excommunicato ſimul oraverit, is pariter " excommunicetur." By Aſſembly 1643. ſeſſ. ult. and Aſſembly 1648, art. 13. ſeſſ. 38. if a miniſter haunt the company of excommunicated perſons, he ſhall be ſuſpended for the firſt fault, and deprived for the ſecond, unleſs he have licence from the preſbytery, or elſe the excommunicated perſon be *in extremis*. No civil penalty, ſuch as eſcheat of moveables or caption, doth now follow upon this ſentence, ſo that the liberty and eſtates of church members are not endangered by it, nor do they depend upon church men. But upon a preſbytery's repreſentation to the privy council, againſt perſons that are contumacious, ſuch may not expect to enjoy their places, or be intruſted with any, as the laſt act made againſt profaneneſs in King William's reign doth inſinuate. By Jam. VI. parl. 11. cap. 27. excommunicate perſons are to be charged by the miniſter to depart from the church in time of miniſtration of ſacraments and prayer, and not to diſobey, under the penalties therein mentioned.

§ 13. The miniſter is to conclude this cenſure with prayer to this purpoſe, that God, who hath appointed this terrible ſentence for removing of offences, and reducing of obſtinate ſinners, would ratify in heaven, what, in his name, and by his warrant hath now been done on earth, and that the ſhuting him out of the church may fill him with fear and ſhame, break his obſtinate heart, and be a mean to deſtroy the fleſh, and recover from the power of the devil, that his ſpirit may yet be ſaved, and alſo that others may be ſtricken with fear, and not dare to ſin ſo preſumptuouſly, or contemn the authority and voice of his church. See Knox's forms prefixed to the old pſalms. Then the congregation is to be diſmiſſed with the bleſſing, after ſinging the laſt part of the 101ſt Pſalm. *Concluſion by prayer, praiſe, and pronouncing the bleſſing.*

§ 14. The 4th art. cap. 30. of our Confeſſion of Faith ſaith, that for the better attaining the ends of church cenſures, the officers of the church are to proceed by admonition and ſuſpenſion from the ſacrament of the Lord's Supper for a time, and by excommunication from the church. The difference then betwixt theſe two cenſures is, ſuſpenſion from the Lord's Supper, which imports, that *The difference betwixt the greater and leſſer excommunication.*

the person so censured is in imminent danger of being excommunicated and cut off from the church; but before that heavy and finishing stroke be inflicted, there are further means to be used, such as prayers and admonitions, in order to his reclaiming, 2 Thess. iii. 6. 14. 15. "Now we command you brethren, in the name of our Lord Jesus Christ, that ye withdraw yourselves from every brother that walketh disorderly: and if any man obey not our word by this epistle, note that man, and have no company with him, that he may be ashamed, yet count him not as an enemy, but admonish him as a brother." Whereas, when a person is cut off by that high censure, he is to be looked on as a heathen man, Matth. xviii. 17. Upon which the church ceaseth to be his reprover, they giving him over for dead or desperate, and will administer no more of the medicine of church discipline unto him, 1 Cor. xii. 13. "For what hath the church to do to judge them that are without? do not they judge them that are within? but them that are without, God judgeth."

Summar excommunication, what, and when to be inflicted.

§ 1... Persons guilty of relapse in adultery, or who are often guilty of other gross scandals, are to be more summarily excommunicate than in ordinary processes, both for the heinousness of the sin, and for terror to others. See sess. 38. assem. 1648. There is no excommunication absolutely summary, that is, without previous citations, admonitions and prayers, but it is comparatively summary, because they are not first suspended, as in ordinary church procedures against scandalons persons. I am sure, where there is no obdurate contumacy, but on the contrary, edifying signs of true repentance, to such *sinus ecclesiæ semper patet:* for the repentance of the greatest sinners is more edifying and grateful than their excommunication, and if the holy One of Israel, who is absolute and sovereign in bestowing of his mercy and grace to whom and when he will, shall think fit, by giving unfeigned repentance to that nottour atrocious sinner, to signify his forgiving of him, and receiving him into his favour; how dare any church upon earth presume to deliver such a person unto Satan.

§ 10. In case the excommunicate person continue obstinate, after the sentence of the presbytery is intimated in all

all the kirks within their bounds, they are to give an account thereof to the synod, who are to appoint intimation thereof to be made in all the kirks of their bounds; and if need be, the synod is to bring the case to the Assembly, that the sentence may be intimate through all the churches of the kingdom, Assem. 1704. sess. 10. Assem. 1648, August 10. Only let this be remembred, that if he come to be absolved, justice be done him, in causing the absolution be intimate, where-ever the excommunication had been, so the plaister will be proportioned to the sore *Intimation of the sentence of excommunication and absolution.*

§ 17. There is in the canon law a church censure which they call *interdictum*, by which they excommunicate whole kingdoms and provinces for the fault of some, whereby they make the innocent suffer with the guilty, through the forbidding the public exercise of God's worship in that kingdom, place, or province. They have a particular *interdictum* by which they excommunicate a number of persons specially designed. By the first of these the inhabitants are only affected and reached with its censure during their abode or residence in the place interdicted. But the particular *interdict* doth reach and follow the particular persons thereby censured, where-ever they sojourn. *Interdictum local and particular.*

§ 18. Calderwood, in his history p. 205. tells us, that anathematization is a censure of an higher degree than excommunication, but the reformed churches generally esteem excommunication to be "severissima disciplina. & ultimum fulmen ecclesiæ," in sect. 16. art. 1 of the directory for church government, as it was printed anno 1647, to be examined by the Assembly, it is said, excommunication is a shutting out of a person from the communion of the church, and it is the greatest and last censure. And, pray, what can a church do more? or, what have they to do more with a person shut out of their communion? The anathematization among the Canonists hath no other effects, but is the same upon the matter with their greater excommunication; only, when the same is inflicted with a number of more solemnities and formatities, because of that parade, it is then called *anathematization*. And we find by Knox's forms, that he useth the words *excommunicated* and *accursed*, as synonymous or equipollent: see the Form of Process both on this and the subsequent title, Assem. 1707. *Anathematization, excommunication, and accursing are synonymous.*

TITLE

TITLE VII.

Of the Order of proceeding to Absolution.

The old and present method of proceeding to absolution.

§ 1. BY the manuscript acts of Assembly at Edinburgh, March 1569, persons excommunicated for their offences, in order to their absolution, shall stand bareheaded at the kirk-door till prayers and singing be ended, and then enter the kirk, and sit at the public place of repentance bare-headed all the time of the sermon, and again depart before the last prayer, which is agreeable to Knox's forms, concluded anno 1567, and ordered to be printed by Assembly 1571, and is not disagreeable to the primitive practice of the church. But now if, after excommunication, the signs of repentance appear in the person excommunicated, such as godly sorrow for sin, as having thereby incurred God's heavy displeasure, occasioned grief to his brethren, and justly provoked them to cast him out of their communion, together with a full purpose of heart to turn from his sin unto God, with a humble desire of recovering peace with God and his people; all which the presbytery being satisfied with, they give warrant for his absolution: but in order thereto, he is to be brought before the congregation, and there also make free confession and express sorrow for his sin, call upon God for mercy in Christ, seek to be restored to the communion of the church; and he must promise, through the Lord's strength, new obedience, and more holy and circumspect walking. Which appearance before the congregation, shall be as often as church judicatures shall find may be for edification and trial of the professing penitent's sincerity.

Absolution in extremis.

§ 2. A minister may warrantably, without licence from the presbytery, haunt the company of excommunicate persons *in extremis*, as is said, tit. præc. And if he shall then find in the dying person true signs of repentance, what is there to forbid his administrating the comfortable sentence of absolution to him, seeing it is due to the signs of his repenance, and his dying condition cannot admit of longer delay. But that ministers might have better warrant, and the tears of dying penitents be more easily removed, I wish there were some church act expressly authorising thorizing ministers to absolve persons in such circumstances.

§ 3. In the preceding title, there is an edict of excommunication mentioned, so, in like manner, and on the same ground, there should be published an edict of absolution, at least a Sabbath before the same, that so the penitent may be restored to the apparent and tacit satisfaction of that congregation who had so consented to his seclusion. *Edict of absolution.*

§ 4. The day being come, the minister is to preach a sermon suited to that occasion: Then, after the ordinary prayers and praises of the congregation are ended, he is to call upon the professed penitent, and make him declare, promise, and call upon God as above: thereafter he is to desire the congregation to join with him in prayer to this purpose, that the Lord Jesus Christ, who hath pronounced, that whosoever by his ministers is bound on earth shall be bound in heaven, and also that whosoever is loosed by the same, shall be loosed and absolved with him in heaven, would mercifully accept his creature this professing penitent N. whom Satan of a long time hath held in bondage, so that he not only drew him to iniquity, but also so hardened his heart, that he despised all admonitions; for the which his sin and contempt, they were compelled to excommunicate him from the society of the faithful. But now seeing the Holy Spirit hath so far prevailed, that he professeth repentance for his sin, that it may please God, by his Spirit and grace, to make him a sincere and unfeigned penitent: and for the obedience of the Lord Jesus Christ unto death, so to accept of this poor returning sinner, that his former disobedience be never laid to his charge, and that he may increase in all godliness, so that Satan in the end may be troden under foot by the power of our Lord Jesus, and God may be glorified, the church edified, and the penitent saved in the day of the Lord. *The minister's behaviour and prayer before absolution.*

§ 5. After prayer, the sentence of absolution is to be pronounced in these or the like words. Whereas thou N. hast been shut out, for thy sin, from the congregation of the faithful, and hast now manifested thy repentance, wherein the church resteth satisfied; in the name of the Lord Jesus Christ, before this congregation, I pronounce and declare thee absolved from the sentence of excommunication *Sentence of absolution & exhortation to the absolved.*

nication formerly denounced against thee, and do receive thee into the communion of the church, and the free use of all the ordinances of Christ, that thou mayest be partaker of all his benefits to thy eternal salvation. After this is pronounced, the minister speaketh to him as a brother, exhorting him to watch and pray, or comforting him, if there be need, the elders embrace him, and the whole congregation holdeth communion with him as one of their own.

How the excommunicated are prayed for before absolution.

§ 6. When the presbytery hath given warrant for absolving the excommunicate person, he is thereupon materially absolved, and therefore may be admitted to church worship, before he be actually and formally pronounced and declared such. The church may pray for excommunicate persons, unless they had certain knowledge, I mean very well grounded, that any of them had committed the unpardonable sin, and that unto death, 1 John v. 16. Matth. xii, 31. 32. and when we do pray for these excommunicated whom we hope not to be so guilty, yet we do not pray for them as Christians, or of our communion, but as if they were Heathens, for their conversation and repentance.

Conclusion of the absolution

§ 7. The minister is to conclude the absolution with prayer, thanking God, who delighteth not in the death of a sinner, but rather that he should repent and live, and magnifying the mercy of God through Jesus Christ, in pardoning and receiving into his favour the most grievous offenders, when ever by his grace they unfeignedly repent and forsake their sins: Thereafter the congregation is dismissed with a blessing, after singing a part of some penitential Psalm.

THE FORM of PROCESS
IN THE
JUDICATURES of the CHURCH of *Scotland*,
With Relation to
SCANDALS and CENSURES.

[Ratified and approved by act of Assembly 18th April 1707, sess. 11.]

CHAP. I.

Concerning Church Government, Discipline, Scandals, and Censures in general.

OUR Lord Jesus Christ hath instituted a government, and governors ecclesiastical in his house, with power to meet for the order and government thereof; and to that purpose, the apostles did immediately receive the keys from the hands of their Lord and Master Jesus Christ, and did use and exercise the same upon all occasions, and Christ hath from time to time furnished some in his church with gifts for government, and with commission to exercise it when called thereunto, and has promised his presence to be with them to the end of the world.

It is aggreable to, and founded on the word of God, that some others, besides these who labour in the word and doctrine, be church governors, to join with the ministers of the word in the government of the church, and exercise of discipline, and oversight of the manners of the people; which officers are called ruling elders: As also, that the church be governed by several sorts of judicatures, and one in subordination to the other, such as kirk-sessions, presbyteries, provincial synods, and general assemblies.

Church discipline and censures, for judging and removing of offences are of great use and necessity in the church, that the name of God, by reason of ungodly and wicked persons living in the church, be not blasphemed

blasphemed, nor his wrath provoked against his people, that the godly be not leavened with, but preserved from the contagion, and stricken with fear, and that sinners who are to be censured may be ashamed, to the destruction of the flesh, and saving of the spirit in the day of the Lord Jesus.

Nothing ought to be admitted by any church judicature as the ground of a process for censure, but what hath been declared censurable by the word of God, or some act of universal custom of this national church agreeable thereto; and the several judicatures of this church ought to take timous notice of all scandals: But it is judged, that if a scandal shall happen not to be noticed in order to censure for the space of five years, it should not be again revived, so as to enter in a process thereanent, unless it be of an heinous nature, or become again flagrant, but the consciences of such persons ought to be seriously dealt with in private to bring them to a sense of their sin and duty

These assemblies or church judicatures before-mentioned have power to convene and call before them any persons within their own bounds, whom the ecclesiastic business, which is before them doth concern, either as party, witness, or otherwise, and to examine them according to the nature of the affair, and to hear and determine in such cases as shall orderly come before them, and accordingly dispense church censures.

If a person be charged with a scandal, who lives within the bounds of another parish, the kirk session of the parish where that person resides should be desired to cause cite that person to answer before the session in whose bounds the scandal happened, and the same course is to be followed in such cases by the other judicature of the church, seeing, for order's sake, they should not presume to exercise their authority without their own bounds.

The minister of the word being an office above that of the ruling elder, cannot be liable to the censure of the kirk-session, but to the superior judicatures of the church.

CHAP. II.

Concerning the entering of Processes, Citation of Parties and Witnesses, and taking Depositions, and anent Fugitives from Discipline.

MEMBERS of kirk-sessions are wisely to consider the information they get of scandals, and consult with their minister thereanent, even before the same be communicate to others, that thereby the spreading of the scandal may be prevented, and it may be removed by private admonition, according to our Lord and Saviour's rule, Matth. xviii. 15. which, if amendment follow, is the far better way of gaining and recovering a lapsed brother, whereas the needless spreading of a scandal does sometimes harden the guilty, grieve the godly, and is dishonourable to religion.

When any business is moved in a church judicature, whether by information, petition, or otherwise, they are in the first place to consider, whether the matter in its circumstantial case be proper for them to enter upon, and whether it be orderly brought in, and proper for them to cognosce and discuss it themselves or prepare it for superior judicatures, and should endeavour to shorten their work as much as with the edification of the church they can, especially as to the head of scandal, but still on all occasions the office bearers in the house of God are to shew all prudent zeal against sin

In proceeding in all causes, where there is any person or parties concerned, the judicature is to see, that before they proceed, these persons or parties be duly sisted before them by a legal and timous citation in write, bearing its cause, either at the instance of a party complaining, or at least by order of the judicature; and if they be residing within the parish, the same may be upon forty eight hours advertisement, and the execution of the summons bearing its cause, and made before two or three witnesses insert, is to be returned by the beadle or officer in writing, and the persons cited called at the door; and this is especially to be observed by presbyteries and other superior judicatures of the church.

Sometimes it may be fit that the party be privately spoken to, before any citation be given, or process begun, for their better gaining, in which case the minister is to exercise his own discretion, and take the concurrence of elders and others with him; but if the party cited as above, appear not, there ought to be a second and then a third citation given by the order of the sessions and presbyteries, either personally, or left at their dwelling house, before the judicature declare the person contumacious, unless the party be cited to appear before a superior judicature by reference or appeal, in which case there is not that need of so many citations, before the superior judicature, the party having actually appeared before the inferior judicature; and being cited *apud acta* to appear before the superior, and the same marked in the minutes, or having been declared contumacious before the cause was brought before the superior judicature.

All citations *apud acta*, are peremptory, and if instructed, infer contumacy, if not obeyed,

If

If the person do not appear on the third citation, or upon a citation *apud acta*, and no relevant excuse adduced and verified, though in that case he be censurable for contumacy, yet it may be fit the judicature proceed to take cognition, either by examining witnesses upon oath, or by other documents of the verity of the scandals delated against him, before they censure him for contumacy.

If the party appear, then the moderator is to inform the person of the occasion of his being called, and to give him, if desired, a short note in writing thereof, with the names of the witnesses that are to be made use of.

There seems to be no need of accusers or informers in ecclesiastic processes, where the same are not raised at the instance of a party complaining formally, but the party, if cited by order of the judicature, is to answer the judicature in what is laid to his charge: yet so, that if the party cited be found innocent and acquitted, those who informed the judicature, whether the party require it or not, ought to be noticed, for either their calumny or imprudence, as the judicature shall find cause.

If there be witnesses to be made use of in the process, a list of their names ought to be given to the defenders some time before, or at least at their compearance, and the witnesses ought to be timously cited to give evidence; and if they refuse, after three citations given, and executions returned, may be proceeded with as contumacious, or if judged needful, after the first or second citation, application may be made to the civil magistrate, that he may oblige them to appear.

Before the witnesses be judicially examined, the accused person is to be called, and the relevancy of the libel discussed, and if the defender compear, he may object against any of them, and if the objection be relevant, and made evident to the judicature, the witnesses are to be cast, but a person's being the delator or informer, doth not hinder him to be a witness, except in the case where he formerly complained for his own interest, or of pregnant presumptions of malice against the person accused.

Though there be no relevant objection, yet the witnesses are solemnly to be purged of malice, bribe or good deed done or to be done, and of partial council.

The witnesses are to be examined in presence of the accused party, if compearing, and he may desire the moderator to propose such questions or cross questions to the witnesses, as may tend to his exculpation, which if the judicature think pertinent are to be proposed; but no accused person is to interrupt the witnesses, or speak during the time of deposition.

If

If the party accufed do before probation offer grounds of exculpation to be proven by witneffes, the moderator and clerk, if required, are to give warrant to cite the witneffes upon the party's charges, the relevancy of the offered exculpation being firft confidered and fuftained by the judicature, and if the exculpation be fully proven as to the fubftance of the fcandal, all further proof of the libel and accufation muft there fift, and the defender is to be affoilzied, and if the libel be fpecial as to the time and place of a fact, and the accufed more pregnantly alledge and clearly prove *alibi*, but if the fubftance of the fcandal be once fuftained and deponed upon, there can be no place for exculpation, unlefs it be as to fome extenuating or alleviating circumftances not contrary to, but confiftent with the depofitions already taken.

If the witneffes cannot fubfcribe their names to their depofitions, the clerk is to mark that they declare they cannot write, and the moderator is to fubfcribe the fame, whether they can fubfcribe or not.

After the depofitions are ended, the parties being removed, the members of the judicature at the fame or fome after diet thereto appointed, are to advife the caufe, and there and then to reafon the affair calmly, fpeaking always to the moderator one after another, without interrupting one another, ufing no reflecting language to, or of one another, nor too long harangues or digreffions.

If any perfon or perfons under procefs for fcandal abfcond, they fhall, after being called before the judicature and not compearing, be cited firft from the pulpit of the parifh where the procefs depends and where they refide, and if they do not thereupon appear before the judicature before whom the procefs depends, they are by order of the prefbytery to be cited from the pulpits of all the kirks within their bounds to compear before the prefbytery; and if they do not then compear, they are to be declared fugitive from the church difcipline, and the fame intimate in all the kirks within the bounds of the prefbytery, defiring, that if any knows of the faid fugitives, they may acquaint the minifter or elder of the bounds thereof, and the prefbytery are to fift there until they get further notice of thefe perfons.

CHAP.

CHAP. III.

Concerning Swearers, Cursers, Profaners of the Lord's Day, Drunkards, and other Scandals of that nature.

IT may fall out that one single act of drunkenness or breach of the Lord's day, disobedience to parents, or of swearing, cursing, scolding, fighting, lying, cheating or stealing, may be clothed with such circumstances as may be a just ground of process immediately, and even bring the persons guilty under the censure of the lesser excommunication, and suspension from the benefit of the sealing ordinances, and require their appearance in presence of the congregation to be rebuked, before relaxation; but the weight of this is duely to be pondered, and church judicatures and members thereof are to consider, whether private admonition of the persons alledged and found guilty of the above scandals, if not cloathed with such circumstances of bringing them to the public, will tend most to edification, and proceed accordingly.

But ordinarily in all such offences, the guilty, for the first fault, would be spoken to in private by the minister or an elder, and admonished, and on promise from a sense of guilt to amend, they may sist there.

But if the person relapse, he should be called before the session, and if found guilty, may be there judicially rebuked, where the session on promise, from a due sense of sin, to amend, may again sist.

But if the person amend not after that, the session should orderly proceed, unless repentance appear, and due satisfaction be offered, till they inflict the censure of the lesser excommunication, and suspension from the benefit of the sealing ordinances, under which the censured are to lie till amendment and reformation.

With respect to scandals, the grossness whereof makes it necessary to bring the persons guilty oftener than once before the congregation, the rules prescribed by the fourth act of the general assembly, *anno* 170., are to be followed.

If the guilty persons continue in this condition, or lie under the censure of the lesser excommunication a considerable time, and yet be found frequently relapsing in these vices they are censured for, it may be construed such a degree of contumacy, and so aggravate the crime, as to found a process of the censure of the higher excommunication, which is to be inflicted, or not, as may tend most to the reclaiming of the guilty person, and edification of the church.

CHAP.

CHAP. IV.

Concerning the Sin of Fornication, Adultery, and scandalous Carriage tending thereto.

IN delations about the sin of uncleanness, it falls frequently out, that when the matter is put to the strictest trial, all that can be proven is but presumptions of guilt or scandalous behaviour, and not the act of uncleanness, the same being a work of darkness; and therefore this should oblige the kirk session to be very cautious how to admit the public entering a process without good warrant, where there is not a child in the case, unless the scandal be very flagrant.

Many of these actions which give occasion to the raising a scandal of uncleanness, are such as are not themselves alone publicly censurable, but to be past by with a private rebuke of admonition.

Yet some of these actions which come under the name of scandalous behaviour, may be so lascivious and obscene, and clothed with such circumstances, as may be as offensive as the act of uncleanness itself, and as censurable.

If a married woman whose husband hath been notourly absent for a considerable time, beyond the ordinary time that women use to go with child, be found with child, this also may give ground to a kirk session for a process against her; but in this case judicatures would be prudent in considering well all circumstances, and whether or not the person hath been always of entire fame before, as also how the public fame now runs.

When an unmarried woman is known to be with child, the same gives ground to a kirk session for a process against her, and after she is cited before the session and appeareth, she is to be interrogate who is the father of that child, and though in no other cases the divulging of a secret may be very imprudent, and indeed the raising of a scandal, yet in this case where there is a child, whereby there is an undeniable scandal, and the keeping secret of the father a ground of greater offence, and of suspecting many innocent persons, if she discover not the father, she is to be looked upon as contumacious.

Prudence may sometimes require that the person she nameth to be the father of the child, be informed thereof, and spoke to privately, and if he deny the same, he is seriously to be dealt with to confess, but if he still deny, then the session is to cause cite him to appear before them.

In this process when the delated father compeareth, he is to be interrogate

terrogate, and if he deny, he is to be confronted with the woman, and the presumptions, as particularly held forth as possible, and all along there should be private treating with him, in all meekness, charity, and seriousness, and if after all this he deny, though the woman's testimony can be no sufficient evidence against him, yet pregnant presumptions, such as suspicious frequenting her company, or being *solus cum sola in loco suspecto*, or in suspect postures, and such like which he cannot disprove to the satisfaction of the session, may so lay the guilt upon him, as shew him, that there appears no other way of removing the scandal, but his appearance to be publicly rebuked therefor; if he will not submit himself to be rebuked as above, it perhaps may be more for edification that a true narrative of the case be laid before the congregation, and intimation given, that there can be no further procedure in that matter, till God in his Providence give further light, to sist there at the time, than that an oath be pressed, and upon refusal proceed to the higher excommunication; but if the person accused do offer his oath of purgation, and crave the privilege thereof, the presbytery may (if they shall judge it for edification and removing of the scandal) allow the same; which may be to this purpose. " I A. B. now under process before presbytery of   for that sin of   alledged to be committed by me with C. D. and lying under that grievous slander, being repute as one guilty of that sin; I, for ending of the said process, and giving satisfaction to all good people, do declare before God and this   that I am innocent and free of the said sin of   or having carnal knowledge of the said C D. and hereby call the great God, the judge and avenger of all falsehood, to be witness and judge against me in this matter if I be guilty: and this I do, by taking his blessed name in my mouth, and swearing by him, who is the great judge, punisher, and avenger as said is, and that in the sincerity of my heart, according to the truth of the matter and mine own conscience, as I shall answer to God in the last and great day, when I shall stand before him to answer for all that I do in the flesh, and as I would partake of his glory in heaven after this life is at an end."

In taking this oath for purgation, all tenderness and caution is to be used, nor is the session to press any man thereto, but they are to deal with him and his conscience, as in the sight of God, and if he offer to give his oath, the judicature are to accept it or not as they shall see cause, and then to proceed to remove the scandal, with the advice of the presbytery, as may be most to edification; but this oath is not to be taken in any case but this, when the presumptions are so great, that they create such jealousy in that congregation and session, that nothing will remove the suspicion but the man's oath of purgation, and when

his

his oath will probably remove the scandal and suspicion, in all other cases this oath is in vain, and so should not be admitted, and never but by advice of the presbytery.

This oath for purgation is to be taken either before the kirk-session or presbytery, or the congregations, as the presbytery shall determine, and if the oath be taken before the session or presbytery, it is to be intimate to the congregation, that such a person hath taken such an oath, and the party may be obliged to be present in the congregation, and may be put publicly to own his purging himself by oath, and so be declared free from the alledged scandal.

After an end is made as above with the delated father, the woman is to be dealt with to give the true father, and if after all serious dealing and due diligence she give no other, she is to be censured according to the quality of the offence confessed by her, without naming the person delated by her, the judicature reserving place for further censure upon further discovery.

If the woman who hath brought forth the child, doth declare she knoweth not the father, alledging she was forced, as in the fields by a person unknown, or any the like reason; in these cases great prudence is to be used, the former behaviour of the woman exactly searched into, and she seriously dealt with to be ingenuous, and if she hath been of entire fame, she may be put to it to declare the truth as if she were upon oath, but not without the advice of the presbytery, and no formal oath should be taken, and if the woman confess she was not forced, but doth not know the man, whether married or unmarried, the same censure is to be inflicted upon her, as in the case of adultery.

If a person doth voluntarily confess uncleanness, and if there be no child, and the case be brought to the kirk-session, the session is to inquire what presumptions there are of the truth of the thing confessed, or what may have moved the person to make that confession, whether it floweth from disquietude of mind, or from sinistrous design, as when a man suing to a woman for marriage is denied, and for revenge, or for to obtain his desire, spreads the report that he hath been guilty with her, they are to be dealt with according as the presumptions upon search are found or not.

If it be found that there is no ground for the confession, and that it is false, the person confessing is to be censured as defaming himself, and likewise as a slanderer of the other party; and withall, application is to be made by the session to the civil magistrate, that he may be punished according to law.

If there be need of witnesses, the directions formerly mentioned (chap. 2.) are to be followed.

When persons guilty of uncleanness live one in one parish, and another in another parish, the process against them, and censures are to be before the session of the parish where the woman liveth, or where the scandal is most notour.

If a scandal of uncleanness be committed where neither parties reside, as if persons having their fixed residence in one parish do commit uncleanness in another parish, or perhaps in the fields, or in the time of fairs or markets; in these cases, they are to be processed and censured where their ordinary abode is, except the place of their abode be at a considerable distance from the place where the sin was committed, and the scandal be most flagrant where it was committed.

When there is a scandal of uncleanness whereof persons are guilty living in different parishes, the session where the sin was committed is to acquaint the other sessions where any of the persons reside, who are *ex debito* to cause summon these persons to appear before that session where the scandal is to be tried.

When a person is convict of scandal by a session of another congregation than his own, and the censure of the lesser excommunication is inflicted, the session is to send an account thereof to that session to which he belongs, but there is no need of any other sentence of his own session, to fix the censure on him, but only a public intimation thereof to be made in his own parish.

When a person is censured and absolved from his scandal in another congregation than where he lives, he is to bring a testimonial of his absolution, which is to be intimate to the congregation he lives in, if the scandal be also flagrant there; otherwise it will be sufficient to intimate the same to the session, and the same is to be done in the case of the profession of repentance, where there has been a sentence of the lesser excommunication.

CHAP. V.

Concerning Appeals from a Kirk-session to a Presbytery, &c.

ALL persons who judge themselves lesed by the procedure or sentence of a kirk-session may appeal to the presbytery, by declaring and protesting at passing of the sentence, and should thereupon according to the eight act of the general assembly 1694, give in the appeal with the reasons thereof in writ, to the moderator or clerk of the session, within the space of ten days after the time of appealing, and procure extracts thereof, and present the same to the next meeting of the presbytery thereafter, if there be a competent time, at least

least ten days free betwixt the time of appealing and the meeting of the presbytery; and should then insist in the appeal, wherein, if the appellant fail, the appeal *ipso facto* falls and becomes null, and the appellant is to be held as contumacious, and proceeded against accordingly by the kirk-session.

When an appeal is brought from a kirk session to a presbytery, the presbytery is to consider, whether the cause is of that nature, as it behoveth at length to come to the presbytery by the course of discipline, before the final determination thereof, as if it be in a process of alledged adultery, or such like, then the presbytery, to save themselves time, may fall upon the consideration of the affair without insisting much upon the *bene* or *male appellatum*, though it seem to be preposterously appealed.

But if the cause be such as the kirk session are the competent and proper judges of, even to its ultimate decision, and if there hath been no cause given by the kirk session, by their breaking the rules of an orderly process, either by the course of the process, or by the incompetency of the censure, the presbytery is not to sustain the appeal.

If the presbytery do not sustain the appeal, and find there hath been some fault, passion, or culpable mistake in the appellant, the presbytery is to inflict some censure, such as a reproof before the presbytery, or appoint an acknowledging of their precipitancy before their own session or such like, on these appealers they find to have been malicious and litigious, thereby to prevent unnecessary appeals, and that besides remitting back to the session, to stand either to the censure of the session, if it be inflicted already, or to sist themselves during the process, if it be depending.

If the appeal be sustained, and yet upon proceeding on the cause the presbytery find the appellant censurable, it is always to be minded, that whatever censure be inflicted to remove the offence he hath given to the presbytery, yet the appellant, if found guilty, is to undergo a censure, either before the kirk session or congregation he belongs to, such as the presbytery thinks he deserves, else presbyteries will be always troubled with appeals.

If, on the other hand, on trial of the process, the presbytery find the kirk session hath unwarrantably proceeded, either in contributing to the raising of a scandal, or inflicting the censure without a sufficient cause, and thereby the appellant lesed; the presbytery is not only to assoilzie the appellant, but to take such ways as may be proper and effectual to vindicate the appellant's innocency, and wipe off the scandal taken at him.

Herein the presbytery is to exercise great prudence, doing justice to the innocent, yet so, as not to weaken the kirk session's authority in that congregation, if in justice it can be avoided.

But such an emergent may very well occasion the presbytery's giving the minister and elders of that session suitable injunctions and rules to walk by, or private admonitions, or to call for a visitation of their session register.

The same method is to be followed in appeals from presbyteries to synods, and from synods to general assemblies.

An appeal being made by parties, should sist the execution of the sentence appealed from, only while the appeal is duely and diligently prosecute, and may thereby be determined, otherwise not, unless the judicature appealed to receive the appeal, and take the affair before them, and in that case the judicature appealed from is to sist until the appeal be discussed.

CHAP. VI.

Concerning Processes, which natively begin at the Kirk-session, but are not to be brought to a final Determination by them.

THERE are some processes, which natively begin at the kirk session, which, for the atrocity of the scandal, or difficulty in the affair, or general concern, the session having the opportunity of frequent meetings of the presbytery to have recourse there unto, do not determine of themselves, such as scandals of incest, adultery, trilapses in fornication, murder, atheism, adultery, witchcraft, charming, and heresy and error, vented and made public by any in the congregation, schism and separation from the public ordinances, processes in order to the highest censures of the church, and continued contumacy; but the kirk session having received information of such gross scandals, they are to weigh the same according to the rules and directions prescribed them in processes, which belong to their peculiar province, and if they find good ground for a process, they are to deal with the person accused to confess, that which now cannot be hid nor amended, till satisfaction be made to the church, which when done, the session is to refer the case, and send an extract of their procedure thereanent to the presbytery.

When there is no confession of the scandals above mentioned, the session are not to proceed to lead probation by witnesses or presumptions, till an account of the matter be brought by reference to the presbytery as aforesaid, and the presbytery do thereupon appoint the session to proceed and lead probation; and after probation is led, the same is to be brought to the presbytery, who may inflict what censure they see cause.

Sometimes

Sometimes it will fall out that the procefs is fo clear, as in a cafe of judicial confeffion, that the kirk feffion may fummon the delinquent when before them *apud acta*, to compear before the prefbytery, without previous acquainting them thereof, but where there is any difficulty, the kirk feffion fhould inform the prefbytery, and take their advice, before a party be fummoned before them.

When the party or parties compear before the prefbytery, if they confefs and profefs repentance for their fin, then the presbytery having gravely rebuked, and ferioufly exhorted the party or parties, are to determine the cenfure, and prefcribe the time and place of the parties, their profeffion of their repentance publicly in the church of that congregation where the procefs began, the fcandal being there to be taken away, or remit them to the feffion, to ftand either to the cenfure of the feffion, to receive orders thereanent.

It is thought more fit that the delinquents be appointed to remove the fcandal in the congregation, where the offence is moft flagrant, efpecially if they refide there, rather than in the place where it was committed, if it be not public there, and that intimation of the removing thereof be made in other places, if the judicature fhall find it needful.

When perfons cenfured for thefe groffer fcandals do apply to the kirk feffion for relaxation, they may both be privately conferred with, and likewife their acknowledgements heard before the feffion, but they ought not to be brought before the congregation, in order to their abfolution, nor abfolved, but by advice and order of the prefbytery.

CHAP. VII.

Concerning Proceſſes againſt Miniſters.

ALL proceffes againft any minifter, are to begin before the prefbytery to which he belongeth, and not before the kirk feffion of his own parifh.

The credit and fuccefs of the gofpel (in the way of an ordinary mean) much depending on the entire credit and reputation of minifters, their found doctrine and holy converfation, no ftain thereof ought lightly to be received, nor when it comes before a judicature ought to be negligently inquired into, or when found evident, ought to be flightly cenfured.

And becaufe a fcandal committed by a minifter hath on thefe accounts many aggravations, and once raifed, though it may be found to be without any ground, yet it is not eafily wipt off; therefore a prefbytery would exactly ponder by whofe information and complaint it comes firft before them, and a prefbytery is not fo far to receive the information, as to proceed to the citation of a minifter, or any way begin the procefs, until there be firft fome perfon, who under his hand gives in the complaint with fome account of its probability, and undertakes to make out the libel. 2*do*. Or at leaft do, before the prefbytery, undertake to make it out under the pain of being cenfured as flanderers. Or, 3*tio*, That the *fama clamofa* of the fcandal be fo great, as that the prefbytery for their own vindication fee themfelves neceffitate to begin the procefs, without any particular accufer: but the prefbytery in this cafe would be careful, firft, to inquire into the rife, occafion, brochers, and grounds of this *fama clamofa*.

All Chriftians ought to be fo prudent and wary in accufing minifters of any cenfurable fault, as that they ought neither to publifh nor fpread the fame, nor accufe the minifter before the prefbytery, without firft acquainting the minifter himfelf if they can have accefs thereto, and then, if need be, fome of the moft prudent of the minifters and elders of that prefbytery, and there advice got in the affair.

If there fhall be ground found to enter in a procefs againft a minifter, the prefbytery fhould firft confider the libel, then order him to be cited, and to get a full copy, with a lift of the witneffes names to be led for proving theroof, and a formal citation in writ is to be made either perfonally, or at his dwelling houfe, bearing a competent time allowed to give in anfwer to the libel, and his juft defence and objections againft witneffes, at leaft ten free days before the day of compearance, and the citation fhould bear the date when given, and the names of the witneffes to the giving thereof; and the execution bearing its date, with the names and defignations of the witneffes fhould be made in writ, and figned by the officer and witneffes; which being accordingly returned, he is to be called, and if he compear, the libel is to be read unto him, and he is to be enquired if he has anfwers to give in to the libel, that they may be read and confidered, in order to the difcuffing of the relevancy, and if the prefbytery find the fame, and that there is caufe to infift, they are to endeavour to bring him to a confeffion, whereby he may moft glorify God; and if he confefs, and the matter confeffed be of a fcandalous nature, cenfurable in others, fuch as the fin of uncleannefs, or fome other grofs fcandal, the prefbytery (whatever be the nature of his penitency, though to the conviction of all) are *inflanter* to depofe him *ab officio*, and to appoint him in due time to appear before the congregation where the fcandal was given, and in his own parifh, for

removing

removing the offence, by the public profession of his repentance.

If a minister be accused of any scandal, and cited to appear before his own presbytery, and do absent himself by leaving the place, and be contumacious, without making any relevant excuse, after a new public citation and intimation made at his own church, when the congregation is met, he is to be holden as confessed, and to be deposed and censured *instanter* with the lesser excommunication; but if after some time he do not return and subject himself to the censure of the church, he may be proceeded against till he be censured with the greater excommunication, if the judicature see cause for it.

If the minister accused do appear and deny the fact after the relevancy is found, the presbytery proceeding to probation, and to find the truth of the matter, all the circumstances are to be exactly canvassed, and the accused heard to object against the witnesses. As also, he should be allowed to be present at the examination, and modestly to cross interrogate, and then the reputation of the witnesses and their hability duly regarded, and the examination considered. If after consideration of all these, the judicature shall find the scandal sufficiently proven, they are to proceed to censure, as advised in the case of confession. See preceding page.

If the matter laid to the minister's charge be such practices as in their own nature manifestly subvert that order, unity, and peace, which Christ hath established in his church, or unsoundness and heterodoxy in doctrine, then great caution should be used, and the knowledge and understanding of witnesses much looked into; and withal, if the errors be not gross and striking at the vitals of religion, or if they be not pertinaciously stuck unto, or industriously spread, with a visible design to corrupt, or that the errors are not spreading among the people, then lenitives, admonitions, instructions, and frequent conferences are to be tried to reclaim without cutting off, and the advice of other presbyteries sought; and unless the thing be doing much hurt, so as it admits of no delay, the synod or General Assembly may be advised with in the affair, and the same intimate to the minister concerned.

If the libel and complaint brought against a minister be a multitude of smaller things laid together, as several acts of negligence, or other insuitable actions, the presbytery in proceeding therein are to make a presbyterial visitation of that parish to which the minister belongs; and at the said visitation, are first to see if any of these things now laid to the minister's charge were committed prior to the last presbyterial visitation of that parish, and whether they were then laid to his charge, and if they were not, it should be tried how they come to be laid to his charge now.

If the presbytery find these things laid to his charge to be committed since the last visitation, or find a satisfying reason wherefore they were not then tabled, they are to inquire what diligence hath been used in acquainting the minister with the offence taken at these things when first committed by him, and how far the minister hath been guilty of giving offence, after he knew offence to be taken.

It should likewise in this case be enquired, whether any of the complainers did first in a prudent private way inform any of the neighbour ministers, of some of these things committed by their minister, who is now challenged, before these offences came to be so many, as to merit a public and solemn trial, and accordingly the presbytery is to judge.

If the presbytery find upon trial, the complaint to resolve upon the minister's having committed such acts of infirmity or passion, as considering all the circumstances may be either amended and the people satisfied, and no such offence taken, or at least not to remain, so as to hinder the minister's profiting the people, and that the offence was taken by the minister's own people only or mainly; then the presbytery is to take all prudent ways to satisfy and reclaim both minister and people, and do away the offence.

But before a minister deposed for scandalous carriage can be restored to the exercise of the ministry, there should not only be convincing evidences of a deep sorrow for sin, but an eminent and exemplary humble walk, and edifying conversation, so apparent and convincing as hath worn out and healed the wound the scandal gave.

Immediately on the minister's being deposed by the presbytery, the sentence is to be intimate in his congregation, the church declared vacant, the planting thereof with another minister hastened, and never delayed on the expectation of his being reponed, it being almost impossible, that ever he can prove useful in that parish again.

CHAP. VIII.

Concerning Processes in order to the Censure of the greater Excommunication.

Since there is a distinction betwixt the greater and the lesser excommunication, it seems that whatever have been the causes of the first process, yet ordinarily all processes that are in order to the greater excommunication are to be grounded on manifest contumacy, or obstinate continuance in scandalous practices; and where there is no

manifest

manifest contumacy, or continuance as aforesaid, the lesser excommunication needs only have place. Yet in some extraordinary cases, the church, according to scripture warrant, hath summarily excommunicated persons guilty of notour atrocious scandalous sins, to shew the church's abhorrence of such wickedness.

Even where there hath been a scandal delated, and contumacy following by not appearing, it would be considered, whether any scandalous practice hath been proven or not; if not proven, then only the simple contumacy is to be proceeded against, for which it were hard to go a greater length than the lesser excommunication.

If the scandal hath been proven, and the censure of the lesser excommunication intimated, as in chapter third, it seems most reasonable that there be no farther proceeding, unless the scandal be gross, or of an heinous nature, or that it is spreading and infectious, as in heresies or schism in the church. In which cases contumacy is to be proceeded against in order to the greater excommunication.

The kirk session having brought the process to an intimation of the censure of the lesser excommunication, before they inflict the same, they are to refer the affair to the presbytery, bringing their whole proceedings before the presbytery in write, that the presbytery may thereby have a clear and full view of the whole affair.

The presbytery finding the kirk session hath orderly proceeded, and that the lesser excommunication is not sufficient, and that the affair is so weighty as to oblige them to enter on the process, they are to cause their officer to cite the scandalous person.

If the party appear, then the presbytery is to proceed in the inquiry at the accused, about the scandal alledged and libelled, and if he deny it, then they are to proceed and lead probation as in other cases.

But if the party appear not, but contemn the citation, the presbytery causeth renew the same, until he hath got three citations, and after the three citations, he is to be cited out of the pulpit: and for the further conviction of all concerned, intimation is to be made, that the judicature will proceed and inquire into the presumptions or probation of the guilt, and this is to be done although the delinquent be absent.

Then the presbytery is to order the minister of the congregation next Sabbath after forenoon's sermon, to acquaint the congregation what proceedings the kirk session first, and thereafter the presbytery hath made in the affair, and how contumacious the party was, and that the presbytery intended to proceed to the highest censure; and the minister is gravely to admonish the party (if present) to repent and submit himself to the discipline of the church, threatning him, if he continue impenitent, that the church will proceed, yea, though he be absent, the minister is to acquaint the people, that the church requires him to repent and submit as above said, under the foresaid certification.

There should be three public admonitions, and a presbytery should intervene betwixt each admonition; and if after all, that person continue impenitent or contumacious, the same is to be represented to the presbytery, who are thereupon to appoint public prayers thrice to be made, in which the minister is to exhort the congregation seriously to join with him in prayer, for the scandalous, impenitent or contumacious person, which he is solemnly to put up to God, humbly begging that he would deal with the soul of the impenitent, and convince him of the evil of his ways.

These public prayers of the church are to be put up three several Sabbath days, a presbytery (where its meeting are more frequent, once a month at least) intervening betwixt each public prayer, both to shew the church's tenderness towards their lapsed brother, their earnestness to have him reclaimed, and likewise to create a greater regard and terror of that dreadful censure, both in the party and in all the people.

If after all, the scandalous person makes no application, but continue impenitent, the presbytery, after prayer, is to pass sentence, and appoint a minister to intimate the same, and to shew the presbytery's resolution to proceed upon such a Sabbath as they shall name, for pronouncing that dreadful sentence solemnly in face of the congregation, unless either the party, or some for him, signify some relevant ground to stop their procedure.

That day being come, it were fit the minister did preach a sermon suited to that solemn occasion, or at least after sermon the minister should shew the congregation what he is going about, introducing the narrative of the process, with a discourse concerning the nature, use, and end of church censures, particularly that of the greater excommunication, if he hath not done it fully in his sermon:

The narrating all the steps of the process in order, shewing the church's faithfulness and tenderness towards the scandalous person, and declaring his obstinate impenitency; and that now, after all other means were used, there remained only that of cutting off the scandalous person from the society of the faithful, and intimating the church's warrant and order to him so to do.

And before the minister pronounce the sentence, he is to pray, and desire all the congregation to join with him therein, that God would grant repentance to the obstinate person, would graciously bless his

own

own ordinance, and make the cenfure effectual, both to edify others, and to be a mean to reclaim the obftinate finner.

Then after prayer, the minifter is with great gravity and authority to pronounce the cenfure, fhewing his warrant from our Lord's command, and the apoftle Paul's direction, and recapitulating the presbytery's warrant in obedience thereunto, and refuming the fcandalous and obftinate perfon's behaviour, whom he is to name; he therefore, in the name and authority of our Lord and Mafter Jefus Chrift, doth, *in verbis de præfenti*, pronounce and declare him or her excommunicated, and fhut out from the communion of the faithful, debarring that perfon from their privileges; and in the words of the apoftle, delivering that perfon over to Satan; which fentence is to be intimate according to the 9th act of the Affembly, *anno* 1704.

If after prayer, or before the cenfure be pronounced, the fcandalous perfon do make any public fignification of his repentance, and of his defire to have the cenfure ftopt, the minifter, upon apparent ferioufnefs in the fcandalous perfon, which he fheweth to the congregation, may thereupon delay pronouncing the fentence, till he report to the presbytery at their next meeting, who are then to deal with the fcandalous perfon as they fhall find caufe.

After the pronunciation of this fentence, the people are to be warned, that they hold that perfon to be caft out of the communion of the church, and that they fhun all unneceffary converfe with him or her; neverthelefs excommunication diffolved not the bounds of civil or natural relations, not exempts from the duties belonging to them.

Although it be the duty of paftors and ruling elders to ufe all diligence and vigilance, both by doctrine and difcipline refpectively, for preventing and purging out fuch errors, herefies, fchifms, and fcandals, as tend to the detriment and difturbance of the church; yet becaufe it may fall out through the pride and ftubbornnefs of offenders, that thefe means alone will not be effectual to that purpofe, it is therefore neceffary after all this, to employ the aid of the civil magiftrate, who ought to ufe his coercive power for the fuppreffing of all fuch offences, and vindicating the difcipline of the church from contempt.

CHAP. IX.

Concerning the Order of proceeding to Abfolution.

IF after excommunication the figns of repentance appear in the excommunicated perfon, fuch as godly forrow, for having incurred God's heavy difpleafure by his fin, occafioned grief to his brethren, and

and justly provoked the church to cast him out of their communion, together with a full purpose of heart to turn from his sin unto God through Christ, and to reform his life and conversation, with an humble desire of recovering peace with God and his people, and to be restored to the favour of God and light of his countenance, through the blood of Jesus Christ, and to the communion of the church, and the presbytery, upon his application be satisfied therewith, and judge that he ought to be absolved, and thereupon give warrant for his absolution, he is to be brought before the congregation, and there also to make free confession of his sin, and sorrow for it, to call upon God for mercy in Christ, to seek to be restored to the communion of the church, promising to God, through grace, new obedience, and more holy and circumspect walking as becomes the gospel; and that this appearance before the congregation be as often as church judicatures shall find may be for edification and trial of the professing penitent's sincerity; and being satisfied in this, then the minister and congregation are to praise God, who delighteth not in the death of a sinner, but rather that he should repent and live; as also for blessing the ordinance of excommunication, and making it effectual by his Spirit to the recovering of this offender, to magnify the mercy of God through Jesus Christ, in pardoning and receiving to his favour the most grievous offenders, whensoever they unfeignedly repent and forsake their sins: But before the minister proceed to absolution, he is to pray with the congregation to this effect: " That the Lord Jesus Christ, prophet,
" priest, and king of his church, who, with the preaching of the gos-
" pel, hath joined the power to bind and loose the sins of men: who
" hath also declared, that whatsoever by his ministers is bound on
" earth shall be bound in heaven, and also that whatsoever is loos-
" ed by the same, shall be loosed and absolved in heaven, would
" mercifully accept his creature N. whom Satan of long time hath
" holden in bondage, so that he not only drew him to iniquity, but
" also so hardened his heart, that he despised all admonitions; for the
" which his sin and contempt, the church was compelled to excom-
" municate him from the society of the faithful; but now seeing the
" Holy Spirit by his grace hath so prevailed, that he is returned and
" professeth repentance toward God, and faith toward our Lord Jesus
" Christ, that it may please God by his spirit and grace to make him
" a sincere and unfeigned penitent, and for the obedience of our Lord
" Jesus Christ unto death, so to accept of this poor believing and
" returning sinner, that his former disobedience be never laid to his
" charge, and that he may increase in all godliness, so that Satan in
" the end may be trodden under foot by the power of our Lord Jesus
" Christ,

"Chrift, and God may be glorified, the church edified, and the penitent faved in the day of the Lord."

Then shall follow the fentence of abfolution in thefe or the like words: "Whereas thou N haft for thy fin been shut out from the communion of the faithful, and haft now manifefted thy repentance, wherein the church refteth fatisfied, I, in the name of the Lord Jefus, before this congregation, pronounce and declare thee abfolved from the fentence of excommunication formerly denounced againft thee, and do receive thee to the communion of the church, and the free ufe of all the ordinances of Chrift, that thou mayeft be partaker of all his benefits to thy eternal falvation."

After this fentence of abfolution, the minifter fpeaketh to him as to a brother, exhorting him to watch and pray, and comforting him as there shall be caufe; the elders embrace, and the whole congregation holdeth communion with him, as one of their own: and the abfolution should be intimate in all the churches where the excommunication was intimate.

THE

THE SECOND BOOK of DISCIPLINE:

OR,

HEADS and CONCLUSIONS of the POLICY of the KIRK.

Agreed upon in the General Assembly 1578, inserted in the registers of Assembly 1581, sworn to in the National Covenant, revived and ratified by the Assembly 1648, and by many other acts of Assembly: And according to which the Church-government is established by Law, *anno* 1592 and 1690.

CHAP. I. *Of the Kirk and Policie thereof in general, and wherein it is different from the Civill Policie.*

THE kirk of God sometimes is largely taken for all them that professe the evangell of Jesus Christ, and so it is a company and fellowship not onely of the godly, but also of hypocrites professing alwayes outwardly the true religion.

Other times it is taken for the godly and elect onely, and sometimes for them that exercise spiritual function in the congregation of them that professe the truth.

The kirke in this last sence hath a certaine power granted by God, according to the which it uses a proper jurisdiction and government, exercised, to the comfort of the whole kirke.

This power ecclesiasticall is an authoritie granted by God the Father, through the mediator Jesus Christ, unto his kirke gathered, and having the ground in the word of God to be put in execution by them, unto whom the spiritual government of the kirk by lawfull calling is committed.

The policie of the kirk flowing from this power, is an order or forme of spirituall government, which is exercised by the members appoynted thereto by the word of God: and therefore is given immediately to the office-bearers, by whom it is exercised to the weale of the whole body.

This power is diversly used: for sometime it is severally exercised, chiefly by the teachers, sometime conjunctly by mutuall consent of of them that beare the office and charge, after the forme of judgement. The former is onely called *potestas ordinis*, and the other *potestas jurisdictionis*.

These two kinds of power have both one authority, one ground, one finall cause, but are different in the manner, and forme of execution, as is evident by the speaking of our master in the XVI and

This power and pollicie ecclesiasticall, is different and distinct in the own nature from that power and policie which is called civill power, and appertaineth to the civill government of the commonwealth: albiet they be both of God, and tend to one end, if they be rightly used, viz. to advance the glory of God, and to have godly and good subjects

For this power ecclesiasticall floweth immediately from God, and the Mediator Jesus Christ, and is spirituall, not having a temporal head in the earth, but onely Christ, the onely spirituall king and governour of his kirk.

It is a titlefalsly usurped by Antichrist, to call himselfe head of the kirk, and ought not to be attributed to Angel, nor man, of what estate that ever he be, saving to Christ the onely head and monarch in the kirk.

Therefore this power and policie of the kirk should leane upon the word immediately, as the only ground thereof, and should be taken from the pure fountains of the scriptures, the kirk hearing the voyce of Christ the onely spirituall king, and being ruled by his lawes.

It is proper kings, princes and magistrates, to be called Lords, and dominators over their subjects whom they govern civilly, but it is proper to Christ onely to be called Lord and master in the spirituall government of the kirk, and all others that beare office therein, ought not to usurp dominion therein, nor be called Lords, but onely ministers, disciples, and servants. For it is Christ's proper office to command and rule his kirk universally, and every particular kirk through his spirit and word, by the ministry of men.

Notwithstanding, as the ministers and others of the ecclesiasticall estate are subject to the magistrate civill, so ought the person of the magistrate be subject to the kirk spiritually, and in ecclesiasticall government. And the exercise of both these jurisdictions cannot stand in one person ordinarie.

The civill power is called the power of the sword, and the other the power of the keyes.

The civill power should command the spiritual to exercise, and to exercise, and to doe their office according to the word of God; the spirituall rulers should require the Christian magistrate to minister justice, and punish vice, and to maintaine the libertie and quietnes of the kirk within their bounds.

The magistrate commandeth externall things for externall peace and quietnesse amongst the subjects: the minister handleth externall things onely for conscience cause.

The magistrate handleth externall things onely, and actions done before men, but the spirituall ruler judgeth both inward affections, and externall actions in respect of conscience by the word of God.

The civill magistrate craves and gets obedience by the sword, and other externall meanes, but the ministrie, by the spirituall sword, and spirituall meanes.

The magistrate neither ought to preach, minister the sacraments, nor execute the censures of the kirk, nor yet prescribe any rule how it should be done, but command the ministers to observe the rule commanded in the word, and punish the transgressors by civill meanes. The ministers exerce not the civill jurisdiction, but teach the magistrate, how it should be exercised according to the word.

The magistrate ought to assist, maintaine and fortifie the jurisdiction of the kirk. The ministers should assist their princes in all things agreeable to the word, providing they neglect not their own charge by involving themselves in civill affaires.

Finally, as ministers are subject to the judgement and punishment of the magistrate in externall things, if they offend: so ought the magistrates to submit themselves to the discipline of the kirk, if they transgresse in matters of conscience and religion.

CHAP. II. *Of the Policie of the Kirk, and Persons and Office-bearers to whom the Administration is committed.*

AS in the civill policie the whole commonwealth consisteth in them that are governors, or magistrates, and them that are governed, or subjects. So in the policie of the kirk some are appointed to be rulers, and the rest of the members thereof to be ruled, and obey according to the word of God, and inspiration of his spirit, alwayes under one head and chiefe governour, Jesus Christ.

Againe, the whole policie of the kirk consisteth in three things, in doctrine, discipline, and distribution. With doctrine is annexed the administration of sacraments: and according to the parts of this division, ariseth a sort of threefold officers in the kirk, to wit, of ministers preachers, elders governours, and deacons destributers. And all these may be called by a generall word, ministers of the kirk. For albeit the kirk of God be ruled and governed by Jesus Christ, who is the onely king, high priest, and head thereof, yet he useth the ministery of men, as the most necessary middes for this purpose.

For so hee hath from time to time, before the law, under the law, and

and in the time of the Evangell, for our great comfort, raifed up men indued with the gifts of the fpirit, for the fpirituall governmeut of his kirk, exercifing by themh is own power, through his fpirit and word, to the building of the fame.

And to take away all occafion of tyranny, hee will that they fhould rule with mutuall confent of brether, and æqualitie of power, every one according to their functions.

In the New Teftament, and time of the Evangell, hee hath ufed the miniftery of the apoftles, prophets, evangelifts, paftors, and doctors in adminiftration of the difcipline; the deaconfhip to have the cure of the eclefiafticall goods.

Some of their ecclefiafticall functions are ordinarie, and fome extraordinary or temporarie. There be three extraordinary functions; the office of the apoftle, the evangelift, and of the prophet, which are not perpetuall, and now have ceafed in the kirk of God, except when it pleafed God extraordinarily for a time to ftirre fome of them up againe.

There are foure ordinarie functions or offices in the kirke of God, the office of the paftor, minifter or bifhop; the doctor; prefbyter or elder; and the deacon.

Thir offices are ordinarie, and ought to continue perpetually in the kirk, as neceffarie for the government and policie thereof, and no moe offices ought to be received or fuffered in the kirk of God, eftablifhed according to his word.

Therefore all the ambitious titles invented in the kingdome of Antichrift, and in his ufurped hierarchie, which are not of one of thefe foure forts, together with the offices depending thereupon, in one word ought to be rejected.

CHAP. III. *How the Perfons that beare ecclefiaftical Functions are to bee admitted to their Office.*

VOcation or calling is common to all that fhould beare office within the kirk, which is a lawfull way, by the which qualified perfons are promoted to any fpirituall office within the kirk of God.

Without this lawful calling it was never leafome to any perfon to meddle with any function ecclefiafticall.

There are two forts of calling, one extraordinarie by God immediately, as was of the prophets and apoftles, which in kirks eftablifhed and well alreadie reformed hath no place.

The other calling is ordinarie, which, befides the calling of God, and inward teftimony of a good confcience, is the lawfull approbation, and outward judgement of men, according to God's word, and order established in his kirk.

None ought to presume to enter in any office ecclesiasticall without this good testimony before God, who onely knows the hearts of men.

This ordinary and outward calling hath two parts, election and ordination. Election is the chosing out of a person, or persons, most able, to the office that vakes, by the judgement of the eldership, and consent of the congregation, to which shall be the person, or persons appointed.

The qualities in generall requisite in all them, who should beare charge in the kirk, consist in soundnesse of religion, and godlinesse of life, according as they are sufficiently set forth in the word.

In the order of election it is to be eschewed, that any person be intrused in any offices of the kirk, contrary to the will of the congregation to which they are appointed, or without the voice of the eldership.

None ought to be intrused, or placed in the places already planted, or in any roome that vakes not, for any wordly respect: and that which is called the benefice ought to be nothing else, but the stipend of the ministers that are lawfully called.

Ordination is the separation and sanctifying of the person appointed to God and his kirk, after he be well tryed and found qualified.

The ceremonies of ordination are fasting, earnest prayer, and imposition of hands of the eldership

All thir, as they must be raised up by God, and by him made able for the work whereto they are called, so ought they know their message to be limited within God's word, without the bounds of the which they ought not to passe.

All thir should take these titles and names onely (lest they be exalted and puft up in themselves) which the scriptures gives unto them, as these which import labour, travell and work, and are names of offices and service, and not of idlenesse, dignity, worldly honour or preheminence, which by Christ our master is expresly reproved and forbidden.

All these office bearers should have their own particular flocks, amongst whom they exercise their charge.

All should make residence with them, and take the inspection and oversight of them, every one in his vocation.

And generally thir twa things ought they all to respect: the glorie of God, and edifying of his kirk, in discharging their duties in their calling.

CHAP.

CHAP. IV. _Of the Office-bearers in particular, and first of the Pastors or Ministers._

PAstors, bishops, or ministers, are they who are appointed to particular congregations, which they rule by the word of God, and over the which they watch. In respect whereof, sometime they are called pastors, because they feed their congregation; sometime episcopi, or bishops, because they watch above their flock; sometimes ministers, by reason of their service and office, and sometimes also presbyters or seniors, for the gravity in manners which they ought to have in taking care of the spirituall government, which ought to be most deare unto them.

They that are called unto the ministerie, or that offer themselves thereunto, ought not to be elected without any certain flock be assigned unto them.

No man ought to ingyre himselfe, or usurpe this office without lawfull calling.

They who are once called by God, and duely elected by man, after that they have once accepted the charge of the ministerie, may not leave their functions.

The desertours should be admonished, and in case of obstinacie finally excommunicate.

No pastor may leave his flock without licence of the provinciall, or nationall Assembly, which if he doe, after admonitions not obeyed, let the censures of the kirk strick upon him.

Vnto the pastors apperteines teaching of the word of God, in season and out of season, publickly and privately, always travelling to edifie, and discharge his conscience, as God's word prescribes to him.

Vnto the pastors onely apperteines the administration of the sacraments, in like manner as the administration of the word: for both are appointed by God, as meanes to teach us, the one by the eare, and the other by the eyes, and other senses, that by both, knowledge may be transferred to the minde.

It appertaines by the same reason to the pastor to pray for the people, and namely, for the flock committed to his charge, and to blesse them in the name of the Lord, who will not suffer the blessings of his faithfull servants to be frustrate.

He ought also to watch above the manners of his flock, that the better he may apply the doctrine to them in reprehending the dissolute persons, and exhorting the godly to continue in the feare of the Lord.

It apperteines to the minister, after lawfull proceeding by the eldership,

ship, to pronounce the sentence of binding and loosing upon any person, according unto the power of the keyes granted unto the kirk.

It belongs to him likewise, after lawfull proceeding in the matter by the eldership, to solemnizate marriage betwixt them that are to be joyned therein, and to pronounce the blessing of the Lord upon them, that enter in at that holy band in the feare of God.

And generally all publick denunciations that are to be made in the kirk before the congregation concerning the ecclesiasticall affaires belonging to the office of a minister: for he is as messenger and herauld betwixt God and the people in all these affaires.

CHAP. V. *Of Doctors, and their Office, and of the Schooles.*

ONE of the two ordinary and perpetuall functions that travell in the word, is the office of the doctor, who may bee also called prophet, bishop, elder, catechiser, that is, teacher of the catechisme, and rudiments of religion.

His office is to open up the minde of the spirit of God in the scriptures simply, without such applications as the ministers use, to the end that the faithfull may be instructed, and sound doctrine taught, & that the purity of the gospell be not corrupted through ignorance, or evill opinions.

Hee is different from the pastor, not onely in name, but in diversity of gifts. For to the doctor is given the word of knowledge, to open up by simple teaching the mysteries of faith, to the pastor the gift of wisedome, to apply the same by exhortation to the manners of the flock, as occasion craveth.

Under the name and office of a doctor wee comprehend also the order in schooles, colledges, and universities, which hath been from time to time carefully maintained, as well among the Jewes and Christians, as also among the prophane nations.

The doctor being an elder, as said is, should assist the pastor in the government of the kirk, and concurre with the elders his brethren in all assemblies; by reason the interpretation of the word, which is onely judge in ecclesiasticall matters, is committed to his charge.

But to preach unto the people, to minister the sacraments, and to celebrate mariages, perteine not to the doctor, unlesse he be otherwise called ordinarily: howbeit the pastor may teach in the schooles, as he who hath the gift of knowledge, oftentimes meet for that end, as the examples of *Polycarpus*, and others testifie; &c.

CHAP. VI. *Of Elders, and their Office.*

THE word elder in the scripture, sometime is the name of age, sometime of office. When it is the name of any office, some time it is taken largely, comprehending as well the pastors and doctors, as them who are called seniors or elders.

In this our division, we call these elders, whom the Apostles call presidents or governours. Their office as it is ordinary, so is it perpetuall and alwaies necessarie in the kirk of God. The eldership is a spirituall function, as is the ministerie.

Elders once lawfully called to the office, and having gifts from God meet to exercise the same, may not leave it again, Albeit such an number of elders may be chosen in certaine congregations, that one part of them may relieve another for a reasonable space, as was among the Levites under the law in serving of the temple.

The number of the elders in every congregation cannot well be limited, but should be according to the bounds and necessirie of the people.

It is not necessarie that all elders be also teachers of the word, albeit the chiefe ought to be such, and swa are worthie of double honour.

What manner of persons they ought to be, we referre it to the expresse word, and namely the canons written by the Apostle Paul.

Their office is as well severally, as conjunctly, to watch diligently upon the flock committed to their charge, both publickly, and privately, that no corruption of religion, or manners, enter therein.

As the pastors and doctors should be diligent in teaching and sowing the seed of the word, so the elders should be careful in seeking the fruit of the same in the people.

It appertaines to them to assist the pastor in examination of them that come to the Lord's Table: item, in visiting the sick.

They should cause the acts of the Assemblies, as well particular as generall, to be put in execution carefully.

They should be diligent in admonishing all men of their dutie according to the rule of the Evangell.

Things that they cannot correct by private admonitions they should bring to the eldership.

Their principall office is to hold assemblies with the pastors and doctors who are also of their number, for establishing of good order and execution of discipline, unto the which assemblies all persones are subject that remaine within their bounds.

CHAP. VII. *Of the Elderships, Assemblies, and Discipline.*

Elderships and assemblies are commonly constitute of pastors, doctors, and such as we commonly call elders, that labour not in the word and doctrine, of whom, and of whose severall power, hath bene spoken.

Assemblies are of foure sorts. For either are they of particular kirks and congregations ane or moe, or of a province, or of a whole nation, or of all and divers nations professing one Jesus Christ.

All the ecclesiasticall assemblies have power to convene lawfully together for treating of things concerning the kirk, and perteining to their charge.

They have power to appoint times, and places to that effect, and at one meeting to appoint the dyet, time and place for another.

In all assemblies an moderator should be chosen by common consent of the whole brethren convened, who should propone matters, gather the votes, and cause good order to be kept in the assemblies.

Diligence should be taken, chiefly by the moderator, that onely ecclesiasticall things be handled in the assemblies, and that there be no medling with any thing perteining to the civill jurisdiction.

Every assembly hath power to send forth from them of their own number, ane or moe visitors to see how all things be ruled in the bounds of their jurisdiction.

Visitation of moe kirks is no ordinary office ecclesiastick in the person of one man, neither may the name of a bishop be attribute to the visitor onely, neither it is necessary to abide alwaies in one man's person, but it is the part of the eldership to send out qualified persons to visit *pro re nata*.

The finall end of Assemblies is first to keep the religion and doctrine in puritie, without error and corruption. Next, to keep ecumelinesse and good order in the kirk.

For this orders cause, they may make certaine rules and constitutions appertaining to the goood behaviours of all the members of the kirk in their vocation.

They have power also to abrogate and abolish all statutes and ordinances concerning ecclesiastical matters, that are found noysome and unprofitable, and agree not with the time, or are abused by the people.

They have power to execute ecclesiastical discipline and punishment upon all transgressors, and proud contemners of the good order and policie of the kirke, and so the whole discipline is in their hands.

The first kinde and sort of assemblies, although they be within particular congregations, yet they exerce the power, authoritie and jurisdiction

risdiction of the kirk with mutuall consent, and therefore beare sometime the name of the kirk.

When we speake of the elders of the particular congregations, we mean not that every particular parish kirk can, or may have their own particular elderships, specially in landward; but wee think three, four, moe or fewer particular kirks, may have one eldership common to them all, to judge their ecclesiasticall causes.

Yet this is meet, that some of the elders be chosen out of every particular congregation, to concurre with the rest of their brethren in the common assembly, and to take up the delations of offences within their owne kirks, and bring them to the assembly.

This we gather of the practise of the primitive kirk, where elders or colledges of seniors were constitute in cities and famous places.

The power of their particular elderships is to use diligent labours in the bounds committed to their charge, that the kirks be kept in good order, to inquire diligently in naughtie and unruly persons, and travell to bring them in the way againe, either by admonition or threatning of God's judgements; or by correction.

It pertaines to the eldership to take heed, that the word of God be purely preached within their bounds, the sacraments rightly ministred, the discipline rightly maintained, and the ecclesiasticall goods uncorruptly distributed. It belongs to this kinde of assembly, to cause the ordinances made by the assemblies provinciall, nationall, and generall, to be kept, and put in execution.

To make constitutions which concerne τοπρέπον in the kirk, for the decent order of these particular kirks, where they governe: providing they alter no rules made by the generall, or provinciall assemblies, and that they make the provinciall assemblies foreseen of these rules that they shall make, and abolish them that tend to the hurt of the same.

It hath power to excommunicate the obstinate.

The power of election of them who beare ecclesiasticall charges pertaines to this kind of Assembly within their owne bounds, being well erected, and constitute of many pastors, and elders of sufficient abilitie.

By the like reason their deposition also pertaines to this kinde of assembly, as of them that teach erronious and corrupt doctrine, that be of slanderous life, and after admonition desist not, that be given to schisme, or rebellion against the kirke, manifest blasphemy, simonie, corruption of bribes, falshood, perjurie, whoordome, theft, drunkennesse, fighting worthy of punishment by the law, usurie, dauncing, infamie, and all others, that deserve separation from the kirk.

These also who are altogether found unsufficient to execute their charge should be deposed, whereof other kirks would be advertised, that they receive not the persons deposed,

Yet they ought not to be depofed, who, through age, fickneffe, or other accidents, become unmeet to do their office, in which cafe their honour fhould remain to them, their kirk fhould maintaine them; and others ought to be provided to doe their office.

Provinciall affemblies wee call lawfull conventions of the paftors, doctors, and other elders of a province, gathered for the common affaires of the kirkes thereof, which alfo may bee called the conference of the kirk and brethren.

Thir affemblies are inftitute for weightie matters to be intreated by mutuall confent and affiftance of the brethren within that province, as need requires.

This affembly hath power to handle, order, and redreffe all things committed or done amiffe in the particular affemblies.

It hath power to depofe the office-bearers of that province for good and juft caufes deferving deprivation.

And generally thir affemblies have the whole power of the particular elderfhips whereof they are collected.

The nationall affembly, which is generall to us, is a lawfull convention of the whole kirks of the realm or nation where it is ufed and gathered, for the common affaires of the kirk, and may be called the generall elderfhip of the whole kirks in the realme. None are fubject to repaire to this affembly to vote but ecclefiafticall perfons, to fuch a number as fhall be thought good by the fame affemblie, not excluding other perfons that will repaire to the faid affembly to propone, heare, and reafon.

This affemblie is inftitute, that all things either committed, or done amiffe in the provinciall affemblies may be redreffed and handled, and things generally ferving for the weale of the whole bodie of the kirk within the realme may be forefeen, and fet forth to God's glorie.

It fhould take care, that kirks be planted in places where they are not planted

It fhould prefcribe the rule how the other two kinds of affemblies fhould proceed in all things.

This affembly fhould take heed, that the fpirituall jurifdiction, and civill, be not confounded to the hurt of the kirk: that the patrimonie of the kirk be not confumed, nor abufed; and generally concerning all weighty affaires that concerne the weale and good order of the whole kirks of the realm, it ought to interpone authoritie thereto.

There is befides thefe, an other more generall kinde of affemblie, which is of all nations, and all the eftates of perfons within the kirk, reprefenting the univerfall kirk of Chrift, which may be called properly the generall affembly, or generall councell of the kirk of God.

Thefe affemblies were appointed and called together fpecially, when

when any great schisme or controversie in doctrine did arise in the kirk, and were convocate at command of godly emperours being for the time, for avoiding of schismes within the universall kirk of God, which, because the perteine not to the particular estate of any realme, we cease further to speake of them.

CHAP. VIII. *Of the Deacons and their office, the last ordinary function in the Kirk.*

THE word Διακονος sometimes is largely taken, comprehending all them that beare office in the ministerie, and spirituall function in the kirk.

But now, as we speake, it is taken onely for them unto whom the collection and distribution of the almes of the faithfull and ecclesiasticall goods doth belong.

The office of the deacons so taken, is an ordinarie and perpetuall ecclesiasticall function in the kirk of Christ.

Of what properties and duties he ought to be that is called to this function, we remit it to the manifest scriptures.

The deacon ought to be called and elected, as the rest of the spirituall officers, of the which election was spoken before.

Their office and power is to receive, and to distribute the whole ecclesiasticall goods unto them to whom they are appointed.

This they ought to doe according to the judgement, and appointment of the presbyteries, or elderships (of the which the deacons are not) that the patrimony of the kirk and poore be not converted to private mens uses, nor wrongfully distribute.

CHAP. IX. *Of the patrimonie of the Kirk, and distribution thereof.*

BY the patrimonie of the kirk, we meane whatsoever thing hath been at any time before, or shall be in times coming given, or by consent and universall custome of the countries professing the Christian religion applyed to the publique use and utilitie of the kirk.

So that under the patrimonie we comprehend all things given, or to be given to the kirk and service of God, as lands, biggings, possessions, annuelrents, and all such like, wherewith the kirk is doted, either by donations, foundations, mortifications, or any other lawfull titles of kings, princes, or any persons inferiour to them, together with the continuall oblations of the faithfull.

We comprehend also all such things, as by lawes or custome, or use of countries, have been applyed to the use and utility of the kirk, of the which sort are teinds, manses, gleibs, and such like, which by common and municipall lawes and univerfall cuftome are poffeffed by the kirk.

To take any of this patrimonie by unlawfull meanes, and convert it to the particular and profane ufe of any perfon, we hold it a deteftable facriledge before God.

The goods ecclefiafticall ought to be collected, and diftributed by the deacons, as the word of God appoints, that they who beare office in the kirk be provided for without care or folicitude.

In the apoftolicall kirk, the deacons were appointed to collect and diftribute what fumme foever was collected of the faithful, to diftribute unto the neceffitie of the faints, fo that none lacked amongft the faithfull.

Thefe collections were not onely of that which was collected in manner of almes, as fome fuppofe, but of other goods, moveable, and unmoveable, of lands and poffeffions, the price whereof was brought to the feet of the apoftles

This office continued in the deacons hands, who intrometted with the whole goods of the kirk, ay and while the eftate thereof was corrupted by Antichrift, as the antient canons beare witneffe.

The fame canons make mention of a fourefold diftribution of the patrimonie of the kirk, whereof one part was applyed to the paftor or bifhop for his fuftentation and hofpitality; another to the elders and deacons, and all the clergie; the third to the poore, fick perfons and ftrangers; the fourth to the upholding other affaires of the kirk, fpecially extraordinary.

We add hereunto the fchooles and fchoolemafters alfo, which ought and may be well fufteined of the fame goods, and are comprehended under the clergie. To whom we joyn alfo clerks of affemblies, as well particular as generall, fyndicks or procutors of the kirk affaires, takers up of the pfalmes, and fuch like other ordinary officers of the kirk, fo farre as they are neceffary.

CHAP. X. *Of the Office of a Chriftian Magiftrate in the kirk.*

ALthough all the members of the kirk be holden every one in their vocation, and according thereto, to advance the kingdom of Jefus Chrift, fo far as lyeth in their power, yet chiefly Chriftian princes, and other magiftrates, are holden to doe the fame.

For they are called in the fcripture nourifhers of the kirk, for fo much as by them it is, or at leaft ought to be maintained, foftered, upholden, and defended againft all that would procure the hurt thereof.

So it perteines to the office of a Chriftian magiftrate, to affift and fortifie the godly proceedings of the kirk in all behalfes; and namely to see that the publique estate and ministerie thereof be maintained and susteined, as it appertaines, according to God's word.

To see that the kirk be not invaded, nor hurt by false teachers and hirelings, nor the roomes thereof be occupied by dumb doggs, or idle bellies.

To assist and maintaine the discipline of the kirk, and punish them civilly, that will not obey the censure of the same, without confounding alwaies the one jurisdiction with the other.

To see that sufficient provision be made for the ministerie, the schooles, and the poore: and if they have not sufficient to awaite upon their charges, to supply their indigence even with their own rents, if need require.

To hold hand as well to the saving of their persons from injurie and open violence, as to their rents and possessions, that they be not defrauded, robbed, nor spoiled thereof.

Not to suffer the patrimony of the kirk to be applyed to profane and unlawfull uses, or be devoured by idle bellies, and such as have no lawfull function in the kirk, to the hurt of the ministery, schooles, poore, and other godly uses, whereupon the same ought to be bestowed.

To make laws and constitutions agreable to God's word, for advancement of the kirk, and policie thereof, without usurping any thing that perteins not to the civil sword, but belongs to the offices that are meerly ecclesiasticall, as is the ministerie of the word and sacraments, using ecclesiasticall discipline, and the spirituall execution thereof, or any part of the power of the spirituall keyes, which our master gave to the apostles, and their true successours.

And although kings and princes that be godly, some times by their own authority, when the kirk is corrupted and all things out of order, place ministers and restore the true service of the Lord, after the example of some godly kings of Iuda, and divers godly emperours, and kings also in the light of the New Testament; yet where the ministerie of the kirk is once lawfully constitute, and they that are placed doe their office faithfully, all godly princes and magistrates ought to heare, and obey their voice, and reverence the majestie of the Son of God speaking in them.

CHAP. XI. *Of the present abuses remaining in the Kirk, which we desire to be reformed.*

AS it is the duty of the godly magistrate to maintain the present liberty, which God hath granted by the preaching of his word, and the true administration of the sacraments within this realm: so is it to provide, that all abuses which yet remaine in the kirk, be removed, and utterly taken away.

Therefore first the admission of men to papisticall titles of benefices, such as serve not, nor have no function in the reformed kirk of Christ, as abbotes, commendators, priors, prioresses, and other titles of Abbeyes, whose places are now for the most part by the just judgement of God demolished, and purged of idolatry, is plaine abuse, and is not to receive the kingdom of Christ amongst us, but rather to refuse it.

Such like that they that of old were called the chapiters and convents of Abbeyes, cathedrall kirks, and like places, serve for nothing now, but to set fewes and tacks, if any thing be left of the kirk lands and teinds, in hurt and prejudice thereof, as daily experience teacheth, and therefore ought to be utterly abrogate and abolished.

Of the like nature are the deanes, archdeacones, chantours, sub-chantours, thesaurers, chancellors, and others having the like titles flowing from the pope and canon law onely, who have no place in the reformed kirk.

The kirks also which are united together, and joyned by annexation to their benefices, ought to be separated and divided, and given to qualified ministers, as God's word craves.

Neither ought such abusers of the kirks patrimony to have vote in parliament, nor sit in councell under the name of the kirk and kirk-men, to the hurt and prejudice of the liberty thereof, and lawes of the realm made in favour of the reformed kirk.

Much lesse is it lawfull, that any person amongst these men should have five, sixteen, twenty or moe kirks, all craving the charge of soules, and bruike the patrimony thereof, either by admission of the prince, or of the kirk, in thi slight of the Evangell. For it is but a mockage to crave reformation where such like have place.

And in so farr, as in the order taken at Leith in the yeare of our Lord 1571, it appears that such may be admitted, being found qualified; either that pretended order is against all good order, or else it must be understood not of them that be qualified in worldly affaires, or to serve in court, but such as are qualified to teach God's word, having their lawfull admission of the kirk.

As to bishops, if the name ἐπίσκοπος be properly taken, they are all one with the ministers, as before was declared. For it is not a name of superioritie, and lordship, but of office and watching.

Yet because in the corruption of the kirk, this name (as others) have been abused, and yet is likely to be, wee cannot allow the fashion of these new chosen bishops, neither of the chapiters that are electors of them to such offices, as they are chosen unto.

True bishops should addict themselves to a particular flock, which
sundry

sundry of them refuse, neither should they usurpe lordship over their brethren, and over the inheritance of Christ, as these men doe.

Pastors, in so farr as they are pastors, have not the office of visitation of moe kirkes joyned to the pastorship, without it be given to them.

It is a corruption, that bishops should have further bounds to visit nor they may lawfully. No man ought to have the office of visitation, but he that is lawfully chosen thereunto

The elderships being well established, have power to send out visitours one or moe, with commission to visit the bounds within their eldership and likewise, after count taken of them, either continue them, or remove them from time to time, to the which elderships they shall be alwayes subject

Criminall jurisdiction in the person of a pastor is a corruption.

It agreeth not with the word of God, that bishops should be pastors of pastors, pastors of many flockes, and yet without a certain flock, and without ordinary teaching.

It agreeth not with the scriptures, that they should be exemed from the correction of their brethren, and discipline of the particular eldership of the kirk, where they shall serve, neither that they usurpe the office of visitation of other kirks, nor any other function besides other ministers, but so far as shall be committed to them by the kirk.

Wherefore, we desire the bishops that now are, either to agree to that order that God's word requires in them, as the generall kirk will prescribe unto them, not passing their bounds, either in ecclesiasticall or civill affaires, or else to be deposed from all function in the kirk.

We denie not in the meane time, but ministers may and should assist their princes when they are required, in all things agreeable to the word, whether it be in councell or parliament, or otherwayes, providing alwayes they neither neglect their owne charges, nor through flattery of princes, hurt the publick estate of the kirk.

But generally, we say no person, under whatsoever title of the kirk; and specially the abused titles in papistrie, of prelates, convents, and chapters, ought to attempt any act in the kirks name, either in councell, or parliament, or out of councell, having no commission of the reformed kirk within this realme.

And by act of parliament it is provided, that the papisticall kirk and jurisdiction should have no place within the same, and no bishop nor other prelate in times comming should use any jurisdiction flowing from his authority.

And againe, that no other ecclesiasticall jurisdiction should be acknowledged within this realm, but that which is, and shall be in the reformed kirk, and flowing therfrom.

So we esteem holding of chapters in papisticall manner, either in cathedrall

cathedrall kirks, Abbeyes, colledges, or other conventuall places, usurping the name and authority of the kirk, to hurt the patrimony thereof, or use any other act to the prejudice of the same, since the yeare of our Lord 1560 yeares, to be abuse and corruption, contrary to the liberty of the true kirk, and lawes of the realme, and therefore ought to be annulled, and in times comming utterly discharged.

The dependances also of the papisticall jurisdiction are to be abolished, of the which sort is mingled jurisdiction of the commissars, in so farr as they meddle with ecclesiasticall matters, and have no commission of the kirk thereto, but were elected in time of our soveraigne's mother, when things were out of order. It is an absurd thing that sundry of them having no function of the kirk, should be judges to ministers, and depose them from their roomes. Therefore they either would be discharged to meddle with ecclesiasticall matters, or it would be limited to them in what matters they might be judges, and not hurt the libertie of the kirk.

They also that of before were of the ecclesiastique estate in the pope's kirk, or that are admitted of new to the papisticall titles, and now are tollerate by the lawes of the realme to possesse the two part of their ecclesiasticall rents, ought not have any further liberty, but to intromet with the portion assigned and granted to them for their lifetimes, and not under the abused titles which they had to dispone the kirk rents, set tackes and fewes thereof at their pleasure, to the great hurt of the kirk and poore labourers, that dwell upon the kirk lands, contrarie to all good conscience and order.

Chap. XII. *Certain speciall heads of reformation which we crave.*

WHatsoever hath been spoken of the offices of the kirke, the severall power of the office-bearers, their conjunct power also, and last of the patrimonie of the kirk, wee understand it to be the right reformation, which God craves at our hands, that the kirk be ordered according thereto, as with that order, which is most aggreeable to the word.

But because something would be touched in particular, concerning the estate of the countrey, and that which we principally seek to be reformed in the same, we have collected them in these heads following.

Seeing the whole countrey is divided in provinces, and thir provinces again are divided in parishes, as well in land-ward, as in townes; in every parish and reasonable congregation there would be placed one or moe pastors to feed the flock, and no pastor or minister alwaies to be burdened with the particular charge of moe kirks or flockes then one alanerly,

And

And becaufe it will be thought hard to finde out paſtors or miniſters to all the paroch kirks of the realm, as well in landward, as in townes, we think by the advice of fuch as commiſſion may be given to by the kirk and prince, pariſhes in landward or ſmall villages, may be joyned two or three or more, in ſome places, together, and the principall and moſt commodious kirks to ſtand, and be repaired ſufficiently, and qualified miniſters placed thereat ; and the other kirks, which are not found neceſſary, may be ſuffered to decay, their kirk yards alwaies being kept for buryall places ; and in ſome places where need requires a pariſh, where the congregation is over great for one kirk, may be divided in twa or moe.

Doctors would be appointed in univerſities, colledges, and in other places needfull, and ſufficiently provided for, to open up the meaning of the ſcriptures, and to have the charge of ſchooles, and teach the rudiments of religion.

As for elders, there would be ſome to be cenſurers of the manners of the people, one or moe in every congregation, but not an aſſembly of elders in every particular kirk, but onely in townes, and famous places, where reſort of men of judgement and abilitie to that effect may be had, where the elders of the particular kirks about may convene together, and have a common elderſhip, and aſſembly place among them, to treat of all things that concerns the congregations of which they have the overſight.

And as there ought to be men appointed to unite and divide the pariſhes, as neceſſity and commodity requires : ſo would there be appointed by the generall kirk, with aſſent of the prince, ſuch men as feare God, and know the eſtate of the countries, that were able to nominate and deſigne the places, where the particular elderſhips ſhould convene, taking conſideration of the dioceſſe, as they were divided of old, and of the eſtate of the countries, and provinces of the realme.

Likewiſe concerning provinciall and ſynodall aſſemblies conſideration were eaſie to be taken, how many and in what places they were to be holden, and how oft they ſhould convene, ought to be referred to the liberty of the generall kirk and order to be appointed therein.

The nationall aſſemblies of this countrey, called commonly the generall aſſemblies, ought alwayes to be retained in their own liberty, and have their own place.

With power to the kirk to appoint times and places convenient for the ſame, and all men, as well magiſtrates as inferiours, to be ſubject to the judgement of the ſame in eccleſiaſticall cauſes, without any reclamation or appellation to any judge, civill or eccleſiaſticall within the realm.

The libertie of the election of perſons called to the eccleſiaſticall function, functions, and observed without interruption, so long as the kirk was not corrupted by Antichrist, we desire to be restored and reteined within this realm.

So that none be intrused upon any congregation, either by the prince, or any inferiour person, without lawfull election, and the assent of the people over whom the person is placed, as the practise of the apostolicall and primitive kirk, and good order craves.

And because this order, which God's word craves, cannot stand with patronages and presentation to benefices used in the Pope's kirk, we desire all them, that truely feare God, earnestly to consider, that for as much as the names of patronages and benefices, together with the effect thereof, have flowed from the Pope, and corruption of the canon law onely, in so farr as thereby any person was intrused or placed over kirkes having *curam animarum*.

And for as much as that manner of proceeding hath no ground in the word of God, but is contrary to the same, and to the said liberty of election, they ought not now to have place in this light of reformation. And therefore, whosoever will embrace God's word, and desire the kingdome of his Son Christ Jesus to be advanced, they will also embrace, and receive that policie and order which the word of God, and upright estate of his kirk craves, otherwise it is in vaine that they have profest the same.

Notwithstanding as concerning other patronages of benefices that have not *curam animarum*, as they speak: such as are chaplenries, prebendaries founded upon temporall lands, annuels, and such like, may be reserved unto the ancient patrones, to dispone hereupon, when they vaike, to schollers and bursers, as they are required by act of parliament.

As for the kirk rents in generall, we desire that order be admitted and maintained amongst us, that may stand with the sincerity of God's word, and practise of the purity of the kirk of Christ.

To wit, that as was before spoken, the whole rent and patrimony of the kirk, excepting the small patronages before mentioned, may be dicided in foure portions: one thereof to be assigned to the pastor for his entertainment, and hospitality; an other to the elders, deacons and other officers of the kirk, such as clerks of assemblies, takers up of the psalmes, beadels and keepers of the kirk, so farre as is necessarie: joyning with them also the doctors, and schooles, to help the ancient foundations where need requires: the third portion to be bestowed upon the poore members of the faithfull, and hospitals: the fourth for reparation of the kirks, and other extraordinary charges as are profitable for the kirk, and also for the common wealth, if need require.

We desire therefore the ecclesiasticall goods to be uplifted, and distributed ftributed faithfully to whom they appertaine, and that by the miniſterie of the deacons, to whoſe office properly the collection and diſtribution thereof belongs, that the poore may be anſwered of their portion thereof, and they of the miniſtery live without care and ſolitude: as alſo the reſt of the treaſure of the kirk may be reſerved, and beſtowed to their right uſes.

If theſe deacons be elected with ſuch qualities as God's word craves to be in them, there is no feare that they ſhall abuſe themſelves in their office, as the profane collector did of before.

Yet becauſe this vocation appears to many to be dangerous, let them be obliſhed, as they were of old, to the yearly count to the paſtors and elderſhip, and if the kirk and prince think expedient, let cautioners be obliſhed for their fidelity, that the kirk rents on no wayes be dilapidat.

And to the effect this order may take place, it is to be provided that all other intrometers with the kirk rent, collectors general or ſpeciall, whether it be by appointment of the prince, or otherwaies, may be denuded of further intromiſſion therewith, and ſuffer the kirk rents in time comming to be wholly intrometted with by the miniſtry of the deacons, and diſtribute to the uſe before mentioned.

As alſo to the effect, that the eccleſiaſticall rents may ſuffice to theſe uſes, for the which they are to be appointed: we thinke it neceſſary to be deſired, that all alienations, ſetting of fewes, or tacks of the rents of the kirk, as well lands as teinds, in hurt and diminution of the old rentals, be reduced and annulled, and the patrimony of the kirk reſtored to the former old liberty.

And likewiſe that in times comming the tiends be ſet to nane but to the labourers of the ground, or elſe not ſet at all, as was agreed upon, and ſubſcribed by the nobility of before.

CHAP. XIII. *The utilitie that ſhall flow from this reformation to all Eſtates.*

SEing the end of this ſpirituall government and policie whereof we ſpeak, is, that God may be glorified, the kingdome of Jeſus Chriſt advanced, and all who are of his myſtical body, may live peaceable in conſcience: therefore we dare boldly affirme, that all theſe who have true reſpect to theſe ends will even for conſcience cauſe gladly agree and conforme themſelves to this order, and advance the ſame, ſo farre as lyeth in them, that their conſcience being ſet at reſt they may be repleniſhed with ſpirituall gladneſſe in giving full obedience to that which God's word, and the teſtimony of their own conſcience doth crave, and refuſing all corruption contrary to the ſame.

Next

Next, we shall become an example and patterne of good and godly order to other nations, countries, and kirkes professing the same religion with us, that as they have glorified God in our continuing in the sincerity of the word hitherto, without any errours, praise be to his name. So they may have the like occasion in our conversation, when as we conforme ourselves to that discipline, policie, and good order, which the same word, and purity of reformation craveth at our hands. Otherwise that fearfull sentence may be justly said to us, *The servant knowing the will of his maister, and not doing it, &c.*

Moreover, if we have any piety or respect to the poore members of Jesus Christ, who so greatly increase and multiply amongst us, we will not suffer them to be longer defrauded of that part of the patrimony of the kirk, which justly belongs unto them, and by this order, if it be duely put to execution, the burden of them shall be taken of us to our great comfort, the streets shall be cleansed of the cryings and murmurings of them, as we shall no more be any skandall to other nations, as we have hitherto been for not taking order with the poore amongst us, and causing the word which we professe to be evil spoken of, giving occasion of sklander to the enemies, and offending the consciences of the simple and godly.

Besides this, it shall be a great ease and commodity to the whole common people, in relieving them of the building and upholding their kirks, in bigging of brigges, and other like publique works: to the labourers of the ground in payment of their teinds, and shortly in all these things, whereinto they have been hitherto rigorously handled by them that are falsly called kirkemen, their tacksmen, factours, chalmerlanes and extorsioners.

Finally, to the Kings majestie, and common wealth of the countrey this profite shall redound, that the other affaires of the kirk being sufficiently provided, according to the distribution, of the which hath been spoken: the superplus being collected in the treasurie of the kirk may be profitably imployed, and liberally bestowed upon the extraordinary support of the affairs of the prince and commonwealth, and specially of that part which is appointed for reparation of kirks.

So to conclude, all being willing to apply themselves to this order, the people suffering themselves to be ruled according thereto; the princes and magistrates not being exeemed, and these that are placed in the ecclesiasticall estate rightly ruling and governing. God shall be glorified, the kirk edified, and the bounds thereof inlarged, Christ Jesus and his kingdome set up, Satan and his kingdome subverted, and God shall dwell in the midst of us, to our comfort, through Jesus Christ, who, together with the Father and the Holy Ghost. abides blessed in all eternity.

www.ingramcontent.com/pod-product-compliance
Lightning Source LLC
Chambersburg PA
CBHW022057230426
43672CB00008B/1206